Return to Paradise

Breyten Breytenbach

Return to Paradise

A HARVEST BOOK
HARCOURT BRACE & COMPANY
SAN DIEGO   NEW YORK   LONDON

Library of Congress Cataloging-in-Publication Data
Breytenbach, Breyten.
Return to paradise/Breyten Breytenbach.
p.   cm.
ISBN 0-15-600132-2 (Harvest pbk.)
I. Title.
PT6592.12.R4R48   1993
839.3'68503 — dc20   93-8721

Printed in the United States of America

First Harvest edition 1994

A B C D E

For Uys Krige

em que espelho
fica perdida minha face
(*'in what mirror
did I lose my face'*)
FERNANDO PESSOA

mise mono ja nai
(*'this is not something we show people'*)
ZEN SAYING

CONTENTS

PREFACE

Although I fondly hope that the following pages will be interesting enough to engage the imagination, it is only fair to provide the unsuspecting reader with the bare bones of a personal history underlying the flow of this story. An introductory note is thus called for.

In earlier times I used to describe myself as an Afrikaans-speaking whitish male South African African temporarily living outside the continent. These characteristics still hold water even if I should add that, given the evolution in perspectives, I am now of the wrong sex and wrongish colour and of an age where time has overtaken me so that I'm getting short of breath, using a wrong language and holding the wrong opinions. Worse – I've run out of convictions!

Nothing original so far: in the latter part of our century many of us are battered by the noises of emptiness and bruised by an environment of hatred, cynicism and corruption. Besides, as a painter and writer living away from my native land for most of my adult life, I have become accustomed to a nomadic existence, moving from page to watercolour and drifting from one *Fata Morgana* to the next mirage.

I first left Africa at the beginning of 1960 to make my way to Paris. The Sharpeville Massacre of March 1960 marked the onset of a reign of state terror in South Africa and the opposition movements were banned and exiled. In Paris I married Yolande Golondrina Sonrisa of Vietnam, thus (as the old law would have it) stepping over the line of immorality into an illegal mixed union. I also became involved in anti-apartheid activities. Henceforth, as an undesirable native, I was twice doomed and twice blessed. All meaning is of course *métissage*, a new mixture of existing truths.

My wife and I were allowed to enter South Africa in 1973 for a three-month visit, an experience which I tried to bring to heel in *A Season in Paradise*. I returned clandestinely to that no man's land in 1975, was arrested and convicted of terrorism, and sentenced to nine years of travelling blindly in the belly of the whale. After seven years I was regurgitated and once more washed up in Europe. *The True Confessions of an Albino Terrorist* flowed from that sojourn.

The present book is the last part of the triptych, an attempt to come to grips with a closing chapter in my life. It is articulated around yet another three-month-long foray into South Africa during 1991. Many things had changed in the meantime. Nelson Mandela had been released and the African National Congress (ANC), with which I'd been associated, was unbanned. In the intervening years I was lucky enough to be of some assistance in breaking down the walls of taboo between 'inside' and 'outside'; this journal touches upon the events I was involved with and the people I met on my journeys. I'd spent time in West Africa and became acquainted with President Abdou Diouf of Senegal and the late President Thomas Sankara of Burkina Faso. This enabled me in 1987 to help organize the first major meeting – in Dakar, Ouagadougou and Accra – between about sixty progressive South Africans from 'inside' and the ANC, which was then still considered diabolical.

To my mind only a fool would pretend to understand comprehensively what South Africa is really about, or be objective and far-sighted enough to glimpse its future course. Since 1991 a middle ground of shared government seems to be emerging down there, occupied by the ANC and the National Party of Mr De Klerk (the present, and now temporary, State President), gradually imposing a 'stability' laced with blood. It is not a revolution, and for the time being it has little to do with democracy. Perhaps the accommodation of power in such an explosive environment cannot really allow for the niceties of democracy. Perhaps, then, history is ultimately stronger than imagination. In order to sleep soundly the dream must be devoured.

The line of my life as indicated here – a warped thread in the complex cloth of a much larger tale – seems to be woven against the woof of Government and State, the Afrikaner establishment and the new politically correct orthodoxy, the exile community of professional victims, and finally the ANC. It has been my pleasure to disagree with the living and the dead.

This book was written on the wing. You should be warned that it consists of many futile paradoxes: the story is neither of the past nor in the present, but winds its way through words in a lost time. It could well be a tissue of fiction stitched together with ruptures, by way of illustrating a parting of the ways. Perhaps I mistook my own rictus for a distorting mirror.

I find comfort in some Tuareg sayings grounded in the wisdom of solitude. 'Death', they say, 'is not like drinking tea.' And: 'Truth is yesterday's spouse.'

Breyten Breytenbach
GORÉE ISLAND, FEBRUARY 1993

Return to Paradise

VOTUM

There is such a thing as an incurable nostalgia. It provokes skin rash, tics around mouth and eyes, long periods of spiritlessness. The pillow becomes a father-confessor listening to stories of the country of the heart. Ancient flames infest the subconscious. Images scald the eyelids. An old man totters from prison and wields a fist. People squat and die like rabbits, with cold shivers. There must be a song that can still be sung.

I sit at a table. It is late night before the departure. The night sings. Sometimes the tune is bumpy, on other occasions thick-throated, then again poignant and thin. Night sings in subtle exhalations like the smell of a nocturnal flower. From planet Urd, through the shafts between buildings, I look upwards through the undecodifiable secret writing of winter-bare branches. The moon is sailing silver and full-throated through the clouds. The Eiffel Tower is spelled out in lights, an icing-sugared rig for launching spaceships. The gold-leaf on the Invalides dome was refurbished last year; it too is shivering with light.

If only we could know of time's circular course, that time is a refrain, a jingle which one repeats so as not to be alone in the dark with one's fears. I have to return to my beginnings. Why does it frighten me so? Could it be because I am my own corpse, and that the smell upsets me?

On the roof, propped up against the chimney-pot is a dark and shapeless form, I imagine the body of an angel. The moon is an ink bottle smashed in the garden of night. At birth all poets are black. Gradually they change colour, they adapt or are bleached through use. Some still know that they carry the night.

These things I jot down in the small hours before leaving, when everybody is still asleep and the few lit-up windows are apertures in the void, my tongue soaked through with the taste of dread. Night-thoughts, notes of oblivion. How to get as far as Good Hope? What happened to the Revolution?

Whales sing and each has its own song. It may have to do with mating anguish, perhaps it is a telling of tides, an ode to green pastures, a kind of sea-book. The score will be appropriated by the herd as a means of mutual recognition and a way along which to relate the surroundings. By the partial sharing of rhythms and scales do we become part of one system. Uttered into the migration pattern from ocean to ocean, mostly from south to north, depending on the seasons and the seaworthiness of the calves, the repertoire is taken along. Other guardian swimmers of the outer limits will copy the original in slightly modified versions. The divas slither through subaqueous cathedrals of light, and they pick up barnacles and mussels and such accretions, perhaps to be influenced by the chanting of other melodies so that the hymn which surfaces after the passing of time and tides will no longer be the same as the birthsong. And yet it remains the narrative of an interaction. The original text is a journey. How far must a song swim before it disappears with cadence and cadaver? To survive with meaning, tracks and notes must slip away in the water.

We are seated in the back of the aircraft. Yolande leafed for a while through a magazine and then fell asleep, exhausted by the preparations for our journey. I am completing a crossword puzzle. To the right the Portuguese coastline with its inlets is falling away. Europe shows a final hunch, and then the small water-bridge to Africa. Below us the earth will turn black. From here, from that cape below, now capsizing in the twilight underneath our wings, adventurers of old set out to 'discover' new worlds – Vasco da Gama, Diogo Cão, Bartolomeu Dias and his brother Etienne, Francisco Almeida, Alfonso d'Albuquerque ... Henry the Navigator (Henri Duc de Viseu) egged them on.

According to Herodotus, the Carthaginians tell of a certain Sataspes, son of Theaspes, who undertook to sail right around Africa. Sataspes had raped the daughter of Zopire, Megabyze's son. King Xerxes wanted the culprit crucified but his mother, the sister of Darius, intervened, pleading for a substitute punishment, namely this impossible mission. Xerxes agreed. Sataspes went to Egypt, had a ship fitted out, took on sailors, set sail for the Straits of Gibraltar. From there he proceeded to a cape known as Siloe, and thence due south. For months they tacked through an empty sea before he turned the bows back to Egypt. To the king he reported about distant lands where small people dwell who go clad only in red. When they saw the voyagers land they abandoned their cities and took to the mountains. Out of kindness he didn't want to do them harm, he just confiscated their cattle, and then the ship didn't want to go any further. Xerxes didn't believe a word of this tale. He had Sataspes nailed to a cross as originally intended.

For a long time we fly over the Atlantic Ocean with her green swells, where wind scratches slate-pencil lines to draw a woman with white combs in her hair. Later we cross other herds of clouds, small, each with a separate dark reflection, so that every green stain in the water would seem to have unfurled its own white vapoury umbrella upon an invisible stalk of writing. But already it is a black memory.

ENTRY

In the middle of the night I come awake somewhere above this inconceivable darkened earth. The few other passengers must all be asleep or lying down with toothache or worries behind closed eyelids. (It is the time of the Gulf War, not many people travel, jet aircrafts are instruments of death.) In her seat Yolande is lying curled like a baby waiting to be born. The reading lights are doused, we are alone in the sky.

A cold death blows over the plane. All lines are already laid out in as yet hidden snares and we are being brought to a fixed destination. My watch shows six o'clock. To the left of the shiny hull of our vessel the first flames are smudging a sea of clouds.

I can do nothing about it. Each time it captivates me again. Like a fly I want to suck up to the glass of the port-hole to stare at the primordial continent being unveiled down below. The cloud cover dissipates, a vagueness is wiped from the eyes, and then I see: endless, timeless – rather, by time drawn to limitlessness. Brown, red, grey. Ridges and carbuncles and groins and fishbones and leaf-patterns – my memory knows those to be mountains, pans, dry riverbeds with all their offshoots. So many rivers. Suddenly a hair-line giving a seam to the nothingness, straight as a ruler. Must have been hewed by human hand, clearly a road, but no sign of life. Maybe that also is but a linking of the sand-silent past to an unknowable future. One could formulate one's flights for ages over such a landscape without ever encountering the impressions of organized settlement.

So often this has been described. There must be the embedded original knowledge. My travels bear the scansions of this continent's rhythms. Always they are characterized by a sense of overwhelming and acquiescence, the coils of experience are not receptive enough to absorb so much beauty. I can become wind-dried above this universe. The sun rises and the earth rolls away and it is as if we hang motionless above an endless expanse. I am the clock without hands. With open eyes I enter a nether world, the eternity of a subconscious. Let go! Fixing the image would mean that I must become an impersonation of myself, a depiction, a substitute. Good morning, oh painted monkey.

Ouagadougou's airport is strict but poor, with brave slogans embellishing the outside wall of the main building: *Ici au Burkina on donne la parole au peuple.* And: *Cette terre de dignité appartient à tous les hommes libres.* Here, in 1987, the Boere got a fright. We arrived after the Dakar meeting, a dishevelled group of pilgrims with an ANC delegation in tow, and had to walk the gauntlet past a guard-of-honour consisting of Revolutionary Youth boys with red berets and yellow neckerchiefs and real loaded AK–47s. Outside, the ANC heroes were mounted on an open military vehicle and with clenched fists held high they led the procession into town along streets where the population massed three-deep to ululate and to shuffle. The Boere followed in small buses, and somebody wise-cracked: 'Here come the liberators with their first prisoners-of-war.'

Dakar's airport is quite spacious. A sea-breeze soothes the hot bodies, the leather armchairs in the VIP lounge are comfortable. The arrivals and departures hall is, however, a court of miracles, with milling passengers and family and friends and gawkers, and porters reeling and lurching under cartons and rope-swathed suit-cases, trying with shrill whistles and cries to make their way through the multitude past the obstacles of luggage piles.

The one at Tripoli is a slightly sinister secret shell of cement, announcements and instructions in Arabic only, green flags every-where. One's passport is confiscated by the Committee of Revo-lutionary Airport Workers; only upon departure will it be restituted, that is if Allah – blessed be His name – wants to help you out of the country. The arriving foreigners working the oilfields have to queue separately to register their whisky; heathens are allowed to soak their damned souls.

In Accra the immigration officials are British-taught toads. To leave the country one has to shell out ten American dollars: nobody warned me about this, so I assiduously tried to change money. They goiter their black throats with importance: they only accept foreign currency, naturally they have no change and as naturally I shall 'lose' on the deal.

At Entebbe one espies in the distance the savannas dotted with thorn trees and the mountain like an over-exposed postcard; often also camouflaged Israeli war-planes, rhinoceroses of metal swatting flies with their tails. On the flight up the eastern seaboard some years back, during night's last watch when the thought of light starts giving shape to the outside boundaries of the imagination but the earth below would still be heavy and sombre like a policeman's hand, a traveller in the next seat questions me on South Africa. He didn't know who I was. Later he talked about a certain Mr B of whom he'd heard – how would he be doing? I conceded that the fellow's name rang a distant bell – bad news needs no messenger – and didn't know what I was going to do once the light of day would be brought to bear on the subject.

In Dar-es-Salaam I had problems when I wanted to take off early one morning. My visa had lapsed, there was a fine to be paid. With great satisfaction the agent wrote out the receipt, and I was lucky not to be taken for a spy. In the air terminal's Indian shops one could purchase wooden effigies stolen from the graves of fore-fathers. Sometimes, at the departure counter, young South Africans who had deserted the ANC's training camps came to beg one's local 'leftover' money: Tanzanian currency wasn't worth a dime anywhere else, and any other coins would also serve the purpose, and the cause.

In Algiers the local security hood had to help me get past the ill-tempered border police with their dark lip-feathers who tried to block my entry despite my Algerian passport.

In Lusaka you are expected upon arrival to pay an entry fee as border grease, but in local currency; since this money cannot be obtained anywhere in the world (Zambian Airlines will not even accept their own money as tender on international flights), we were obliged to request a customs official to go and kindly change some 'beyond the border', and obviously he had to have his cut. Outside we entered with sighed relief a taxi which turned out to be so despondent that my spine registered every bump and cough in the road.

At Abidjan a scrounger awaits me right by the immigration official's glass cage to 'help' me fill in disembarkation forms, 'help' me sign my name. Each 'helper' marks down a client and if a competitor tries to entice him away a fight will start up immediately. Outside the clothes will be torn from my body by a pack of young men who as a matter of life and death insist upon carrying my empty briefcase even if only for three yards, or summon a taxi or help me into the bus.

In Nairobi's men's rooms there are cleaners who offer to assist in the noble art of unbuttoning the fly, to dust shoes, to pull a chain or to open a tap, and they will smile with the cupped hands of cherubs to show how hospitable they are. On the first floor there's a sad corridor for transit passengers where all manner of *touristeries* can be bought; in the basement a space where the poor and the patient slouch in clapped armchairs to sleep away the heat while a sluggish propeller circles against the ceiling.

Lagos, the city of lakes, is known in Africa as a robbers' den. Airlines with Murtala Mohammed International Airport as destination prefer to offload and fly on to Cotonou where their crews can spend the night. On the way there a black fellow passenger, when he learns where I'm heading, clucks his tongue in pity and squeezes my hand with much sympathy: 'Oh, my dear sir . . .' My friend Hugh Lewin once had to change planes here: his suitcase was stolen from the conveyor belt in the transit area. In vain he ran after the culprit and hollered: 'T'ief! T'ief! Dere he goes, catchem!' A while later he looked on helplessly while his clothes sauntered through the airport on the frame of a swaggering fellow. When I arrive my passport is taken possession of by a shady official. I wait an hour or more to get it back in exchange for a dash of appreciation. It will be stamped with the expectation that I contribute towards the labour costs: we are in the land of the free market. I reclaim my baggage under similar restrictions. There a Swiss couple hired a car upon arrival. A kilometre from the airport they were held up by armed soldiers, robbed and shot dead.

In Harare I have to report in writing whether I've ever been imprisoned and why. When I put down 'terrorism' the officer winks a conspiratorial eye. One gets processed quite rapidly, but be sure that your currency declaration has been duly stamped by competent quarters inside the official area or else you'll find yourself let loose in the country without ever being allowed to buy money legally.

So many fly-palaces, so many dreamers who have to hit the jackpot, so many portraits of dictators dirtying the walls, so many panels carved from precious indigenous wood, so many impatient ministers with fat bellies and swollen rings and hangers-on with imitation club ties and empty briefcases, so many Indian and Lebanese trading posts, so many flocks of passengers apparently already in camp for days, who at fixed times unroll their prayer-mats to prostrate themselves in the direction of Mecca like angry geese stretching their necks close to the ground to hiss.

Monday, 11 February, Jan Smuts Airport, Johannesburg, South Africa ... Ever since I started coming to South Africa at shorter and sometimes longer intervals spanning many years, legally or clandestinely, alone or with Yolande holding my hand, under my own name or with a stolen one, barefaced or masked, there has been a flunkey with white shirt and shoulder-tabs who identifies me from afar. Over the years his head has become a silver dog. At the top of his voice he exclaims: 'Hello, old B! You back? How's things?' I shrivel with embarrassment. He's my home-grown Peter, he knows my sins, he keeps check. At this airport they always lie in wait for me, the grey security hounds, to pick up the spoor, or else to nab me on the way out.

This time around I pass the time of day with the flunkey while I wait for my wife's papers to be stamped. I notice the strategically posted Greys who have already turned me inside out with their pebble eyes. Flunkey wants to know if it is a long visit, this one. No, well, not quite for a dance but for longer than a mere song. And my impressions of this New Sarth Efrica? No, well, encouragingly improved, still somewhat mixed up, we shall see what we shall see. Yes, he confirms gravely, no really, ah yes, enjoy it then, y'hear?

Ukwezi Star, our faithful friend of many years, is there to fetch us. Her face is a happy torch. She has changed so little; her hair makes a half-hearted attempt at being grey, she wears sandals and her feet are brown. We are still white and slug-like from the European winter. Yolande's cheeks blossom with joyful excitement.

In front of us, walking their luggage to the parking area, are groups of men visibly and nonchalantly at home; I hear German and Portuguese and English being spoken. What right have these 'foreign intruders' to strut so arrogantly, as if this country belonged to them, even if they have been living off the fat of the land for years? But then, since when is this 'my' country? Who am I? I and my kind, those who look and speak like me? And the blacks? Of course the country is theirs, that's what the struggle has been all about and am I not black too? Yes, but actually the land belongs only to those who are locked in a battle for life and death. Can there be degrees of nativeness? Black and Boer and brown, OK. Indian? Come now, do I really see them as fully South African? And the Anglo-whites? Wait a minute there, don't ask all these uncomfortable questions. The other white immigrants then – Greek, Dutch, Polish, Italian, German, Portuguese? How long before they can qualify as African? And the black immigrants from Mozambique and Botswana and ever further north? Should they have a better claim than the pale Europeans?

On a previous occasion I changed planes here on my way to Cape Town and found myself in the air wedged between a bearded Jew with *kippah* unknotting a Hebrew text on my left and on my right a youthful Chinese with a book of inverted insects in his lap. In the arrivals hall at Cape Town I saw a traditionally dressed Pakistani family with glistening brown mussels for eyes. Isn't it 'their' country also? And I, after all, bent past fifty, with but half of those years spent here? Am I the stranger, with nothing to do and nothing expected of me? Is this a No Man's Land? Everybody's Land? Reason understands and accepts, the heart is clearly much more narrow-minded. My country, 'tis of Thee . . .

Ukwezi Star and Yolande have a lot to say to one another. Over the years they have grown ever closer. It was in her Johannesburg flat that we spent the last night before leaving upon my release from prison; the moon had a brackish taste. How is it with her Bushveld farm? There was a burglary, she relates. She is quite upset because a relationship of mutual trust with the workers now lies shattered. The elephant tusks collected by her late father were thieved. Also a firearm. It was quickly established that a son of one of the oldest inhabitant families was the one who had done the deed together with an accomplice, and to think he'd been hand-fed in the house. The police caught them and locked them up, but they escaped from custody. One was shot dead, the other is still running. Now there's blood in the farmyard.

We go along the speedway towards Johannesburg, then round to the right to Randburg where we are to lodge with Van Zyl 'Freddy' Slabbert and Jane. The estate where they live is an oasis of quietness on the verge of the metropolis. We drive up through the gates and stop under lofty trees. Jane is there to welcome us. Slabbert is still at work. It's time for a stiff drink.

3

BEGINNING

Meadowbrook Farm belongs to Dick Enthoven. Years ago he and his family left the country, returning only for residual business; it is awkward to survive honourably in an environment of naked exploitation, and on top of that boycotts and sanctions and uncertainties. He put house and belongings and staff at the disposal of his old friend Slabbert so that the latter could exercise his politics from that base. (At one time the two were together in Parliament when there were still white pipedreams of decency in the land.)

The house is comfortable, spacious. There are fresh tropical fruits for breakfast, bottles of alcohol in the cabinet, a television set for the news, paintings (including French Impressionists) on the walls, telephones which ring incessantly, kindling in the fireplace in case the evenings should get cold. The grounds are landscaped in green lawns bordered by flowerbeds and indigenous shrubs. Big trees were planted to cast shade, birds with opera-trained voices flicker in the foliage, a dog scurries from trunk to trunk to bark at the turtle doves, the laughing doves, the red-chested cuckoos, the black cuckoos, Klaas's cuckoos, the red-faced mousebirds, the black-eyed bulbuls, the willow warblers, the red-backed shrikes. At morning and at night beaked hadeda ibises traverse the sky above the house and shriek their diabolical laughter. Roses climb up the arbors. There's a swimming pool like a flowing mirror. Screened off behind some trees is the cottage where Jennifer, Slabbert's blonde Girl Friday, works night and day. Chisi and Timothy are in charge of the kitchen, the fireplaces, the tables, the bowls of nuts, the bedrooms. Chisi also doubles as driver. Under a lean-to and in the be-ribboned shelter of the willow tree by the driveway five cars are parked. Lizzie takes care of the washing and ironing. Three or four further employees move from task to task: someone is washing the chariots, Josiah the gardener is on his haunches planting flower bulbs. The sun shines.

We have been guests here on a previous visit. Early in the morning, before it got too hot, I would go running with Slabbert. Beyond the ring-wall around the estate is a bluegum plantation and Slabbert could point out where squatters had dug in. Shreds of plastic like flags on a conquered battlefield indicate the dwellings hollowed into the soil or burrowed under culverts and in drains. Nobody knows how many they are. With the Highveld thunderstorms some must get washed away. Sometimes one sees a fellow emerging from the bush to stride off to work. He or she won't greet you. Locally it is apparently considered a weakness to be the first to salute – it may even be insulting. Only a headman greets his subjects first.

All over South Africa, from north to south, masses of people are on the move, raising shacks as close as possible to the cities. They are looking for food or work or a little something to steal or some medicine for death. We are becoming more nomadic. The history of this country is a pattern of shifts and displacements, a raw war between settlers and disinherited. In copses and in hedges, in backyards or on vacant plots people hide like moles in the earth or like hares behind leafy curtains. Whenever there's the chance they will overnight strip an unguarded house down to the foundations and carry it off brick by sheet of corrugated iron by doorpost by frame. On smallholdings the Boere are using firearms as if they're chasing weaver birds from the fruit trees. Recently Jennifer's cottage was burgled and everything was swiped. The whites live in a state of siege, burglar-proof systems are installed, walls are built higher and topped by broken glass or spikes, private security firms patrol the neighbourhoods. Slabbert tells of people streaming blood from knife and bottle wounds knocking for help after a Saturday night's tiff. Last time we were here we woke one morning to find all the cars with smashed windows and the radios gone. Chisi clicks a bitter tongue against the roof of his mouth and says it's all Mandela's fault. What is one to do? Where do you start? How do you reconcile liberal instincts with the preservation of property? It doesn't help sending for the police: they reproach Enthoven for not wanting to act more forcefully, reluctant as he is to deliver the 'illegals' on his property.

Some violence gets exposed in the country's newspapers, as blood seeping through bandages. Not that the moral authorities, the church leaders and the journalists – politicians know nothing about morals – could until recently be bothered about the massive bloodshed. The 'hard politics' of inhuman laws and repression, the pragmatism needed to live on this continent, made everybody insensitive to the worth of human life, or simply to suffering.

The ANC cannot admit that some of its militants are involved in intimidation and murder, even if only in retaliation to attacks upon the organization, or that they helped bring about the present climate through the policy of 'making the townships ungovernable' and the mythical expectations of 'armed struggle'. Now they don't have the means to protect their own supporters. A stone was thrown into the bush but we didn't really see our way open to an uprising.

By a planned, induced and white-coordinated campaign of terror, the Inkatha Freedom Party is claiming a blood-besmirched chair in the first row around the table of national negotiations. Government rubs its hands at the spectacle of 'tribal wars' which it prophesied, and of blacks who, if they ever come to power, will lead the nation to the knacker's yard. (During our stay Christiaan Barnard, the ex-surgeon, will threaten to emigrate and become a Swiss national, oh woe to us! The spreading mayhem is too disquieting for the future of his children, he declares. Since he moaned to the papers President De Klerk must grant him an audience; after a long chat Barnard will emerge to rub his hands: no, the President calmed his anxieties, the violence is not aimed at 'us', it's only tribal warfare. In the meantime the Swiss authorities will let it be known that it is impossible to obtain their citizenship just like that – 'Please rather stay home as long as you can send us your money.')

Government is hand in glove with Inkatha. How else? Isn't my enemy's enemy the spear-carrier who can do the dirty stabbing for me? Top echelons in the State clearly decided: if we have to be brought down we shall topple the pillars of Babylon with us. Dogmatists and theorists and robbers, niched within the shadowy reaches of occult structures and operations and secret funds,

continue their corrupt machinations and incitement to murder –
even though there's no longer an ideology to underpin the policy –
for the sake of 'survival', like mad dogs who go on biting even
without orders to do so.

At a gathering in Johannesburg a little more than a year ago – was
it the Five Freedoms Forum? – I ran into a seasoned Pharisee, the
Reverend J. A. Heyns. He hailed me with one of those obscure
hand-grips intended as a mutual form of recognition among the
chosen ones, and said: 'Welcome back. The doors have been
opened! Now there's a future for everybody. Of course we still have
a little violence on our hands, but that's just . . . birth pains.' This at
a time when every week took its toll of a hundred or more people
killed. New Jerusalem!

All of the above I knew before coming here. These deductions
one does not read in the newspapers. One can't just go into the
streets and shout such things. It would be malevolent speculation,
politically misguided. On whose side am I anyway?

In the papers I read the story of a gang of boys who on Christmas
Day broke through the ceiling of a girls' hostel in Soweto to rape
them. In the papers one sometimes sees as a strip the photos showing how individuals depart this vale of tears – beaten, stoned,
stabbed with sharp objects. The rapid movements of the hunters,
a certain gracefulness even, as if performing a ballet with mortal
steps. A kinetic fate as flames squirt from the backs of writhing
victims, like the death-shout of a mythical dragon. Already the
hands are stumpy claws once again, like those of a foetus. Later a
foot protrudes from under a negligent blanket. A dead lies down as
if he (or she) were exhausted. But nestled close to the earth to
coddle agony.

South Africa is the photographer's paradise: undefiled desert
landscapes, cloud-towers of fancy in the electric heavens, rubbish
dumps where women and children scratch for sustenance; the
sombre shifting shapes of galloping buffalo, an *impi* (group of warriors) surging over a crimson horizon, soldiers with soot-daubed
faces somewhere in the bush along the border; a wild buck when
the fatal bullet snaps his breath in the heart of an elegant jump, an
athlete breaking the ribbon, a man in full flight pinned down by an
assegai, white joggers with pink fat-rolls shuffling along to burn off

the excess, hungry blacks trotting to work; faces living incestuously with cream and eye-liner, the toothless mouth and the small hate-eyes of the civil servant, the crumpled faces of poverty, the black glasses and the thin snarl-moustache of the security dog, faces from the mirror and faces from the bottle, the thick snout of the power merchant, the self-satisfied countenance of the liberalist, the newspaper editor's visage dripping with good intentions, the all-knowing face of the returned political exile, the army officer's mask of death, the dead mug of the prisoner, the absent face of the migrant labourer, the upper lip and the inflamed neck veins of the suburban housewife, the ancient used-up face of the farmwife, the worried blind look of the writer.

The day after our arrival I have lunch with John Miles in town. Yolande is unpacking and looking for her feet. With time it has become customary – at least since President De Klerk's February speech of two years ago opened the portals to the country so that I too could come and steal honey more often – that I should break bread and pour wine with Jonna when in town. Not only is he a first-class writer, he is also friend and counsellor. Over the years his beard has taken on the silent colour of wisdom – it must be all the laughing and the smoking; his eyes however are ever more mischievous. Now he is thin. It is because he has finished his novel at last. This is the way a cow should be once the calf has been weaned.

During a previous visit I deposited in a local United Bank account the portion inherited from my father's estate. It wasn't much, my father was a poor man. Abroad South African money is not worth the paper it is printed on, it's a hassle to try exporting it, and I thought I might need something for a song and a dance during our sojourns in the country. But no, life is never this simple. On a subsequent trip, when I thought about using some in Cape Town, I was informed that my account had now been blocked: for any further transactions I was henceforth to fill in forms, turn my face in supplication to Head Office, wait for arbitration if not abso-lution. The bank manager in Cape Town explained this in detail with Dutch accent and teeth, then produced two of my books from a bottom drawer and requested me to sign them please, 'for the wife and the kids'. Back in Johannesburg I closed down the account and opened a new one with Jonna as co-signatory so that he could deposit my income during my absence. In Paris I received an uncouth letter from United Head Office informing me that my action had been cancelled: as a foreigner I had no right to open an account, nor to close an opened one, let alone give signatory rights to anybody else; they first want to know much more about me.

And so, after lunch, I ascend with Jonna John to the loftiest spheres of United – that is, after the two of us were frisked by armed guards on the ground floor, were let in through a bullet-proof portico, were each given a laissez-passer to pin to the chest. The executive dame on the next-to-last floor withholds the small mercy of a smile. Please surrender yourself completely to the following questionnaire. Your status? Well now, what am I in reality? A 'returnee'? In that case, if you have been away at the fleshpots for longer than twelve years you will be entitled to repatriate a given sum (plus your furniture) as financial Rands, which is to say at a more advantageous rate of exchange. Your last fixed abode in South Africa? I write 'prison'. No, rather make that 'lodged by the State'. Your assets at the time? Nil. Your assets at present? She explains that if I were to 'normalize' my situation the State would oblige me to liquidate whatever I have accumulated and now possess abroad to repatriate same. The origin of your local money? Father's estate. His name? Write down, Johannes Stephanus Breytenbach. Why did he die? Good question, ms. Do you perhaps know the answer? She promises that all information will be passed on to the Reserve Bank and within days I am to be informed about the decision. Seems like Jonna is going to have to continue paying for the lunches.

In the evening we have dinner with the Slabberts. Yolande is wearing a buttercup dress; she has already renewed her friendship with the flowers outside. It is a going-away meal for Slabbert's daughter, Nathalie, and for André Sow. They will be leaving for the island of Gorée, off Senegal, in the morning to open there an office for the Institute for Democracy in Africa. Over the years many of our initiatives germinated on that island in the bay of Dakar.

I first met Van Zyl Slabbert when he came to visit me in prison. At the time he was Leader of the Opposition in Parliament. Yolande had enlisted his help in trying to have me released. (Right near the end of my stretch the Minister of Justice and Prisons, Kobie Coetsee, still suggested to Slabbert that I could have my freedom if he would prevail upon Yolande [Vietnamese by birth, thus 'non-white' according to South African race classifications, and probably considered a 'born communist'] and myself to divorce – a manoeuvre which Slabbert rejected with spluttered contempt.) I emerged, left and shook the dust of Babylon from my shoes, and when I next saw Slabbert it was in Paris and he was thinking of quitting the dead-end chamber of 'Whites Only' Parliament. He did so, we became friends, we started dreaming together.

I helped in having Slabbert invited to Senegal. This place in West Africa was where the healing of the rift between white and black South Africans must start. We knew we were tendering for trouble. Any meeting between 'passport holders' (South Africans from inside) and the 'terrorist' ANC would be considered treason. I was involved in Paris with Daniëlle Mitterrand's France-Libertés Foundation; with her help I could smooth the way with Senegal's President Abdou Diouf for such a meeting to be held in Dakar – there was after all also a taboo in Africa on allowing in the white devils from the south.

Slabbert, together with his fellow ex-parliamentarian Alex Boraine, started organizing the meeting from inside. It all had to be kept confidential. We were coming home to Africa. We were putting in motion a process that would decisively alter the history of confrontation between black and white . . . One of the unforeseen results was that Slabbert (and to a lesser extent Alex) fell victim to the success of the enterprise. Once the ball was set rolling the intermediaries and facilitators became sidelined. In later years I often teased him about this, encouraging him to strike out and establish a new political base. Maybe my nagging was getting on his nerves . . .

The first time the ferry took me to Gorée it was filled to the gunwales with people. Stepping ashore on the island a young man tottered up. 'You are Monsieur B, right?' he insisted. When I admitted to there perhaps being some peripheral truth in the assumption, he triumphantly turned to a companion: 'What did I tell you?' With me there were Benoit Ngom, Sahli Feti, Charles

Longname and other members of the Association de Juristes Afri-
cains (AJA). A white lady with straight grey hair and a voluminous
African garment, a magistrate by trade, waited for us at the landing
place, the quai des Boucaniers. Firmly they fobbed off the nuisance.

Gorée, Devil's Island, Zanzibar, Cape Verde, Poulo Condor,
Robben Island, Alcatraz . . . Low-water marks of human conduct,
terrible warts on the history committed by some upon others. Gorée
was perhaps the most important black market and shipping point for
slave trade on the west coast. During centuries the silent genocide
grew into an undisclosed holocaust. How many went into damnation, torn away from family and soil – six, eight million? Dark
ages of brutalization which have never been adequately explained.
The place bears the name of an island in Holland – a distortion of
goede ree, good anchorage. The Dutch were practical people.

We walked to the slave house. The inebriated youth tagged
along, staggering. 'Psst! Psst! Monsieur B!' he tried to catch my
attention, but again he was chased away. The buildings date from
Portuguese colonial times, painted in pastel colours now flaking.
Behind street doors one sensed overgrown courtyards. Baobabs and
palm trees and fig trees grew all over the place, bougainvillea and
flamboyants made splashes of colour. Joseph Ndaye, ex-sergeant in
the French colonial forces, with a face like a relic carved from
ebony, is the curator and the guide of this terrible place of pilgrimage which he keeps up all by himself.

Giving on to the walled court were the low-ceilinged cells,
smaller than animal stables. A hundred and fifty men, women and
children, chained and with heavy iron balls around neck and ankles,
were stuffed in there, sometimes to languish for six months before
being sold and shipped. Then there were two cages with furrows in
the soil for sanitary purposes, where women were separated in
groups of above and below sixteen years. The young girls, worth
more than their mothers, had only one chance of not being
swallowed by the ocean: to get heavy with child by one of the
dealers or buyers. Under the staircase there was a 'dark hole' where
recalcitrant captives were brought to their senses by being deprived
of water and food. In one angle of the courtyard was the weighing
room with scales and measuring sticks. Sixty kilograms minimum;
less than that and the produce lost its merchant value.

A double staircase swept from the yard to the merchants' quarters bordered by a veranda from where prospective buyers could evaluate the harvest with expert eyes. Henchmen in the area below had to verify the quality of the articles: upper arms were tested and lips prised apart to inspect the teeth; much sought-after 'studs' or 'breeders' could be judged by the breadth of the chest and the weight of the testicles; women were pinched to test the firmness of breasts and the generosity of hips. Man, wife and children of the same family were sent off to different destinations as a matter of policy.

Upstairs were the rooms of the dealers with hairy faces and pig-thoughts; these had wooden floors and windows and one assumes that the cotillion was sometimes stomped with heavy boots so that the floorplanks creaked above the heads of the multitude packed into the underworld.

Finally, in the wall directly opposite the heavy portal gates, the Alley of No Return. Through this corridor the bartered ones left Africa. A door at the end opened directly above the sea where the ships waited. Waves tipped over the basalt rocks. Guards were posted on either side to prod along the timorous travellers and to shoot those who saw fit to jump into the water with their heavy weights. 'There used to be a lot of sharks around here,' Joseph Ndaye says. 'They knew, and usually the corpses of those who succumbed in captivity were also thrown out.' Ships were overloaded. Merchants calculated that up to 40 per cent of the cargo might go bad during the crossing and they compensated accordingly by cramming ever more people below deck.

The door was open that day, a square of blinding light with the two blue fields of ocean and sky beyond. A wind often paints a grey mask on the sea's face. To come up after months in a dark cave and to see the free heavens – how the eyes must have hurt!

Walls can retain the stench of death agony. Raids would have been carried out deep in the interior; the coast served as catchment area. The buyers were Europeans and Arabs, the sellers alas only too often black chiefs. Many slaves were in fact prisoners-of-war captured during tribal wars. People were exchanged for mirrors, cloth and safety-pins. The go-betweens received gunpowder, weapons and liquor from the wholesalers.

Many island-dwellers are descendants of emancipated slaves, those who had children by the merchants. One can understand how this gave rise to a matriarchal society. Some of these ill-fated ladies, known as *Signares*, later became slave-owners themselves. Joseph Ndaye reminded us of the example of Joséphine, Napoleon Bonaparte's first spouse, a Creole of Caribbean origin, herself a mulatto. It was she who badgered her consort to re-introduce slavery for the sake of the economy when some misguided revolutionaries managed to have the practice outlawed. She had the reputation of dealing particularly harshly with her human chattel.

We walked around the bay to a restaurant named after a French knight who served as governor of the island, the Hostellerie du Chevalier des Bufflers. We sat outside under the pergola to feel the breeze of relief on our foreheads. Small children with snotty noses came to beg at our table, a young boy with a voice like a silver string played the *kora*, and the drunken supplicant of just now again tried to penetrate the circle. A fierce exchange of words flared up between him and my companions. He wanted nothing from them, he said, he only wished to lay a few words in my ear.

I went to talk to him. Tears trickled from underneath his dark glasses and left a wet web on his blue cheeks. Suddenly he removed a heavy yellow-copper bracelet from his wrist (the token of the slave?) and slipped it around mine: 'Now we are brothers.' (While I write these words the bracelet is still accompanying the skiff of pen and fist over the blackened ocean of paper.) His name, he said with hand over heart, is Ka'afir. Poet, student, world wanderer, stray dog, dealer in thises and thats with North America. Deeply saddened and offended and angered by the fate of the brothers and sisters in Azania. Little did I know that my life was to become entwined with that of this poet.

Flies came in choirs to harmonize over our food. Taken in tow by Ka'afir, we again entered the town, and now we proceeded to a slight promontory on the highest part of the island. Here among the ruins of what might once have been a fort, a group of young *Talibes* lived. They are known as *baye fall* and consider themselves the disciples of Cheik Ibra Fall, the bosom friend of Cheik Ahmadou Bamba, the founder of mouridism, an Islamic doctrine which took root in Senegal during the nineteenth century. Up there against the remains of a wall a slogan was painted in crooked letters: 'FREE NELSON MANDELA AND HIS WIFE WINNIE MANDELA'. A little further on: 'AFRICA MUST RAISE AN ARMY TO COMBAT APARTHEID'. We are poor and impotent, why then shall we not dream? Solemnly a few mute *baye fall* brought a bougainvillaea plant and a bucket of water. A hole was dug. Ka'afir stumbled around, blinded by tears, and inadvertently nearly filled up the hole again. Together, with hands clasped around the same roots, we planted the symbol, and swore an oath to do everything we could to get Mandela free before this little tree became big. We held one another close to the heart and then it was time to catch the ferry back to Dakar. Ka'afir wanted at all costs that we should return with him to his house for a drink. Benoit Ngom remarked ironically: 'In such a way every person sooner or later encounters his disciple.'

Here in foreign parts – because I am a foreigner at home – Gorée island becomes a fixed point of reference to help me from being washed away by new impressions. I ask André Sow to go and see if the bougainvillaea has grown much. Now that Mandela is free. In fact, the old man himself is due within a few days to travel to West Africa. During the meal there's a call from Dakar. Hamidou, a friend of Benoit Ngom, is ringing to ask if we can help prevent the coming of Nelson Mandela to Dakar. They want a month more to organize a great reception for him. In reality they are keen to put together a sort of Wembley concert, probably hoping to hit some jackpot.

I remember attending the big Wembley concert with Yolande. It was Easter 1990. A cold rain flew its soggy flags over the stadium but this in no way could quench the delirium of the thousands of dancing enthusiasts. Funny how few black people there were in the crowd. Part of the pavilion was cordoned off for guests, and there Neil Kinnock sat puffing at a pipe, trying to look as people as possible. Jesse Jackson was also present with shiny hair and shiny moustache and a camel's-hair coat and a nose for the television-lens like a fly for shit: each time the camera looked his way he was on his feet with clenched fist held high and a pious tear in the combative eye; when the camera swung away he was back to supercilious boredom.

There were opportunists and arse-talkers and boot-lickers and pop singers and banana politicos and exiles who'd grown white in these foreign climes. A reception room had been prepared for the guests to guzzle unperturbed. As befits such an occasion (or any other), most expatriate South Africans were already visibly moved. Donald Woods told me of how he had a special ANC tie made and delivered to Mandela (he wore a similar one), and will you believe it: the great man himself phoned to say thank you! 'When you join the ANC,' he jested half-seriously, 'I want to be just behind you in the queue to hang on to your shirttail – together it will be easier.'

The ANC courtiers tried to look important. Essop Pahad collected his 'guardians of the innermost truth' off to the side in a smaller hall to harangue them in strict confidence, perhaps about historical perspectives, the enemy is everywhere, or maybe only to bond the exclusiveness of the insiders, and Sam Ramsamy, filled to the brim with the importance of his task, stood to attention in the elected circle. And then Mandela entered and strode through the hangers-on like a tree-trunk being carried along by a flood. He rose head and shoulders above everybody else, his face beaming, his fist like a shield in the air.

Later Father Trevor Huddleston in his purple cassock appeared far below us on a stage, small like a figure from a Punch and Judy show: some John the Baptist bent double from sucking locusts, ready now to announce the coming of the Lord – or was he the Pilate who had to hand Him over to the mob? And if he were to cry: 'Who should I deliver unto you, De Klerk or Mandela?' – what would the rabble's answer have been? But no, he was there to welcome a crony as old as he.

All at once the white-haired Easter lamb appeared in the spotlight. The myriad-tongued crowd rose as one man, for five six seven eight minutes we cheered and chanted his name rhythmically. People lifted their children high to catch a sight of the man. Old exiles and total strangers wept on each other's shoulders. I had difficulty swallowing my tears. Yolande held my hand very tightly. Then, after a long moment, he started reading his stilted and hackneyed gospel while the icy wind fluttered the sheets of paper in his hand. It was as if he was clutching a dove.

André Sow promises he will throw the asked-for spanner in the works relating to the planned Mandela visit. I am of an opinion that they're going to come undone – the ANC leaders are untrustworthy, one has to break one's back to get them to be anywhere more or less on time, all the world wants to carve their pound of flesh from Mandela – it would have been preferable to take what you can get.

After supper Pierre Cronjé arrives with an MK commander, Mzi M. (Umkhonto we Sizwe [MK] is the ANC's military wing.) I am glad to see Pierre – this Philistine rocker with the Senegalese copper bracelet around the wrist is one of the most unassuming South African strugglers I have the pleasure of knowing. Mzi K has the powerful build of a panther, he talks softly and carefully, he got his degree on Robben Island. They speak of a shooting in Natal, several people dead, mostly Inkatha. 'But it's all your fault,' Slabbert accuses. 'No,' Pierre denies, 'it was an ambush prepared by Inkatha and then some of their shooters got separated from the others. The bus left them behind – that's when the victims chased the assassins into the bush and finished them off.' It is clear that Pierre has moved much closer to the ANC in the years since I first met him in Dakar with the home delegation. Mzi K listens softly, taking care not to let a glimmer of his feelings shine through.

The two visitors and Slabbert and Sow retire to Enthoven's study to plot quietly; Nathalie angrily flounces off into the night because she feels excluded from Dad's 'men's business'; on my way to bed I make sure nothing of the good South African wine is left unattended to go sour.

4

MOUNTAIN

Early in the morning Slabbert and I leave for the airport in his white Mercedes. He has two Graces – this white one and a bigger whale in blue which the bosses of Mercedes-Benz foisted upon him after he facilitated an end to a strike in their East London plant which came to within an inch of closing down Mercedes-Benz in South Africa. (Workers in the same factory had given Mandela a red one as a liberation present.) Slabbert, with his heart as roomy as a Mercedes, has offered us the white Grace for our intended trip through the country.

We are booked on the morning flight to Cape Town. As trustees of *Die Suid-Afrikaan*, a political magazine, we are to attend a meeting in the mother city. Slabbert is also a director of the Institute for a Democratic Alternative for South Africa (IDASA).

That I and Yolande should be in the country at all is thanks to Alex Boraine and Freddy Slabbert, the Institute's two godfathers, and their efforts to help me come in from the cold and break free from the vicious circle of a decaying conscience. IDASA adopted our visit as a 'project' for which they canvassed financial assistance. In return I promised to stop off at their regional offices and several universities to exchange sanguine thoughts with people with sombre brows.

The Cape and its surroundings seem grey after the lush greens of the Transvaal Highveld; I've forgotten that the Colony with its winter rainfall will be brown in summer. A fire in the brushwood and the pine trees a few days ago has once more laid waste a large panel of Table Mountain. This too I have forgotten: that people here live cheek by jowl with crackling vegetation and sputtering mountain slopes, the deeper fire of gnawing droughts, winds like the huge fiery breath of passed-away generations, thunderstorms as white papers against a slate-coloured sky. At D. F. Malan Airport we pick up a rented car. What will the future names of all these airports be? At present the albino elephants are all named after white premiers.

First stop – IDASA's head office in Rosebank. Alex is as elated as a defrocked parson to see us. We have been chums for a long time. I embrace his ribs – higher I cannot reach: he's a blond giant with a twinkling nose, the prototype of all sun-and-salt-tanned beach bums. I meet Paddy Clark, his right hand, and the five or six left hands who keep the offices humming.

There are framed cartoons on the walls, from the time newspapers shat so liberally over the 'Dakarites'. Some participants were victimized upon their return to the country. In East London the Greys murdered an IDASA representative: he was thrust with a sharp object under the wing right into the heart, *chouf*, then manacled with hands behind the back and left sitting with bowed head in his car; another, who used to be a trade-union leader, was tied up in a police station and, under personal supervision of a warrant-Boer, swung from a stick passed behind the knees in the 'helicopter' ritual, all the while being walloped so brutally that parts of his body could later only be described as 'raw liver'; his sisters, detained also, got away with electrodes attached to vagina and nipples; a young pastor from Pretoria found his wife and school-aged children discriminated against, was himself savaged in Parliament by PW 'Crocodile' Botha, the then State President; another participant was promptly disinherited by her parents; others lost jobs and commissions. And today, a mere three years on, it is admitted that Dakar helped unblock the road to national reconciliation . . .

A quick cup of coffee and into town. The aestival South-easter is bowling through the city streets, blowing away all cobwebs but all reflections as well, delineating images, flattening noses, waltzing grey-bearded ladies, changing the sex of dogs.

Franklin Sonn is the chairperson of the council of trustees of *Die Suid-Afrikaan*; he has his offices on the highest floor of Mobil House. After a while I notice only brown people working there, and it is a fine idea, it means at least that Franklin is trying to provide his 'own people' with job opportunities. It is after all the same *helpmekaar* (help one another) methods that allowed the white Afrikaners during the 1930s and the 1940s to liberate themselves from British blood-sucking. Trevor Manuel of the broad shoulders and the blue eyes comes to grip me in his arms; ever since the ANC has been legalized, with Trevor playing a key role in the Western Cape apparatus, it has become difficult to remember the fire-eating and flame-spitting activist behind the shirt and tie.

The chairman is still occupied by his calls and callers. Chris Louw and André du Toit enter, both of them meek and lowly in heart and modestly attired. André has a forehead like a library full of philosophy manuals; now and then his hand runs over this dome, doing research. We shall have to constitute a quorum; the other ladies and gentlemen trustees are out of town. When Franklin walks in at last it is to say with glee: 'No, look you people, now they must rather bring back apartheid, things are really getting too screwed up.' He's had a heavy morning.

Chris – he's the man who conceptualizes the magazine, who writes most of the copy, who goes hunting for advertisers, who does the page-setting, who then sells the product – informs us that we are bankrupt, as ever, and that we risk becoming even more bankrupt soon. We solemnly take note. The question arises, what would *Die Suid-Afrikaan*'s calling be in this new dispensation? Who is the public? Why would people want to buy it? From a given point of view, the magazine's task has been completed. A mouthful of decency is no longer subversive, the Establishment don't shudder any more when they see the contents, what we write can now be found in all kinds of publications, people wipe their hindquarters on it, we only do it more tediously. Silence.

Beyond the glass wall the mountain rears grey from the heat, over the top crest the white flow of wind-words spills. Franklin says perhaps we ought to think about being more De Klerk-friendly. De Klerk also has his troubles. One must listen carefully when Franklin Sonn speaks – he knows on the fingers of his two hands the cadences of Cape society. Silence.

Then too there are problems. André delivers a meticulous report concerning a scabrous feud between factions of the staff, about who should control subsidies intended for the training of rural journalists; the Swiss sponsors may pull out unless the discord is resolved. Franklin knows more about the matter than he's willing to let on – not for nothing is he the Principal of the Peninsula Technikon and boss of the Cape Teachers' Professional Association. Cape politics are Byzantine and all the main actors know one another in this parochial community.

We are still caught in an epoch where people try to outbid each other with populist posturing, where credibility is established by one's connections to the civics and people's organizations – *de people de people, whaddabout de people*? André is clearly of the opinion that a genuine and logical argument ought to be binding on all parties. Through his opaque glasses of honesty he doesn't even discern the sharks devouring the whales. Franklin says, look here, all decisions must be taken democratically. You must throw them with democracy. Take my campus now. Take the unreasonable demands that the African (meaning 'black') students are trying to push forward. I insist that we should have a vote, but with everyone taking part, the gardeners included. And if the vote goes against you? Slabbert asks. Then we vote again, Franklin retorts. Anyway, real democracy is knowing when the time is ripe to let people vote, not so? I, for my part, am wondering whether this is a pre-revolutionary or a post-revolutionary phenomenon.

The meeting is adjourned because Slabbert claims to have an urgent business appointment. We drop our travel bags at his house in Newlands, then I drive him to the cricket field where a provincial game is being played.

The last time we were in Cape Town, Yolande and I stayed behind this mountain. Each visit is an initiation, a searching for the oracle. We long for the trance of burning laurel leaves, the purification of the subterranean weep-hole so that we may figure out the riddles. The only prayer-beads we have are a string of names and they too are fading, the topography of an experience going back so far that perhaps it never existed. The syllables have weathered to a smooth sheen from being told through the fingers: Riviersonderend, Bredasdorp, Swellendam, Stormsvlei, Halfaampieskraal, Buffeljagsrivier, Leeurivier, Voorhuis, Karringmelk, Soetmelkrivier, Reisiesbaan, Dekriet, Suurbraak. Listen, there's a story buried behind each and every one of them. Whose? My forebears with the deep eyes of injured baboons and the cumbersome hands and the dark chintz dresses? My other ancestors in their borrowed clothes and the ostrich feathers in their hats? Those who had the memory of rocking ships in their gait? Those who roamed for centuries behind flocks of beasts, from oblivion to an inaccessible skyline?

Here, in that fold of the mountain, we stopped over in Alex and Jenny Boraine's beach house – Witsandbaai, Perdekloof. In the morning I went for a run. The mistiness hadn't cleared up yet, the mountain was a carillon of pure notes. Bush-tick berry, heather, pincushion (*Massonia candida*), sugar bush, waggon tree (*Protea grandiflora*), monkey apple (*Royena pubescens*). Now and then there was the hollering of squatters deeper in the bush. Birds jotted down their errors with nozzled sounds. I took into my mouth the well-known and unused words, like pebbles to suck against a stitch in the side, with the bitter taste of ex-votos: *snoek, volstruisnek, mebos, murasie, parskuip* (baracouta, ostrich-neck, dried and sugared apricots, dilapidated walls, wine-press . . .) Downhill I ran singing at the top of my lungs: 'A-fri-ca, A-fri-ca, I am thi-hine, thou art mi-hine, A-fri-cot, A-free-qua . . .'

Now it is the morning of 13 February. Together with Slabbert I go walking on the mountain above Rondebosch. The first students are already jogging with concentrated miens along the border between the pine forest and De Waal Drive. South Africans rise early: by 6.30 a.m. streams of cars and small buses leave the suburbs for the inner sanctum. But they also go to bed early. The sun drops like a coffee-bag into the kettle and soon night is stained black. Here you do not have long evenings like in Europe. Now the morning sun flashes and flirts in the windows of vehicles flowing in canals from south and east. Heliographic signals spear the morning haze. Store-fronts are rolled up with a rattling noise, people are on their way to the office, children with scrubbed faces are driven to school, sandwiches are in the lunch-boxes.

In other African countries the dream may be more alluring, but what is the condition of the roads? What will you find on the shelves? Do the telephones work? (Between brackets I ought to add that I am smitten with white-sight here against the mountain flank, with blindness: along the edges of the well-to-do estates a disorderly metropolis of poverty is gnawing its way through – with its own internal structures – and there the communal taxis, the Zola Budds [Toyotas] and the Mary Deckers [Nissans] would have been stacked full while it was still night with tattered people living more than an hour away from their workplaces. If they have jobs, that is. If their huts weren't burnt down last night. If they haven't been done in by knife or pickaxe handle.)

Wind takes the words from our mouths, trees shake from tip to toe as if taking part in some demonstration. Slabbert sweeps a hand comprehensively over the vista at our feet, the gardens and the parks and the shopping centres, the rivers of flickering metal: 'All of this will be yours, and much more, if you are willing to worship me,' he says ironically. We have to laugh.

A little further we meet an early hiker coming from the opposite direction. He wants to know if there's a path that will take him up as far as the old blockhouse. He says he doesn't know this wing of the mountain. It seems more likely that he's looking for company. He's young, his beard is unfinished, he's carrying a thick book – a Bible or a considerable novel. He describes how he scales these heights from time to time to exchange some thoughts with God up there (he points an arm). One hears so much more when one is alone. It is only in the Cape that you still find people spaced-out enough to take a morning off work to spend by the sea or along a mountain track. We warn him that it may be dangerous, clouds descend rather suddenly, stones slip away under your feet, one becomes a blethering sheep, each year a saint or two freeze to death up there in the seething fog or plunge into the void leaving just a howl like a streamer in the air. Why, the only things left of Van Hunks, the retired pirate, and his visitor the devil, when they sat on the mountain top trying to out-smoke each other, were a burned-out pipe, a pair of horns and the recurrent cloud.

I remember one of Peter Blum's most beautiful poems had this theme: a man loses his way in the labyrinth of Table Mountain's cloth, his life hangs by a thread, then when he has lost himself as well he hears the clanging of bells and below his feet a wonderfully peaceful but unknown township fans open.

The young Blum arrived here from the haziness of Central Europe as a German-speaking Austrian (Jew?) who'd grown up in Trieste. He learned English at school in the Free State but because the tongue stuck in his craw he went to Stellenbosch University to study agriculture. Within a few years he was to re-invent Afrikaans poetry with two slim volumes of biting verse, and just as mysteriously he disappeared, taking with him his sharp eyes and his red moustache, his glasses and his paunch. He and his Afrikaner wife left for England. Some gossip-mongers would have it that he left for a madhouse. One picks up death in this country. His crooked publisher tried to rob him of his work ('because he must be of unsound mind to refuse to have his books reprinted').

At nine o'clock we have an appointment at the Holiday Inn in Woodstock with IDASA's top management, who are to meet Sweden's International Development Agency. The council is nearly at full strength: Elizabeth Mokotong, a social worker; Reverend de Villiers Soga with a serious waistcoat; Peter Vale, who is fond of shadows; Canon Mcebisi Xundu of the expressionless pock-marked pallid face; Nthato Motlana, Mandela's house doctor, with the deft hands of a pianist, white teeth, lively eyes, a laugh like a bodyguard; and Beyers Naudé. Oom ('Uncle') Bey – without his permission I've adopted him as pater – must be the closest to a white saint we shall ever have in this country. In one lifetime he struggled from the privileged position of Broederbond-preacher (he was named after Christiaan Beyers, a Boer general and Rebellion leader, and his father was a founding member of the Broederbond) through all the declensions of 'traitor to the *volk*' and all the articulations of resistance against the Beast, until he became the living conscience of the 'people', a man who could string together a vertical prayer but who would not hesitate to fight the Boere with their own underhand methods. The price he paid for many years was State-imposed loneliness.

The leader of the Swedish delegation, Karl Tham, is a young humanitarian cadre with a high-pitched blond accent and a no-nonsense jaw. Per Wastberg, number two, is alarmed to find me here, his quiff standing on end like that of Kierkegaard and his face heavy with meditations; for the first time since decades back when he was forbidden entry he has again been able to obtain a visa. Slightly more than a month ago Yolande and I visited him and his wife Anita in their Stockholm home; it was night, through the windows of their flat high up against a hill snowflakes could be seen to flutter – 'It is the doves in heaven shucking their shadows,' Per said. The third member of the team has the golden fleece as beard, the cigarette and the files; he knows his story.

Alex Boraine touches his nose with circumspection, bats his light lashes and delivers a layman's sermon. Slabbert sketches a synopsis of the political players' options in this crush-pen of transition. Nthato Motlana tells of the catastrophic decay of black community mores – parents have lost all influence with their offspring, young boys chase teachers away from school and take over, 'but don't let our fathers know or else they'll beat us.' Questions are asked and answers are cogitated. Per Wastberg takes notes, perhaps in view of a poem. Karl Tham asks what can be done about senior military commanders who may be holding up progress. (He has had experience of comparable Latin American situations.) I offer the suggestion that the Swedes may be of some help in this matter by making old-people's homes in their country available to the generals; in my mind's eye I already see them tending the reindeer. (But something tells me they won't easily be seeking my assistance in any further discussions of such momentous issues!)

When we break for tea Oom Bey informs me about his anxious second thoughts. The exiles are quite simply not up to the job, and it is difficult to get through to Madiba (Mandela's tribal name) himself with proposals; 'there's finally a line which the white man cannot cross,' and the old men clinging to power, that's another headache: one can understand it, after a lifetime in the struggle – jail, banishment – what are they to live from if they retire now, no provision has been made for the future. I propose that they can perhaps go to live with the generals in Swedish old people's homes – just think of the tales of subterfuge they will tell one another and all the meat and mealie-pap they can share. Motlana laughs.

Lunch at the French ambassador's residence together with the council, so that Joëlle Bourgois, the recently appointed envoy, may from the very beginning of her term be in contact with some of the better souls in this region of damnation. Palm trees and fancy shrubs outside, mountain looming close in the background, by each plate on the table a name. The important thing is to recognize your own. Gibson, a waiter who's been working here for years, brings his mouth to my ear when he offers the meat dish and asks: 'How is madame?' I put him at ease: all is well with Yolande, she's more at home in South Africa than I am. He knows her from all those years when she came to visit the country while I was still hiding in prison. Alex offers to have the ambassadorial couple escorted on a tour of the townships – they should be exposed to more pressing realities. Life is not just wine and sun. Foreigners will meet these courteous and convivial South Africans and perhaps not surmise the decades of surviving with clenched teeth veiled now by smiles and eye-winks. (Not that there's anything amiss with the French wines.)

The wind makes bigvoice in the treetops; it is as if I were buried under sea-sounds. I dream I'm back in the country, in my home town, in the house where I lived so long ago. I lock myself in a white room, I don't trust the peace. I cut an opening in the door, with a shutter that I can close from within. This is where they can pass me my food from outside. But dangers lurk, one can never be too careful. I start all over and open a smaller square in the wood. What if the enemy were to enter? Would I recognize the name? I must reduce the risk. At last I'm down to a small aperture right at the lower portion of the door, practically level with the threshold, too tight for even a cat or a crayfish to wriggle through, and this I block off with a hatch. I go on my knees, swinging low like a chameleon. I put my ear to the hole to hear if there be life still outside.

5

NORTHWARDS

Early in the morning Slabbert and I leave for the airport. Although the shrubs already flower their shadows, most people are still indoors. In hot countries one learns how to farm with shade. Wind is going to run up its flags again today. We stop off briefly at André du Toit and his wife Maretha's place. The tin roof is painted red, the green garden shows luxuriant and fat type pages, the rooms must house many whispering books. André emerges barefooted in striped pyjamas; he wants to give me a book. It is a thick anthology of essays on violence in the country – its history, the structures, the devouring nature, the implications, the reactions, the desperate analyses. As an afterthought he has inserted the few typed pages of a study prepared by an ex-student of his who now resides somewhere in a border district of the Eastern Cape – you absolutely must go and look him up. Look, he explains here how traditional superstitions are exploited by 'modernists' for the vicious control of a community. (It is in fact an account of nominal Christians – 'civilized' because Westernized – terrorizing and disrupting a rural community by killing to obtain human ingredients for witchcraft, and by manipulating 'Western' facilities such as tractors and water-pumps for power.)

On the flight back to Johannesburg I read the newspapers. At black schools in the Orange Free State white teachers are chased away; they are pelted with stones and spat upon. They refused to take part in protest meetings where demands for an 80 per cent rise in the wages of their black colleagues were to be discussed, as well as the dismissal of white educators. Two policemen are accused of having tortured an old man. They took him into custody when he was drunk and in the courtyard of the police station they hosed him down with all his clothes on. When he started shivering and lost consciousness they chucked him from their van on the street in front of his own house, but they aver that he was still alive at that stage and they have no idea how his arm got broken. Under public pressure the weak defence of General Malan, the gruesome mortician who is considered the initiator of the Civil Co-operation Bureau, the Government's semi-clandestine death squads, is: 'And what about the others?' meaning the means employed by the ANC. Death and destruction in Natal. A man complains of having suffered headaches for years. During a medical check-up the broken tip of a knife-blade is found in his forehead. A band of white schoolboys from one of the foremost educational institutions in the Eastern Cape beat to death with sticks and stones a black drifter who's had the cheek to spend the night on their rugby field. A man's mother passes away. For a month he goes to visit her grave every day, then a shaft of lightning short-circuits him right there in a kneeling position.

Back at Meadowbrook Farm, Chisi is to take us into town to fetch our visas to Swaziland. We intend spending this coming week in the north, then moving down through the Kruger National Park into Swaziland where we shall join Slabbert and Jane. Jane is a Swazi girl; they have had a house built for themselves on her father's farm.

I sit in front next to Chisi, Yolande in the back to keep an eye on the urban landscape sliding by. Whenever we are together Chisi will sound off the same jeremiads: this country is going to the dogs, in the townships murder and mayhem and robbery and poverty, just look, it's all the fault of that Mandela, he must be put back in prison. He carefully navigates the white Mercedes through the rising tide of vehicles. I listen with a mouth stuffed with tongue and teeth, knowing beforehand that I'm not going to deflect his disgust with liberal or leftist arguments. Chisi has only limited patience with the feeble humanism of greenhorns like myself.

He's been working for Enthoven for years. He and his twin brother Timothy are from Malawi, true 'Nyasa Malawians' as Chisi expresses it, and Banda, he says, is not such a bad leader. It is peaceful up there, only very poor. Before coming here he worked in several African countries – the former Rhodesia, Zambia,

Tanzania, Kenya, right up to the Congo. Everywhere a fuck-up. Just observe now what happens when the white people leave. Money is finished. Blacks cannot govern themselves, he says. They may be soldiers yes, but the officers must be whites. Blacks do not know about democracy or administration. When the one takes over he eliminates all the others to eat up everything all by himself. Hendrik Verwoerd, now there was a true man, he had the right idea. This here isn't England. Parliament and such may be all right over there, but the English are teaching you the wrong things. Just watch the townships – the children have no more discipline and everybody lives from stealing. He knows what he's talking about, will show me if I want to see. Now this Mandela blighter. You can't make him President! Big fuck-up, I'm telling you, he says.

Chisi's head is practically bald, his eyes see without looking, his mouth with the deft little moustache – as mobile as a mouth which knows about eating mangoes – says loud and clear: nobody messes with me. He's a burly man, standing straight in his own body. He and Timothy regularly return to the home country. Wife and children up there. Birds of a feather will flock together, you can't just go and mate and mix any which way, people ought to be kept apart. Slabbert has told me how he once talked over this subject with Chisi and Timothy and when it got to the 'birds of a feather' bit, Slabbert asked Chisi, 'And what have we now – don't you also keep a wife and kids here and isn't she a Zulu?' Timothy, it would seem, laughed so much that he fell over.

At the Swaziland Consulate in town – security guards at the entrance with carbuncles of fat like hand-grenades strung around their midriffs – a swarm of applicants is waiting to be helped. They are young Mozambicans. Must be looking for transit visas.

We spend Saturday with the Slabberts. In the afternoon we slouch like real South Africans on a couch in front of the television, our legs slung over pouffes, to watch sport on the box, any old sport. White South Africans often go barefoot in the house; one distinguishes little Afrikaners from their English counterparts by the fact that they are always without shoes in shorts and short skirts. Man and woman invest a coccyx in a deep armchair, the legs are stretched and preferably deposited on a low bench; often they embed their arms in the air with the hands resting on their heads;

sometimes they clutch a cushion to the belly. When they sit in upright chairs it is with thighs crossed – thighs are anyway old hands at temptation.

Upon occasion black South Africans may also sit relaxed, but leaned forward with elbows on knees. Then they will thoroughly dry-wash their faces with flat hands. Black women prefer lower chairs. At table they will discreetly kick off their shoes. Black men, when sitting down with shins kept in check, will juggle a foot rhythmically, but it is a minute movement. Sometimes they appear to be sullen or bored. White men laboriously fill their pipes from labiate pouches, with loose lips; they have meek shoulders and they often bend their heads as though talking to people shorter than they are. White women have utterly discontented mouths. When white people smoke they mostly prop an elbow on the table to hold the cigarette between the index and long finger of an upstretched fore-arm. The glass of alcohol they will hold in both hands by way of reverential complicity, especially when talking to black people. Brown people take the cigarette between thumb and index. They prefer wearing glasses and look you quietly and steadfastly in the eye (but not at one another). They are stiff until unexpectedly shaken loose by a spasm of laughter. Nobody blows out smoke through the nostrils any more.

Black South African women often have a fold of sceptical aston-ishment between the eyebrows, and when they are not from the city they may cup a chin in the open palm with fingers spread support-ively over throat and cheek – 'Now, look, one doesn't get to see this every day' – the other hand holding up the elbow. White men smile continually and say 'Yah-yah'; they touch their own faces and the arms and shoulders of other people a lot. Often they grow their hair just long enough to comb it forward to cover the tip of the ear, preferably with a careful curl.

South Africans who are politically or socially aware and who assume that they belong to the 'left intellectual establishment' qual-ify all definitions (at times even all concepts) by quotation marks sketched with two antenna-fingers on either side of the head. The secret police and/or other Pretoria *nouveaux riches* wear grey shoes. All official white males go ensconced in the same striped suit and tie. Television presenters have weak eyes and they emit a language of their own – the Afrikaans a fulsome Germanic strain of throat-terrorism. They swore an oath on John Vorster's grave to speak this way. The English comes from redundant BBC issue – they utter it with neutered faces wearing striped political garb. There are gloomy shades of brown and green that you only find woven in South African garments. South Africans have a sweet tooth for clichés, but the unwiped bottom line is nevertheless that the settler white minority racist regime will hand over power to the democratic masses at the end of the day.

The Afrikaans for 'bourgeois' is *boershow* or *bowjoys*; these days this condition is largely a brown and Indian prerogative. Young South Africans think it cool to be as deadpan as possible. People speak slowly, loudly and with emphasis, as if their listeners are hard of hearing. South African Jews have a sort of superior sympathy for the Boers. The word *naturel* (meaning human-like native) has ceased to exist and cannot be revived because it is without any conceivable application.

Black men do not wear shorts and long socks unless they work in game reserves. Most black people suffer from high blood pressure and/or diabetes. Many brown people have their front teeth pulled – it is believed to enhance sexual desirability. Most white people have café teeth which underline their jawbones and make for hungry dimples in their cheeks. One doesn't see as many Adam's apples as in olden days.

Wines have the most pretentious names in a mish-mash of languages. All South Africans have a drink problem. After a certain age the skins of white women, particularly the English, look like those of plucked chickens which got hurt. Warders and policemen and other civil servants are born with moustaches. Black and brown males have a weakness for going to prison.

It is habitual for youngish Afrikaners to wipe out their entire immediate families in one go, usually with a firearm. Sometimes the woman of the house will do it. Poison may also be used. Most white dominees sooner or later will sleep with a black woman or a white boy so that they may go through the Christian experience of forgiveness. South African Chinese are invisible but rich. The church is a breeding ground for politicians. Many white people have red eyes, from drink and sun.

*

Not for nothing do desert people wrap their faces in cloth until only the nose-bridge and eyes show, then they still use *kohl* (a black eye make-up consisting of antimony) around the eyelids to tone down the sharp mineral reflections. The blue people (Touaregs or Tamacheks, also known as Kel-Adrar – they are 'blue' because the ultramarine dye of their clothing gives off on the skin) are swathed from head to foot. The Berbers, Africa's white people, have their footsoles and palms tattooed in blue as well, supposedly to limit perspiration. The indigo nomads carry swords and knives which are forged, just like their jewels, by slaves, called Bellah, who roam with them from one star's place of dying to that of the next. It is said that the wanderers have a hundred different names for the camel, the way one's hand is always new every morning. At times they will dance with the animals.

In 1668 an illustrated *Description of Africa* was published in Amsterdam. Although the author, Olfert Dapper, had never left Holland, through his reading he knew everything there was to know. According to him the camel has a hump on its back and one on its stomach to rest on when it lies down. The procreation organ, he wrote, is so nervous that it is used in the making of strong crossbow strings. The camel has small buttocks, it has no gall bladder and bile courses through its veins.

Dapper provided a run-down of the descriptions given of the camel by various ancient authors – Aristotle, Pliny, Suidas and Solin. It brings together a fascinating mixture of lore and observations. They disagreed about practically everything: the mating habits, the period of gestation, the lifespan. What interests me now is that the people of the time lived in a world defined by these beliefs. The confines of our environment, as we perceive of it, change all the time. We situate ourselves and act according to the images which we take for reality. And wasn't the world of Aristotle, or that of Dapper, richer than the one which we inhabit?

In his book Dapper describes how camels are taught to dance. They are locked up in a place where the floor-tiles are heated; first they lift the one paw then the other. In the meantime a drum is thumped rhythmically just outside the door. This continues for a year. Thereafter they are so conditioned that they start dancing at the sounds of percussion. When they tire, they are encouraged by song. To keep a cow in milk the Tamacheks will use a stuffed calf.

These migrants are the substance of their own lives and death is a hem which pleats the horizon. At times, by a different light, death has the long face of a pale baboon. You ride astride the imaginary in order to hunt down the real – once you've killed that real you no longer need a mount, but until such time it will be too fleet-footed and too devious for you.

Africa is the domain of the spoken word. Words have a magic dimension, they are spun to ensnare time, to delay it, to annul it, to perpetuate it. Words constitute the nearly visible tissue of relationships, the creation of patterns of congress. Although speaking is patterned and ritually stereotyped, it leaves room for subtle shifts, adaptations and accentuations. It is furthermore an activity which can cast a spell and physically take on shape through structure – a reference field, a history, finally a reality.

The small aircraft flying from Bamako to Timbuktu touched down at Mopti. It was an Andropov, Thomas Nkobi said: you can always recognize it with closed eyes just by the sound of its engines. Thomas ought to know – as treasurer of the ANC he often visited the Soviet Union to beg for money at a time when the ANC was still *persona grata* there. And indeed, above our seats the instructions were in Russian and in French. We were in one of the last two Air Mali planes from a fleet of six that could still take to the air.

We were in that part of the world to participate in a week-long manifestation of solidarity with the oppressed South African people, organized by Moussa Traoré's Mali government. Delegations of the ANC and the Pan-Africanist Congress (PAC) – rival liberation movements – had been invited. They weren't really speaking to one another and I had to act as go-between, dining with the ones and supping with the others. When Johnny Makatini, leader of the ANC component, had to proceed to Lagos for another empty meeting, he entrusted me with the important political task of keeping Willy the Laughing Revolutionary Poet sober.

Mopti is the chief urban centre of the Bambaras. The Dogons live in strongholds of myth and mystery higher in the cliffs, but the Bambaras are agriculturists, although they too have all manner of

39

secret brotherhoods for hunters, ironsmiths, sculptors, healers . . . , each with its own initiation rites, rituals, magicians and language.

In this ancient world with its profusion of deities magic comes to light when the soil is tilled. Along the banks of the Niger water-spirits are still looked after and initiates dance themselves into a convulsive trance to exorcise maladies. Islam tolerates these traditions; the animists are in fact considered to be subcontractors who can propitiate inexplicable forces. The lonely god, Unum, is an eclipse of the sun; in a monotheistic creation man gropes for other ambient and buried worlds. Judaism, Islam, Christianity – these are in reality only codes for expansionist power.

Timbuktu is a strange closed city, now cracked open like the skeleton of a prehistoric beast in the sand. It used to border on the river banks, but with time the Niger shied off. The desert mystery is captured in light and absence, it is a blinding. Perhaps the past is a mirage which existed in another place. You know it's all there, the glorious empires, the epic battles, the sieges, the armies raising a history of dust, the mosques built in the Sudanese style by Andalusian architects paid with gold from the caravans using Timbuktu as staging-post in their trade from the African coast to distant Damascus, in salt, precious stones, skins, spices, silk, slaves and knowledge. There was once a concentration of wisdom and research and education (from the twelfth to the fifteenth century, more or less) that has never since been equalled in Africa. Masters of learning understood the secrets of the eye – they could slice it open and focus the image again; they knew about the origins of words and could read them in the wing-tracks of bird flights; they systematized the names of plants and animals and thus could extrapolate the geography of winds; they introduced the nought into mathematics so that one plus one could for ever afterwards add up to two (give or take a few).

All gone. Mankind's history is the long fall of oblivion, a dolorous detachment from the Empire of Simplicity where demarcations between human and animal and tree and stone and water were lines of integration. We became afraid of our own remembering. It gives us squamas and eczema and migraine, unusual anxieties and asthma and nightmares, and sometimes we wake up all wet with perspiration because we have smelt the moon.

Nothing much remains of Timbuktu. The legendary warrior-king Sankore's great mosque from sand-drippings; a small Unesco documentation centre in a building where books from the thirteenth century can be inspected, with above the door the winged words of the exiled Ahmad Baba ('Oh, you on your way to Gao: go by Timbuktu, go murmur my name to my friends and bring them the perfumed greetings of the exile who sighs for the earth where his friends, family and neighbours reside'); broad sand avenues with mud houses behind walls of clay, and in the courtyards the rough shelters of squatters from the desert.

Before lunch our hosts with dark glasses and flowing garments took us in jeeps to a high dune outside the agglomeration. There was no road, just wheel tracks in all directions. Butterflied over poles in the sand were colourful tentcloths, and the local population congregated in the pools of shade – children and elderly people, a mix of Arabs (or Moors) and black Africans (Songhay, Fulanis, Bambaras, Markas, Bozos, Somonos, Dogons, Toucouleur, Fout-anke, Kountas . . . – along the Niger one encounters all the migrant remains of previous civilizations). A shade in the desert is something you carry with you like a home deity, a family treasure, the bones of a hero, and you will open it like a prayer or a whispering of water. A man without shade is an outcast.

A youth told me how grateful they are because of the sand; they even use it for cleansing their bodies. White sand will make your skin black and clean. The women don't wear veils; except for North Africa (and sectors of South Africa) the continent is still quite free from the narrow vision of modern-day Islam. Far away, where the skyline shivers between a *Fata Morgana* and ancient memory, a large number of black specks appeared abruptly. Gradually they grew until we could distinguish the riders mounted on camels. With thudding hooves like the announcement of heavy weather the war-riors sped by and engaged in mock battle with flashing swords. To one side sat two horsemen holding up a banner: 'THERE ARE TWO VIRUSES IN AFRICA, AIDS AND APARTHEID: LET'S KILL THEM.'

Afterwards a festive meal of whole sheep grilled on the spit was laid on for us in the local inn. We were amazed by the fresh green salads so far from any garden soil. We sipped small cups of thick black coffee. Hard by the windows of the hotel, high 'walking' dunes were shadowing the walls. Big yellow bulldozers are used to scrape the streets clean.

I want to return for a moment to Dapper's encyclopedia. He attempts a list of African tribes. The *Gymfasantes*, he reported, went completely naked and knew nothing about weapons; that's why they ran away whenever they saw a foreigner and talked only to people of their own nation. The *Cynocephales* had the heads and paws of dogs and barked. The *Sciapodes* were very light and could run like the wind; they knew how to protect their heads against the sun with the shadows of their feet. The *Blemmyes* had no heads; their eyes and mouths were attached to their stomachs.

In antiquity, our scribe notes, Africa consisted of seven parts: Egypt, Barbary, Biledulgerid, the Sarra Desert (Sahara), the land of the Negroes, Upper or Inner Ethiopia (the Abyssinian Kingdom, also known as the land of Prester John), and Lower Ethiopia. Egypt was made up of Upper, Middle and Lower. Barbary embraced six parts of which one, Barca, was a province; the other five were kingdoms: Tunisia, Trimisen, Fez, Morocco and Dara. In Biledulgerid there were three kingdoms – Targa, Bardoa and Goaga – and four deserts – Lempta, Hair, Zuenziga and Zanhaga. In the Sarra Desert there were neither kingdoms nor provinces. Only sand. The land of the Negroes had nineteen kingdoms: Gualate, Hoden, Genocha, Zenega, Tombuti, Melli, Bitonin, Guinea, Temian, Dauma, Kano, Kassena, Benin, Zansara, Guangara, Borno, Nubia, Biafra and Medra. Upper Ethiopia was also divided into twenty kingdoms or provinces: Dasila, Barnagasso, Dangali, Dobas, Trigemahon, Ambian, Kantiva, Vangue, Bargamandiri, Beleguanze, Angote, Balli, Fatigar, Olabi, Baru, Gemen, Fungi, Tirut, Esabella and Malemba. In Lower Ethiopia one would have found Congo, Monomotapa, Zanzibar and Ajan. To these must be added the seas and the islands.

Willy the Laughing Revolutionary Poet listened to my evocation and asked for a drink. Together we dreamed of the day a gathering of African poets could be brought here to Timbuktu, even if only to pay homage to the passing of knowledge. Our guide told us there were thirty-three tombs of holy men in the city and its vicinity. Against one wall, nearly engulfed by sand, we read the inscription:

I am here
this my body
here I go.

We flew back all along the river. The sheet of water, dozing its broad way through a world that might as well have been of ice, was now a blind mirror of metal for the invisible stars and moons above us. Back in Bamako my bodyguard and that of Thomas waited on the airfield (the plane had been too small to take them along), their pants damp with excitement – they were so happy to see us back intact that they nearly shot us by accident. My sergeant wanted to know if I had missed him also. He addressed me as Bourema Diarra, the name he'd bestowed upon me. (Bourema is one of the many derivatives of the Prophet's name; one of the biggest Bambara clans is called 'Diarra', which means 'lion'.) They insisted on piling into the same car as us, just about sitting on our laps.

It is Sunday, 17 February when we go to have lunch with Piet Henning and his family. They live in one of the older quarters, nearer to the centre of Johannesburg. The better-off white people have moved to the suburbs and around every shopping centre a town has sprung up so that white housewives now only very seldom venture into the city. They feel unwelcome there, perhaps even threatened. With the *de facto* demise of the Group Areas Act, black families started occupying some of the older buildings around Joubert Park. Washing is drying on the balconies and people can be heard singing ho-lo-lo-lo. In the daytime the streets of Jo'burg are like those of any other African city, alive with hawkers, messengers, *mlabalaba*- or chequer- or card-players, pickpockets, good-time ladies and drifters. The crime figure is phenomenal. Cars are hijacked left and right. People are robbed in broad daylight. Even Oom Bey was mugged and turned inside out. Guests in the Carlton Hotel who wish to go for an early jog are accompanied by minders.

The Hennings' house is protected by a garden of trees and shrubs and bright flowers shooting up to heaven. As an apron the house has an old-time deep stoep. Inside there's a friendly dog and light falling through windows. Against the walls are paintings and photos of Namibia. Piet took the photos himself; the enlargements give one a sense of that vast world to which he lost his heart, where everything looks dry and where the light lies in shards. All over low tables and on shelves there are souvenirs. The walls of his study are covered with rows of impressive files and lawbooks bound in marocain leather. Hung in between are framed photos of family and friends with old-fashioned knees.

On his desk he has a thick document: together with a study group he is preparing a conceptual framework which they want to submit to the Minister of Justice, and which will argue that it is already perfectly possible to legislate for a non-racial state of law. Piet Henning, with the vulnerable blue eyes, the straight eyebrows, the lock of hair falling over his forehead, has something of a monk about him. If the constitution is right and affords protection, then surely the rest can't go wrong? There must be democratic guarantees. He is happy about the changes which have come about and which are in the offing; it's nice to take pride again in one's Afrikanership, to move away from the filthiness. There's a tremor coursing through the land – if only it hadn't been for the unacceptable violence. De Klerk is heading the right way, his hands ought to be strengthened. An old farmer in the country said to Piet that he could hardly wait for this 'New South Africa'. Seeing is believing.

Yolande is happy to be with the Hennings. There is much tenderness in the way she speaks to Piet and Elbie. Piet was faithful during all the years of quandary and quarantine when she had to come to the country alone. Often he also helped her financially, discreetly slipping a closed envelope into her hand, and he refused even to discuss it. We must say goodbye, we must leave.

Northwards. On Monday morning we pack our bags and study the map. I have a luncheon appointment with the Swedish delegation in the Sandton Sun Hotel. Chisi will bring Yolande to meet me there.

Sandton borders on the Johannesburg township of Alexandra, a rotting ghetto for blacks, but for the sake of decency the smoky cancer is hidden from the sight of whites. The future is nevertheless at hand. People have to rethink their options. Quite a number of Sandton's rich white citizens have been recruited into the ranks of Inkatha. To them Inkatha is an anti-communist organization of noble natives living in quaint huts in faraway places.

The hotel is a dream of glossy pages callously come to life: subservient 'good' blacks with red uniforms and headgear open and close doors, the concierge is a 'clever' Indian in his black outfit with the golden keys, the empty-headed receptionists are white, white-bloused, white-bosomed, with pollen-powdered cheeks; water laps at fountains, chrome and marble glitter, lifts made of glass slide up the walls, there are layers of restaurants, cafés, drinking places and bars; there's a shopping centre where guards patrol with batons and walkie-talkies.

I compare notes with the Swedes. They are shocked to within the deepest recesses of their *naïveté*. The single hostels in Alexandra are concentration camps, surely. This very morning they were taken on a tour of a squatter camp. What hit them between the eyes was of course the squalor and the promiscuity. Somewhere they came upon row after row of deep-drops in the veld, the shithouses like graves for food that nobody was ever going to get to eat, no dwellings anywhere near, but squatters had already set up house in some of the conveniences. The visitors were stopped by a patrol of aggressive cops, black and white, so informally dressed and so heavily armed with automatic rifles and shotguns that they thought they were being confronted by a gang of dirty plunderers. The singing of the poor people, everywhere and at any time – that is what was so heartbreakingly beautiful.

6

BLOW-HOLE

Last time we were in the country we came for a meal in a Pretoria
suburb at the house of the writer Marti 'Green' du Plessis and his
wife Hettie. After dinner Marti took us through his garden.
Between the fig and the red ivory there was a strong shrub-like tree
with the name of puzzle bush (in Afrikaans, *deurmekaar*, 'through-
each-other' or 'mixed-up', the *Ehretia rigida*).

In a subsequent article I used the puzzle bush as metaphor for
the South African Communist Party (SACP). Later still, Marti
wrote us a letter with more information. The bush can grow to a
height of 6 metres but is dependent on a neighbouring tree to keep
upright and twine towards the sun. In the absence of a host, it will
stay close to the ground. The wood is hardy and flexible even when
dry. People use it for *knopkieries* (knob-headed fighting-sticks) and
slangstokke (snake-sticks) and the Bushmen make arrow-shafts from
the twigs. The powdered root is applied to cuts in the skin above the
abdomen and chest to relieve pain, and sometimes to treat biliary
sickness in cattle. Mixed with the hairs from a goat's head, this
powder is dusted over hunters to bring them luck, while a foul-
tempered ox is said to become docile if its enclosure's gate is made
with the branches of the bush. Sometimes a branch is dragged
around the homestead for protection against hailstorms. The puzzle
bush has attractive pink and white flowers and the bright-red fruit
are greedily gobbled up by mousebirds and black-eyed bulbuls,
which is why the shrub is found in so many places. The SACP is
indeed exactly like this, I thought, spread by twittering intellectuals
with their powdered bung-holes.

For Pietersburg, where we're heading, one bypasses Pretoria.

Gradually the scenery becomes prettier, with dramatic hill formations to the left and to the right. Big trucks rumble towards us, going by in a whoosh of warm wind. The national highway stretches all the way to Messina, then crosses the Limpopo at Beit Bridge into Zimbabwe. (When I was still active in the underground organization Okhela, our plans for blowing up Beit Bridge were quite advanced; a Dutch comrade had even been to do the necessary ordnance surveys.)

A few dusty vineyards – must be of the katowa cultivar. Remarkable the way Afriquas walk: where you expect it least, along a stretch of deserted road, you suddenly see somebody striding out; before sundeath he has to be with the in-laws somewhere the back of nowhere. On through Warmbaths and Nylstroom. The trekkers ostensibly believed they'd reached the source of the Nile here. No water.

Heartland of the Far Right, the Boere hereabouts have *sjamboks* (whips of dried hide). They'll easily beat the daylights out of you. Fields with an eruption of anthills. The skies above the veld become more spectacular. Expanse is silence, even country sounds are but a tissue of omissions. Naboomspruit, the Waterberg watery blue on the skyline to the left.

Potgietersrus. The Afrikaner towns (*dorps* as the Anglo-whites call them) seem to be clones of American mushrooms – false shop-fronts with enormous billboards, filling stations like ocean liners decked out in flags. Deeper into town are the big houses with tin roofs and big gardens with big trees with big bats and grown-up boys wearing shorts riding their bikes through the twilight streets, whistling. The petrol jockeys address you as 'sir' so as not to have to say 'baas'.

Somewhere to the right in those hills will be Modjadji the Rain Queen's territory in a forest of succulents, some petrified. Modjadji (it means 'Sovereign Over the Day') rules LoBedu (Land of Sacrifices), but the white folk call it Duiwelskloof (Devil's Canyon) because of rainclouds permanently gathered over the abyss. The story of this matriarchy is one of exile and incest and magic powers. The rain secrets are stored in clay pots to which Modjadji alone has access; it is said that inside them can be found human skulls, the skins of predeceased Modjadjis and counsellors, the fat of the aardvark, specific parts of a kudu, seawater, the feathers of a lightning bird, black and white shells, all manner of roots and bark. When rain is made the *gomma*-drums are beaten. The present Modjadji is the fifth. She lives in seclusion where no one is supposed to lay eyes on her except for very intimate subjects. She cannot marry, although she does have children and dozens of 'wives' (offered to her by her liege headmen), who live inside the royal enclosure. The fathers of her children, as also of those of her wives, must remain anonymous.

Beyond Potgietersrus we stop under some tall marula trees to eat the provisions (*padkos*) which Yolande has prepared so lovingly. For her a big part of the fun of travelling is preparing *padkos* and then stopping to eat. Darkness comes, the wind is hot, heavy blue clouds put their heads together, occasionally shuddering a streak of lightning.

Here and there impressive farm gates set in white-painted walls with the names of owner and life's companion written large. Nirvana is in the Pietersburg district. Eerstegoud, Soetdorings (First Gold, Sweet-thorns). Night has donned its black raincoat by the time we turn into 'The Ranch' a few kilometres before Pietersburg. Jennifer had us booked in under the names of Mr and Mrs Slabbert. Maybe this will only make us all the more suspect. The young black fellow behind the reception desk recognizes me. With a smile he asks after Slabbert, who grew up on a farm just over there.

The rooms are bungalows scattered over the property. Dinner hotel-English. Waiters dressed as cowboys. A stiff drink (offered by the management) in the deserted bar. Walls decorated with motley references to aeroplanes, aerial photographs and propellers and trophies. A stuffed swordfish above the door. The black barman says the previous owner was a pilot from the wars, hence the decorations, ran through the place in no time, had to sell. Then he returns to hearkening the black language of night on his radio.

Television news. Indifferent mention with twitching facial muscles of so many killed here and so many there, buried under fatuous reports of crops and graft. The national newspapers which I bought before leaving Johannesburg bring echoes of the cauldron of strife and slaughter all over the country. In Lebowa there is tension between, on the one hand, the *sangomas* and *inyangas* (traditional

48

healers and witchdoctors) and, on the other, the 'comrades'. It is affirmed that all the major black leaders, and some whites as well – like Verwoerd and Vorster – regularly got advice from the *sangomas*, and they still do. *Inyangas* continue sprinkling *muti* (potions concocted by the witchdoctors) over black warriors to make them immune to bullets. (Dr Motlana says these people are charlatans; it's whites who romanticize them, thus insinuating that black culture is rubbish. 'Comrades' put the torch to magicians.) A warning sign at the periphery of Bekkersdal states: 'It's dead stupid to cross this line' – battles rage between opposing factions, heads are bashed in, houses burnt down. An ANC lawyer, Bheki Mlangeni, involved with an inquiry into atrocities committed by death squads, is murdered in gruesome fashion. By mail he receives a Walkman and a cassette, supposedly with secret information. He goes into a room to listen to it, switches on the instrument, an explosive charge in the earphones is detonated and blows out his brains. The parcel was apparently intended for Captain Dirk Coetzee, the 'renegade' policeman who first revealed details of the death squads' dirty doings. The trial against Winnie Mandela, accused of complicity in the murder of a young activist in her house, slides deeper into muck – witnesses disappear or are eliminated, the defence tries to elicit sympathy with the cheap argument that the 'detainees' (the activists) in Winnie's house had had carnal knowledge of a white priest. What happened to the Revolution? I also have so often mistaken turds for figs.

The early morning – 19 February – catches us beyond Soekmekaar and Bandelierkop. Yolande's eyes are swollen from the darkness. Towards eleven o'clock we are in Louis Trichardt. In the background the Soutpansberg. That's where Eugène Marais, our morphine-addicted national poet, went to talk to the baboons and contemplated their long pale faces.

In the café where we stop off a young white is clearly in no hurry to be served; he's swopping small-talk with the red-faced saleslady, looks surprised at us, stretches a pig's ear when he hears us exchange words in a foreign tongue. Outside there is a row of black men. When we walk by, a delegate speaker steps out of line and asks if the 'baas' hasn't got a job for him? I say no, we don't farm in the area, we're just passing through. He changes his song: I wouldn't perhaps have some money to spare? On the way back to the car the thin white of just now catches up: 'Excuse me, you aren't Mr B by any chance?' I feel faint; already I anticipate the whip snaking across my back. I mumble that it may be an indistinct possibility. No – what a surprise to see us in Louis Trichardt. He just wants to shake hands – everything of the best, y'hear? In the car Yolande turns up the air-conditioning.

All along the mountain range, nearly due east, runs the road to Thohoyandou. It becomes more mountainous, the vegetation subtropical. We notice paw-paw trees, banana groves, avocado orchards. There must be parrots. What language do they imitate? By the roadside we eat the last of the *padkos* under a tree heavy with birds. The day is blue, all about us Africa. The soil becomes redder, there are bright flowers. Somewhere we must have crossed the invisible border between the Republic and Venda. No more vast plantations and citrus orchards now, but smallholdings with clustered huts sometimes linked by a low wall.

Just before entering Thohoyandou (the name signifies 'Elephant's Head', after Thoho ya Ndou, the legendary ancestor of the Vhavenda [the region's people]; it's not quite a town, more a settlement – the administrative capital is actually called Sibasa), there's a tourist complex, Ditike. Here we stop to look at local items of wood and metal. Venda is known and romanticized for its wizards, its music and its sculptors. Some pieces are daubed with colour, many express a religious motif, a few are cracked. The brown lady behind the till says it's because the artists are in a hurry: the things are worth money nowadays, they won't wait any more for the wood to dry out properly. What kind of wood it is? No, good local wood. Fanie Vriolie, head of the Arts Faculty at Thohoyandou University, has written that the sculptors work up high in the forest; they don't bring the wood down the mountain – 'they go to the wood'.

Among the cowhide-shields and spears and spoons and shoes are several attractive works. We buy the bust of a man with a long head and a bearded mouth. His face is painted red, bulging eyes glare sternly, he grimaces as if he's about to take a bite out of death. He wears a tie; if he had arms he could have clasped an empty briefcase under the elbow. We decide to call him Mr Ixele. I carry him in my

50

arms to the car and it feels as if the head is getting heavier at every step.

Outside Harare's Art Museum there are a number of impressive statues. Some are life-size and fashioned to resemble humans exactly. They loiter underneath the tree-canopy in small compositions, and young men dressed exactly like the sculptures often come to sit or stand among them. It could be a meeting, a lecture, the jobless having a date with passing time.

Two years ago Yolande and I passed through after a week-long get-together at Victoria Falls of ANC expatriates (among whom were a few writers) and young Afrikaner authors in need of conversion. Albie Sachs, whose arm had been ripped off in a car-bomb blast in Maputo, was present as well. He resembled a broken-winged bird. We were over-awed by his gentleness.

The last tired evening was spent in determined festivities; exile danced with passport-holder, people looked deep into the bottles of the past and the future and into a few others as well, just on the off-chance of there being anything left; hands were linked and *'Nkosi Sikelel' iAfrika'* sung from one throbbing throat, to the obvious distress of white guests in the hotel and with the equally obvious approval of the black staff. When night was already on its ear Steve Tshwete and Neo Mnumzana, two ANC commissars, took me aside, both of them darkly gleaming from the liquor but loyally propping one another up: three white assassins had been arrested in the hotel grounds earlier that evening by the Zimbabwean security police, they told me. Two were booked into a room next to Steve's, the third with the explosives was waiting in a car outside. The intention was to blast our whole show to hell, but please don't say anything to the others, they requested with fingers of silence before wildly yawning mouths.

Suddenly I realized again: these people have walked all these years of exile with violent death ever at their heels. Discreet enquiries the next morning confirmed the information. Later we were to learn more about South African death squads consisting of members of Military Intelligence (*sic*), the security police, National Intelligence (re-*sic*), 'Askaris' (ex-ANC soldiers who'd been turned around) and other detritus and random psychopaths.

It was tough to take leave of the unsuspecting conferees. Many wept. Who'd have thought that the ANC was to be legalized barely a year afterwards and that exiles were to start returning home, albeit some with tails between the legs?

Thohoyandou lies spread over a large area against the background of green mountains. The soil is Venda red. The university is ringed by lawns and trees, the scattered brown-brick buildings low but functional. We ask for Fanie Vriolie's office. He's sitting in on a meeting just now. Ian Raper, a colleague, intense and finely strung, his mouth busy with a cigarette, invites us to make ourselves at home.

A Nigerian gentleman comes to introduce himself. He is attached to the Law Faculty. He looks like a crook; one eye must have been damaged in a car smash or else been wounded by knife or broken bottle. He tries to impress with a clutch of Afrikaans words and is annoyed when nobody takes up the tune – it just goes to show how blacks are looked down upon, he says. We speak French. He insists that I should visit his office while Yolande enjoys a cup of tea. There he draws my attention to a blown-up photo pinned to the wall of himself with the Pope. Completed his studies at Awksferd, he says, lectured at Harfhard, now here, but doesn't know whether he's going to stay on: the South Africans are mind-locked, a little backward. Natty in his dove-like French-African attire, his pointed black shoes. He embeds name, titles and address in my notebook.

Afterwards I hear of several more 'foreign' Afriquas employed by the university; many originate from Ghana. A similar tendency can apparently be noticed at other universities in Apartheidstan. Also numerous students from Zaire and elsewhere. South Africa will draw more and more people from Africa.

Fanie arrives, his smile so big he cannot tuck it into his mouth. We proceed to the staff's dining quarters for a latish meal of English colonial food – colourless, boiled to tasteless death. Somebody at least had the heart to provide a bottle of wine so that the mouth doesn't have to leave with too many regrets. Around the table we have teachers from the Afrikaans Department and some from Theology (religion plays an important role in the wilderness). The table-language is Afrikaans. The conversation hiccoughs and splut-ters – can it be because they expect me to perform? Also: what makes you think these people are refugees, isolated in an outpost? A bashful lecturer with big blue eyes – one is jumping in an unsettling way – tells me about her dissertation: she went to the Far East to research Buddhist concepts which may just be applicable when studying local traditions. This I'd like to hear much more about.

We'll spend the night at Fanie's. But first he must show us this autonomous state. A tarmac road snakes over the mountains. Green slopes are decked with tea plantations. There are also lychee orchards, fields of watermelon, stretches of tobacco. It has always been a closed area with customs and a language totally distinct from those of neighbouring tribes. A country of kings. Nobody seems to know quite where its people the Vhavenda came from; perhaps they emigrated here from the lake areas of Central Africa. The bones of history go robed in the flesh of the supernatural. News is a mixture of myths, rumours and facts.

Somewhere there's a sacred grove. To the left of the road head-ing towards the northern border is a holy mountain. It is said that generations of baboons guarded these valleys against invaders from Zimbabwe; they were the watchmen on the walls. Ritual murders occur frequently. There are waterfalls to be found higher up – the country is sometimes referred to as 'the Land of a Hundred Streams'. The Funduzi is a sacred lake. Victims designated by witchdoctors wade into its waters to drown themselves; perhaps they are hypnotized. The whites dwelling among the blacks are quite safe though – they are deemed unfit for *muti*.

Boere at this end of the world live intimately with the Vhavenda in a relationship of mutual parasitic dependence. Whether they're racist? Naturally, but they share the same direct interaction with nature and will never leave. Road signs point out turn-offs and crossroads: Bylsteel, Ledig, Witvlag (Axe-handle, Idle, White Flag). Space weaves a sound of silence. Contact between people is slowed down to retain control. Everybody is terribly polite to cover the absence of moral considerations. You can sense that the eyes of Afrikaners here in the far north must have grazed over these expanses with the possessive sentiments of recognizing a promised land. Many whites who came in here, that is with time, did so with a missionary mentality.

The brigadier in power, Ramushwana (he used to be in the South African Army and fought the guerrillas, now he's close to the ANC), is the third head of state since 'independence' – in other words since Venda was proclaimed a Bantustan. (The Bantustans, created in terms of apartheid policy as 'independent states', more or less mirrored the traditional rural homelands of the various ethnic groups.) The previous two leaders were deposed for incompetence, corruption and dictatorial tendencies. This one has also become unapproachable since he increased his own salary. Governments are changed by coups d'état.

There are undercurrents of reprisal and a whiff of liberation euphoria. Black staff saw to it that the Dutch doctors who had been active for years in a local hospital were chased away: the result is that medical services have largely collapsed; there are quite simply not enough qualified people to replace those who've been sacked. The student council has an ANC majority but their positions are those of the PAC even if they don't know it. Frustration can easily focus on the presence of whites in the educational structures. (It's true that it used to be planned Broederbond practice to place their operatives with the black shoes in the 'bush colleges', hoping to ensure the deployment of 'separate development', and many of these grim white oxen are feeble teachers with entrenched contracts.)

Everybody who wants to be somebody in the country now lays claim to having been in the resistance movement; we are all of the ANC. Rumours of heroic feats abound. In fact there was very little infiltration, as the people hereabouts constitute a well-knit community and penetrators would have stood out. What will happen to Venda in the New Sarf Efrica? God alone knows. The Vhavenda are homogeneous, they definitely have their own separate identity, it may well be that they prefer not to be assimilated into a new dispensation.

Evening is already falling when we drive towards the forestry station (Timbadola) between Thohoyandou and Louis Trichardt where Fanie Vriolie has rented a house. The earth road takes us through forests and plantations into the foothills of the mountain range. Inside the fence around the station we pass by sawmills and arrive at a row of houses. Fanie's lies obscured behind a garden overgrown with tropical vegetation. Dark hills rise against the late sky on either side.

The interior of his house is one enormous book collection from floor to ceiling: his wide world of studies in The Netherlands and of travels all through the sub-continent, the many trips of the heart and the mind too through civilizations and epochs, all bound here black and white. The old dog he used to have, a colony for fleas, has gone over to the other side – a snake bit him; now there's no one waiting for him at sundown with a friendly glass to ask what kind of a day he had.

We sit outside in the half-light with a bottle of better red. Mosquitos are droning their Tibetan evening prayers. Fanie enthuses about the many snakes in the environs. Puff adders, cobras, mambas, pythons, tree snakes. Some time ago a boa constrictor nearly throttled to death a nine-year-old cowherd from the native kraal (village) up the hill. By the time foresters delivered the boy from the coils he'd already lost consciousness; one can still see the bruises and weals all over his body. Here, just underneath that hibiscus bush, there lives a puff adder. Very cordial. Lazy. Hasn't been seen for a long while. But then, he himself gets so little chance to burrow in the garden. The foresters even brought snakes in to keep down the rat population gnawing at the roots of the seedlings.

Sometimes there are fires. Spectacular manifestations from another world. Just imagine: on that skyline not so long ago, flames trippling all along the tree-crests (like news of ghosts); suddenly they stop, tumble down the branches and ignite the rosin. An explosion! Wind scoops up the fireball and throws it a hundred yards away, a tongue of the last days. Nothing can stop a fire. The last time, Fanie hurriedly borrowed a neighbouring farmer's lorry to cart away all his books.

We talk about Aristotle, the cultural boycott, language policy, Joe Slovo (now President of the SACP), but then it's time to get away from under the swooning mosquitos and the heavy stars. We close the screen door behind us.

Sometimes the electricity dims and bulbs get haloes of obscurity before flaring up once again. In the bathroom there's an

55

old-fashioned tub. I didn't interpret the snake story for Yolande – it's better she doesn't know – but just the same I glance nervously at every nook of darkness.

Guests arrive. A Dutch biologist with his nursing wife. He speaks French, used to work in Mali, now he's looking into an aspect of the digestion in the gemsbok's colon. He is at ease here, in no hurry to return to Holland. His wife is much more upset: the poverty and the bloodshed get her down, she feels there's no progress, it's growing worse and she's not appreciated (because white). She works for a project called Operation Hunger, the only outfit which stands between life and death for thousands. And to top it all there's Aids. More by the day. She wants out, back to Europe.

A hefty Anglo-white historian enters with a flask of wine. (These people are all neighbours of Fanie; they drop occasional remarks about snakes and fire.) This historian with the beard and the sandals is originally from the Cape. He's a consultant to the Gazankulu authorities further south. He starts questioning me on the links between the ANC and Okhela. It seems that he knows all there is to know about my disastrous political involvements. He's laughing up his short sleeve.

In the morning we return to the university. This is going to be a boring day for Yolande. My first assignment at the university is to read poems in the dying language. This happens in a lecture hall without acoustics. People enter and leave, doors bang. There are a few ladies from town in the audience (the wives of missionaries?), with happy dresses and high heels; it must be curiosity to hear Satan that brought them here. I declaim solemnly. Nobody hears a damn word. The black students look at me in surprise; some get up to go. I'm wearing my black Dogon shirt from Mali, the one that feels as if it has been woven from ropes. I read a Bamako poem.

In Bamako I made the acquaintance of a young teacher who at that stage had received no salary for six months. He came to our hotel to discuss literature, then he invited me to his home. The compound behind a clay wall was on the opposite bank of the river towards the outer rim of the city. The young teacher sat very straight on a chair in the yard, his shirt spotlessly white. On his lap there was a book, sunlight over the pages. Perhaps it was the sun's life story. His father came to shake hands; he used to be the ambassador of his country in Accra. Even though he wore no shoes now his smile was dashingly formal. The mother was lying on a mattress by the front door in the shadow which a tree in the court-yard had painted on the wall. She was too ill to get up but put out her limp hand to greet mine. The sisters squatted on their heels with a group of friends in one corner of the yard. This was the weekly meeting of their circle to pool all their money, and each one would get a turn to borrow from the pot. The youngest sister's gums were dyed a bright blue, enhancing her attractiveness. I caressed the thought that she was fondling the sky in her mouth. Inside the house the eldest daughter poured water from a kettle over my hands and offered a clean piece of towel for the drying. Then they brought a big glass of *bisap* (the juice of the hibiscus flower).

The only pieces of furniture in the room were a sofa, two chairs and a covered television set. We had a serious conversation about nothings so as to give politics a wide berth. Still later I was intro-duced to a humming of aunts and nieces and nephews. The meal was prepared on an open fire behind a shelter outside. Fire gave tongue in the gathering dusk. We ate with our fingers from a communal bowl. They were Songhays from up Timbuktu way, and not all that happy in the south.

The day before my leaving, the painfully correct schoolmaster rode his bike to the hotel to bring me going-away presents: a whole goatskin tanned and put together as a tuckerbag, to carry the necessary through the world; a smaller hand-painted leather pouch to be hung by a thong around my neck so as always to have at hand dope, *gris-gris* and vaccination certificate; and this shirt. Teacher wrote his name and address in my notebook.

After the inaudible reading (Yolande has put on a black frown woven from the short ropes of her eyebrows) we are escorted to a hall where a number of academics lie in waiting. With Fanie and Ian Raper I confront the chaffers from behind a table. An elderly man in a wheelchair asks barbed questions. The young representa-tive of a local civic gently guides me back to the cages of reality whenever my tongue starts flying too high. I wish to say something about the *silences* in the South African situation and history – that there are perceptions which we refuse to face, of which we've

57

practically made taboos. What do whites really think of blacks? And blacks of whites? And that 'reconciliation' can only take place once we're ready to lay these suppressed hind-thoughts on the table.

Using the Gulf War as image I attempt to draw a picture of our shared collapse. (*Baghdad delenda est*.) For nothing is now unthinkable. At each step the horrendous opens up under our feet. All catastrophes, absurdities, aberrations of the spirit, the transgression of moral norms and the violation of the most elementary human values have now become acceptable. I declaim seriously about man wiping his powdered backside on the law, about the fatalism of power equations that must lead to the elimination of the weak, and how painfully new limits must be identified.

Perhaps the listeners secretly laugh at my moral posturing. Gondwanalanders have a habit of giggling with closed mouths. I'll never know what they really think.

From the auditorium I'm led like a leashed bear to Buljan de Bruyn's office. Behind beard and moustache his eyes are wide with innocence. Books are scattered over his desk like litter in a Baghdad street. A callused thumb fusses over a scorched pipe-bowl and a tobacco pouch. Ian Raper sits on a chair with the drawn face of a gunfighter, breathing through a cigarette. We discuss the fabrication of poems, about how much gets lost (stillborn, disorientated, chucked away). Buljan proposes: 'Paradise must be a place where one finds all one's lost poems.' Ian resists with a nervous cigarette: 'Oh God, just imagine, who'd want that?' Buljan huffs: 'Paradise is not necessarily a nice place.' (I also have a wisdom to contribute: 'As long as there exists an alternative to paradise, the people up there will be peevish.')

A little later Buljan adjudicates: 'Big poets throw works away, the little ones are constipated.' He has lost so many of his own. For instance, he wrote a magnificent verse for me the day I was clapped in chains. He was scrutinizing his own face in the looking glass, shaving brush in hand, and begad, some agent swiped the thing. The poem, not the brush. Hang on, a line or two come to memory: 'I am here / this my body / here I go . . .' Do I want to hear more? No?

We proceed to the student cafeteria. Yolande, bored stiff with these poetical speculations, makes snapshots of our earnest mugs.

The food is an improvement on yesterday's – at least one can get *mealie* porridge. At the table I ask how they get along with the white farmers of Louis Trichardt – isn't this rightist territory? Buljan explains that it is worth the effort to get to know better the Afrikaner Weerstandsbeweging (AWB, Afrikaner Resistance Movement); one must effectuate an intertwinement, they're not all hairy-faced hooligans. The grid of forbearance is shared interests in the local conditions of the district.

Raper lights a cigarette with trembling hands, since we're discussing tolerance now, and remembers a story about N. P. Van Wyk Louw, the poet whom we all revere. At the time Raper was teaching at Wits in the same department as the master. Van Wyk Louw was always close to Baboon Grové, a proto-fascist literary godfather from Prehistoria (Pretoria). This Grové had written an article in which he'd really gored me, B, stringing my innards from his pen. Van Wyk Louw was on his deathbed when the hatchet job came to his attention. He wrote an angry letter to Grové, breaking all ties with him, and insisted on mailing the missive himself to make sure that it would reach its destination.

Yolande is startled by a shadow. A hand falls on my shoulder and a familiar voice says: 'But is this not Mr B?' I look up into slightly bloodshot eyes, see the sparse beard, the vaguely remembered features. Could this be Jean, or Jan, Walker? It is indeed. I'll be damned.

I excuse myself from the table, wipe my speechless mouth on the napkin. We move off to one side. He hasn't changed much over the years, although he, who always had a bland expression, has apparently succeeded in growing a face. He laughs when I say this, then pulls back a shirtsleeve to show me that the hand which he'd laid on my shoulder is in fact an imitation; it fits into a leather sheath fastened to the arm. 'I lost on the roundabout what I won on the horses. Yes, the hand you knew rotted. This one is of wood – a local sculptor made it for me. Exactly like the real job, hey?'

What on earth is he doing in South Africa? Smuggling, he says, as ever. Travels through all the black areas. Buys up bones, horse skeletons and such – there's a lot of bones to be had in this country, even if some little horses are two-legged – which he then sells to glue factories. On the other hand he sells nags to the blacks. He says he also has his contacts in Europe and Latin America. From there he imports second-hand statues of Lenin and Stalin, seeing as how these votive objects have no more value; locally there's a big demand. He hopes soon to be able to offer a few Castro and Ho Chi Minh heads as well. The wheel is still going to be invented in South Africa.

And besides (he drops a small cough in the wooden prosthesis), he's also 'recruiting' black girls for abroad – people are dying of hunger around here after all. In Europe there are impotent old men who believe they can be 'cured', that they'll recover their virility, you know, if they can lay their hands on the curves of these supposedly submissive maidens.

Back at the table my wife tugs at my shirt and asks who this man is. I whisper (in French) something about an adventurer, somebody out of the past, a bird that would shit in any tree. I'll tell her all about it later.

We say goodbye to the three poets, to the woman with the eye that flutters like a blue bird, to the uneasy Nigerian, to the man in the wheelchair. The bird-eye lady has brought us a jar of marula jam. It's getting late. Our travelling bags go into the boot. When I open it Mr Ixele is lying there grinning at me. We must still reach the gates of the game reserve and then the first camp. We turn the nose of the white Mercedes to the east. We see the first baobab trees, the earth is made of dry fire, the mountains fall away, grassy expanses are dotted with thorn trees, it is getting to look more like Africa. No more towns now, just a store from time to time, sometimes a market, women with bright dresses and headcloths by the roadside.

Walker? Yolande asks. The car buzzes and sunlight is burning the veld to dust. You'll have to explain. Look, I got to know him in Paris, years ago. Not all that well, to tell the truth. He belonged to Okhela. I remember it was intimated to me that the man had been recruited because he was so anonymous, faceless one could say, and because he had a knack for falsifying documents. We called him 'Walker' – who would know now what his true name was? She surely understands.

When he was young, it is said, he had the habit of stealing Christ statues from churches, 'to give them a proper burial'. He even spent time in prison for theft; that must be how Okhela got a grip on him. But he persisted in his endeavours to liberate the martyred deity until he realized that these Christs were only butterflies pinned to crosses to show the wingspan. Thereafter he became a gigolo. Out of compassion, he claimed. A faceless stud-ram for old ladies with sour breaths or younger ones with scarred throats. The story goes that he used to clamber over rooftops – some of the women had impossible fancies; he told of how he sometimes met angels with wings burnt black huddling behind chimneypots. Actually one can say he was an exile, somebody who had fallen out of society's bag.

Then, after I was arrested and with the eclipse of Okhela, he really went to the dogs. In the end he had neither home nor identity documents. And thus no identity. But he had already been bitten by the Africa bug. Could it be that he conceived of Africa as paradise? In order to get there he managed to obtain a false passport, from Ghana or the Ivory Coast. As was to be expected, he was stopped on the street one day with his forged papers. The French police couldn't care less: to them he was just a clandestine immigrant, and they deported him to his country of origin. That's what he'd hoped for. How else was he ever to get there?

And the hand? No well, I only have the story at second hand as it were, and cannot swear to its veracity. (I won't put my hand on the block.) When I met him again in Ouagadougou after many years – it must have been one of President Thomas Sankara's generous gestures to allow such a man into Burkina Faso – that's when he told me about the hand. Even showed me the hunk of pinkish flesh.

He's supposed to have worked for a while on a Liberian cargo vessel, as fireman down the boiler room. In Romania acid from the engines dripped on his hand. It started swelling and became infected. In Algeria he went to see a doctor, pills and ointment were prescribed, they didn't help. In Brazil he looked up an expert hand-and-foot man, got injections, no joy. By the time the Chilean landfall was bobbing on the sea-line he was frothing with pain; he wanted only to return to Europe to have the agony amputated. In Santiago the chief engineer, a Cretan, talked him into giving the local doctor one last try. This quack was known up and down the coast for his skills with fractures and abscesses.

With the chief he went straight from port to the hospital. There they were directed to the 'professor's' house – which was, according to Walker, a palace with parapets and dogs and portals. The doctor, an old coot, had them wait a long time. They were finally shown into the consultation rooms by a blonde with buttocks and boobs. When the doctor, grey as a monkey, learned that the chief (who had to interpret) was from Crete, he was so excited that he started jumping and singing. He had wine and cheese brought in and insisted on talking about the island. They had to put their hands on each other's shoulders and hop about in a semicircle, like goats. Poor Walker was writhing in agony. It was late that night, after hours of merrymaking, that the doctor carried out an operation right there in the house. By then the blonde's bust had come unslung. The 'professor' was so glad to be with civilized people again. And within a few days the hand was as good as new!

The tail to this tale was that the 'professor' was a Nazi refugee who'd learned his skills experimenting in a concentration camp. At some stage during the war he had been with German occupation troops on Crete – *ach*, he so much loved Mediterranean culture!

Walker regained the African continent, got off at Lagos and struck out for the interior. He told me how friendly he became with all kinds of powerful potentates in West Africa. Also that he had the intention of making use of this selfsame miraculous hand to write his life story. That's when the limb was still whole. What had happened since I don't know. How he got from there to here is a mystery.

She only hopes this kind of incident will not be an excuse for getting lost in inessentials, Yolande says. 'If you must write, keep it short and readable.' It really makes me angry. She can't realize how difficult it is to close a life and conceive of a country. The skull is a dead bell. How can one write succinctly about Africa? Even Western culture cannot imagine an end to counting. The spirits come along endlessly, like birds.

How are you going to get Thomas Sankara into your journal, my wife asks. Yes, the man is entitled to a decent grave, I admit. I'll have to find a point of contact, perhaps a flashback, to ease him into the story through the telling of the first meeting. It must have been 1984.

*

Maybe I could start in Ouagadougou. That occasion when I and Tobe, a mixed-up Paris exile, also from Gondwanaland, were attending an official reception and a certain Diallo called us out: somebody wanted to talk to us.

It was night. Across the road, on a fenced-in terrain, there was a low construction, a radio station, Diallo said. We noticed all the soldiers at the entrance. But they were unarmed. Inside we were introduced to Captain Thomas Sankara, head of state of the Land of Irreproachable People (Burkina Faso). He was dressed in a striped cotton gown, his eyes were mischievous, his forehead shiny and clever, his mouth full of witticisms. He called in the soldiers and had them stand in a row ah-ing a note. He walked his ear from mouth to mouth and pulled out the false voices. The remaining ones had to learn a song he himself had composed earlier in the day. The song made fun of his Minister of Foreign Affairs, who'd just returned from Teheran where he'd been begging arms from Ayatollah Khomeini. Sankara asked Tobe and me to act the parts of the minister and a journalist in a spoofed interview. The minister was to be commended for his 'death-defying mission' and asked whether it was true that he'd offered a signed copy of the Koran to Khomeini. Wasn't it true, furthermore, that some weapons were actually intended for the ANC? This was all taped and the unsuspecting minister duly heard the fun-poking broadcast the next morning.

Sankara was a good man, my wife says. Yes, he knew how to dance, I concur. But he was also a restless ruler who had to invent and embody his own opposition.

A day or two later he summoned Tobe and myself to the palace – bullet holes of the coup d'état that brought him to power still pockmarked the walls – and asked if we would help bring some of the Métro musicians from Paris to Burkina Faso – they must surely be without haven or income. He would have the streets closed off once a week so that these artists could give music lessons to the people. The whole population, right up to the fattest cabinet minister, already had to participate in Wednesday afternoon sports.

Then, a week afterwards – does she remember? – Diallo, on the instructions of Sankara, arranged for us to be driven to the military base at Po close to the Ghanaian border. I was to lecture the officers on the problems and perspectives of South Africa. The camp commander was Sankara's bosom friend and adopted brother – together they'd made the revolution – Captain Blaise Campaoré, *le beau Blaise*. The two were as different as fire and water. Sankara was a half-blood and an extrovert, Campaoré clearly of noble Mossi stock, tall and dark and withdrawn. Sankara liked his fun, Campaoré was a teetotaller, probably a pious Catholic.

Of course it leaked out in Ouagadougou that I'd been to Po, the 'base of the Revolution', and Walker (who was in town) asked me one night if this meant that I was becoming politically active again, if we were going to dig up Okhela. I said: 'No, no, not in the least. May God (praise His glory) protect me against the death of the heart.' I even meant it.

As we drive through this country so reminiscent of Burkina Faso Yolande says she'd like to believe me – it's such a waste of time, it does eat out the heart.

We enter the Kruger National Park at Punda Maria. A young game-warden with starched shorts and blond down on his brown forearms enquires by radio-telephone whether there'd be accommodation available for Mr and Mrs Slabbert at Shingwedzi. It's still another 70 kilometres away. On a shelf in his office there's a glass container. Inside, small and white and wrinkled and uncannily human, is an elephant foetus. It is something out of an ancient memory, a thought of slow lightning. We pay and buy roadmaps and postcards and books. An old black gamekeeper lets us in through the gates.

The afternoon has the colour of gauze. At first it is strange to have to drive so slowly. It takes time before the eyes are attuned to the registering of animals. We probably won't see too many – it's the rainy season, grass and shrubs are tall. Then one sinks into the hypnosis of this quiet world.

At Shingwedzi the Milky Way is spun over the camp, a sprinkling of stars. Old acquaintances like Venus Big-eye in the west, the saucepan full of darkness, the Southern Cross an anchor above the sombre etched tops of the mopanes.

I sleep with my face to the wire netting over the window underneath a waterfall of stars and dream I've left a woman in the lurch.

Maybe I've broken her heart. Joe Slovo, President of the SACP, was in love with the same woman and he's so touched by her dying that he's in the process of committing suicide. I lean over the sea and see him standing under the water with a small white dog. His grey head is bent in prayer. A comrade is lying on a pebbly beach with a rope in his hands. He wants to pull Joe Slovo from the water. I want to help but my offer is turned down because I am now the traitor. It is too late in any event. Joe is drowning on his feet. We're not going to have a revolution.

When I wake up it is dusk outside. On the grass a lesser blue-eared starling (*Lamprotornis chloropterus*) is looking for crumbs. In a tree there's a yellow-billed hornbill (*Tockus flavirostris*) going tok-tok-tok-tok-tok-toka-toka, and two olive woodpeckers (*Mesopicos griseocephalus*) with carmine quiffs say chweet-chweet-chereep-chereep.

7

SHADOWS

On 21 February we wake up in Shingwedzi. Today we shall roll at 40 kilometres per hour through the game reserve, going south. The streams, the rivers, the dams and waterholes, the rocky outcrops have evocative names imparting journeys, outspans, deaths: Mooigesigdam (Beautiful Face Dam), Wik-en-weegdam (Stop–go Dam), Kanniedooddam (Diehard Dam), Bububu, Olifantsbadpan, Twisappeldammetjie (Little Dam of Apple of Discord)... In places there are surely graves, the rare ruins of cattle farms from the previous century now long since recovered by green thickets, the beasts of burden killed off by tsetse flies, the people succumbed to malaria and other fevers.

To our left as we drive is the ever-present undulating barrier of the Lebombo Mountains. Beyond them lies Mozambique. Apparently it often happens that small bands of fugitives come across trying to reach South Africa through the game park. Many are caught and eaten by lions. Those who succeed sometimes find slave-work with Transvaal farmers. A few tougher ones escape and make their way deeper into the country – some even get as far as the squatter camps around Cape Town.

In Mozambique one of the continent's most abominable wars is dragging on. Maiming and killing can no longer be computed. Some adult Mozambicans have never worn clothes; they live like animals in the bush and go covered in bark and grass. Children are forced to do away with their own parents, men are castrated, women have their breasts chopped off.

South African agents – diplomats, security pigs, politicians – have created a terrorist force, Renamo, train them, procure weapons for them, egg them on, protect them. The result is a dislocated country, barbarism, hundreds of thousands dead, more hundreds of thousands without feet or arms or eyes, hundreds of thousands of fugitives, millions of famished people. We know and yet we don't want to know.

Death is a silent environment. Do you still remember how excited we were during the early 1970s when Portuguese colonialism was toppled in Mozambique and in Angola and Guinea-Bissau? I'd met Mozambican President Samora Machel in Dar-es-Salaam, an exuberant man with a beekeeper's beard and a pistol on his hip. (Dead.) Yolande and I got to know Vice-president Marcelino dos Santos, his South African wife, their daughter; together we sat in the sun on a beach by the Indian Ocean. Together with the poets José Vieira and Antonio Guebuza and Wole Soyinka and Boutros-Ghali, at a congress I dreamed that Africa may perhaps be united around two or three major languages, Swahili and Hausa, and what then? We even drew up documents to argue for the preservation of what had been gained, to say that a language is not of itself colonialist or racist. Frelimo's (the Mozambican Liberation Front's) revolution was going to be cultural.

Revolution? Well now . . . It was a no-go. From exile and out of the bush the dreamers came with gun in one hand and poems and paintbrushes in the other. One became Vice-president, another chief of the security police, a third Minister of Defence. Blood, blood. Years later the South African State President, Crocodile Botha, with a black homburg on his double-dealing head, signed a peace accord with Mozambique on the Nkomati border. Dry blood became ink. The official and non-official warring against Mozambique – 'destabilization' was the name of the game – with Renamo as go-between, was to cease. It still continues.

Not so long ago, in broad daylight, South African Military Intelligence agents in a car with tinted windows gunned down David Webster in front of his Johannesburg home. David Webster was a gentle academic activist and researcher. He'd made a study of the on-going dirty tricks of MI in Mozambique; soon he was going to publish the irrefutable documentation. Dead.

The thousands of AK-47s distributed by South African underminers are now finding their way back across the border. Hungry soldiers are swopping arms for food. In shanty towns on the Reef factions settle their scores with Kalashnikovs. Town-centre banks are robbed with these assault weapons. Death.

It is still early when we see a few waterbuck, then reedbuck. A little further along a kudu with inquisitive eyes and proudly curving horns, hatracks for the hunting caps of ancestors. The gnu is an ancient thought which has lost its drift. The impalas cannot be counted. Birds are coagulations of blue imagination. Some also give sound a short shrift.

There are kingfishers and swifts and kites and hawks and falcons and plovers and bee-eaters and barbets and woodpeckers and larks and tchagras and herons and eagles and woodhoopoes and honey-guides and shrikes and orioles and starlings and widows and weavers and common sparrows and sunbirds and vultures and bul-buls and rollers and crows and waxbills and firefinches and wagtails and marsh warblers and chats.

Mostly we see a reasonably dense screen of trees and scrub on either side of the road. Game-paths going nowhere fork off into the undergrowth. These must lead to a world of gorging and guzzling and foraging and copulation and breeding, of stalking and being stalked, and of hiding.

So many of the authors I look up to have handed in their pens over recent years. They are now for ever behind the curtain. Jean Genet is buried somewhere on the parched lip of a North African desert with a view over a prison. I once spotted him sitting in a car in Paris, scarf around the neck pulled up to the beak to keep warm the cancer in his throat, a Jacobin cuckoo (*Clamator jacobinus*). When I was still inside my friend Tobe tried to contact him to solicit his signature on a petition for my release. Tobe was received by an oldish lady in a nondescript rooftop flat and interrogated at length on the merits of the request. Then she repaired to the adjacent room 'to telephone Genet', there was a whispered consultation and finally Genet himself (who'd all along sat listening next door) emerged and croaked his approval. Another friend, Kalbsauge, tells of how he had to escort Genet through the Hamburg streets to pick up a sailor. Genet would then make love the whole afternoon in a broken-down rocking chair in the upper room of an abandoned dockyard shed while ships groaned mournfully. This empty room was occasionally used as a recording studio for jazz bands; a few instruments were left behind – one doesn't know whether they picked up the vibrations – and neon ads flashed through the naked windows.

Mysterious bacteria he'd come by in the Far East put an end to Bruce Chatwin's life. I met him in a television studio in England. We looked at the chit-chatting intellectuals around us and he whispered in my ear: 'Did you ever get a degree at university? No? Thank God, neither did I.' In a Paris café he explained to me how impressed he'd been with the white soldiers he'd encountered in Namibia. Under their helmets they had the rigid faces of youths from a twilight world.

Sam Beckett was an African hawk eagle (*Hieraeetus fasciatus*). Like a spectre he threaded the streets of Paris. When one wanted to contact him one deposited a note as bait in an anonymous letterbox. On occasion he could be encountered unsteadily engaging a sidewalk in the wee pee-faded hours of night. Graham Greene was an owl blinded by light, the hand warmed by a whisky glass used to flutter. Henri Michaux was a hooded vulture (*Necrosyrtes monachus*) with a plucked red head and a brown scapular. He passed away in the obscurity of a hospital when the streets outside were black with cold, and his last exclamation was 'More oxygen!' as he pushed away the mouthpiece. The most beautiful words he ever threw away were: 'Hell is the rhythm of the Other.'

Amadou Hampaté Bâ was the last in a line of African storyweavers, 'When an old man dies in Africa it is a library burning down.' Towards the end he was blind and paralysed. At night one still hears his voice in the gurgling of the Niger. When he passed over to the other bank friends put a spray of fresh jujube leaves in his mouth to make the words immortal.

Dirk Opperman came to visit me in jail with a rope around the neck as tie. He wanted to pilot me back to the pathways of poetry. Brandy killed him and then he resuscitated and wrote in coma-script with a bamboo stylus about the silkworm which is actually but a maggot, and then he died again.

James Baldwin died in southern France. He was a marabou stork (*Leptoptilos crumeniferus*) with the pate and the sombre shoulders of a sacristan. When we argued about the world and its ways (drunk as a sexton with a head filled by the shouting of church bells) he said it was all the fault of whites like myself, and I retaliated that the evils were to be ascribed to Americans such as he.

He'd also been invited to the mayor's congress I attended in Senegal. During our sojourn a concert was organized on Gorée island with musicians from all over Africa. Johnny Clegg stomped energetically, Miriam Makeba was slightly worn-out in a nightclub number with two befuddled female prancers. There was a crush of spectators, the indigenous population plus thousands from the mainland. All the island was a stage with spotlights on the roofs and coloured bulbs in the trees and the children could not be kept down. With Matsemela Manaka and Maishe Maponya and Ptika Ntuli and other South African writers I also read a brief text. We were accompanied by a nine-year-old *kora*-player with the fluted voice of an angel. He was of a family of *griots* (traditional court singers), trained from birth in the lilting art of his forebears. The calabash of the *kora* was nearly as big as he was.

Afterwards we strolled through the sandy alleys, shadows shuffled. Everywhere in the courtyards eating places and beer gardens had sprung up. We went into one: Yolande, Slabbert and Jane, James Baldwin. We drank beer until we could drink no more. Baldwin's eyes were big and soggy, he was negotiating for balance and at odds with his city suit. What strange thoughts must have crossed his mind. (But then, every thought must come to mind sooner or later.) Dames with bright headcloths twisted to look like pointed hoods, distinguishing them – the *Signares* – as descendants of the inter-breeding between slaves and slave-dealers, brought more food and drink.

A Senegalese came to our table. He was far gone, the moon was in his throat, he wanted to know who these *toubabs* (whites) might be. To the best of my ability I explained and when he learned that Slabbert was a down-South politician he burst into tears. He couldn't credit it: then there was some hope for our continent after all. Peace! Peace! A dirge of bitterness and of sweet dreams. The very next day he was going to proceed to the mosque to commit us with sacred formulas to the protection of Allah (praised be His name). In fact, he promised to give Slabbert a potent formula of protection right away, on condition that we sacrifice a few notes to help defray the costs of the ceremony. We bought more beer. Baldwin was blown over by a wind which had escaped our attention. Our initiator's memory was too wet to remember the magic phrase.

With the black dog star we sailed back to Dakar in the ferryboat, the island a volcanic mountain behind us, the oily waters of the bay reflected the pulse-beat of many bands. Long after the tunes had died away one still heard the rhythms. Baldwin took off his jacket and leaned over the boat railing. In the city there were as always the mixed smells of fish and sea and oil and rubbish and decay and faeces and sweet flowers and incense.

I remember standing high in the hotel and looking out over the sea. The sky was often opaque, greyish. The city – its teeming docks, the port with its graveyard of dead ships, the baroque-pretty station building, the president's palace with the high-stepping mannequin-like guards in their baggy black pants and curly-toed shoes and red pom-poms, the streets shaded by flamboyants, palm trees, banana trees, bougainvillaea, pink hibiscus bushes, the markets with their multitudes, the big mosque built with Saudi money, one of the finest Arab libraries in the world, the halt and lame beggars in the vicinity of the Ministry of Foreign Affairs, the men in their *boubous* (loose gowns) sitting in schools around braziers on the pavement, the hip-rolling beauties with shape-enhancing dresses and neat matching headgear, the Koranic classes under trees practically on the street, a master and boys with wooden slates and slate-pencils, their sandals and shoes in neat rows, the rhythmical recitations – the city slept.

First light spread over the sea, glinting the contours of my field of vision. On the sea-line Gorée Island lay washed up like a dead whale in the shallows. Down the coast road a pack of dogs came, perfectly silent apparitions of skin and bone, and systematically they ransacked every dustbin and black plastic refuse bag. This image remained with me.

I remember a conversation I had at the time of the Dakar meeting with H. Adam, who was with us as an observer. This German Africanist had long been delicately de-boning the South African imbroglio. We talked about the difficult relationship between 'apostate' and 'group' when one is an Afrikaner. It's all very well to see yourself as a transformative agent, but when you are outside and

71

purposefully use that self as an instrument for cutting in upon your people's problems, is that not alienating? To break away from your group means after all that you are being deprived of a certain existential dimension, that you lose your sense of direction and perspective and become sullen like a bull pushed out of the herd. Will this lead to a private cave-in of values? Does one inevitably become rogue, embittered and unconnected? Adam laughed and remarked that when one Afrikaner terminates another it is not because of revenge or reprisal, not even as punishment; it is rather an ultimate 'helping right', the 'healing' of a 'sick' member. And he added: the agent killing you probably considers it a way of helping you out of the misery of being human, seeing that the Afrikaner's cosmogony is a vale of tears flooded with sour pessimism.

How we love Africa! In the dark we are all Africans. But completing life is to fill remembrances with collected death. The mongrel is a non-citizen, by nature a slave, someone speaking an incomprehensible language, imitating birds.

Over the years we returned to Gorée. Once, in March 1989, we came to participate in the reflections of philosophers from Europe and Africa on the theme 'Identity and Differences'. I was already a 'Frenchman'; we French stayed in a students' hostel near the central mosque. One could measure the impoverishment of Dakar with a naked eye: there were still a myriad small shops and tiny workplaces where Mauritanians with swathed heads forged iron, but also many more beggars than ever before, some of them small kids with cracked feet, and bigger children roamed the city for hours on end to sell a shirt or trousers suspended from a clotheshanger.

The students were restless. During our stay there was agitation in the streets; people would suddenly start running, tear-gas was fired, soldiers on troop-carriers were visible everywhere. The slogan of the demonstrators was '*Sopi!*' ('Change!') – anything, as long as it could be *different*. Their hero was Abdoulaye Wade, a demagogue with a flashing pate who'd been plotting for years for his share of the dividends of power.

Africa is in need. On the campus students pleaded for books. All wanted addresses, somebody to correspond with, a reference, as if the link could prove that they weren't stranded in death's empire of not-knowing; all wanted group photos to staunch the despair of the temporary. On pavements and in streets there were turds. In the mosque area, among crowds moving back and forth, holy men sat on prayer-mats with strings in their hands and beaded words in the mouth, to be counted with a long tongue and rolled in spittle. In front of them were open books in Arabic script.

Down by the sea, where I went to trot early in the morning, more men were on their hunkers to stare at the blinding waters. Out in the bay was a long low island called Madeleine, considered the dwelling-place of the deceased. Nobody lives there, it is infested with snakes. Some believers (of an older religion?) still row out to re-enact obscure ceremonies.

During our stay I realized that my passport had expired and would have to be renewed for me to leave the country. I duly went along to the French Embassy where I was issued with temporary travel documents describing me as a '*Français de passage*'. (Indeed, I am but a momentary Frenchman passing through.)

With us in Dakar were a few German philosophers, lodging in the student quarters of the Cheik Anta Diop University. One was from Berlin; his name was Kurtz, he wore a monocle. Inevitably he managed to get himself mugged, thrashed and robbed of whatever he had, including watch and eye-glass. The next morning before we were due to start the day's proceeding's, the leader of the German group, Herr Spückbeutel, looked at his fellow thinker – who was covered in bumps and purple bruises, the one eye considerably smaller than the other – and announced existentially: 'Kurtz, he no dead.'

Some of our meetings took place on Gorée in rooms of the Université des Mutants. Palm trees groaned under the weight of the wind of ages. Seldom before was I so aware of all the bodies bobbing just below memory's surface, some turned to water and others to dust, nearly as if an attempt had been made to build from corpses a dyke against a foreign sea.

The theme of our meeting – 'Identity and Differences' – obliged me to situate myself. Perhaps the deciding factor is not *who* you are, but *where* you find yourself. Which already implies that identity is circumstantial and relative, an idea which only gets fleshed out in the search for positioning in relationship to the Other. In other words through the recognition of differences.

It is through shifts and attempts at fixing, as in olden days when one tried to plot a course with an eye on stars which themselves were always on the move, that you realize you are alive. This eternal journey does not stop with death: physically you go on scattering the self, and the image similarly continues changing with the washing of memory. Cheik Anta Diop is not dead, he's moving around under the sand here.

Here on this island I again met my acolyte, Ka'afir the poet, who explained to me that one should use illusion to pin down reality: and self-evidently there was talk of 'moving sands', of 'mirror' (also the buried one), of 'light' and of 'moon', of 'gestures', of 'conventions', of 'conditioning', of 'history', of 'aesthetics' and of 'ethics', as also of 'birds'. You ought to know there are no poets, he said, only people who make use of poetry as *pense-bête* (think-thing) to liberate themselves from thinking. Language eclipses the word. Put differently, the poem is an Other which fashions silences. 'Only that which has no history can be defined.'

Fernando Pessoa has claimed: 'To live is impossible; to travel perhaps . . .' But there must be a point of departure. I entitled my remarks to the attendant philosophers: 'The Stranger and the Bastard'. I am the nomadic nobody, I said. Sure, I could define myself – in absences and hollows, although clearly in opposition to my arch-enemy the State, as also to its sidekicks like the bankers. This much is certain: I'm not the State and I'm not a philosopher. Like a mirror I'm the lair of a collection of impressions, sentiments, afterthoughts. Since there is memory, however unreliable and given to improvisation, and dead in places, there must be a collector. It is argued that the collection makes sense only through the collector. I shall go no further. Indeed, I'm convinced of the Buddhist observation built around the radical impermanence of the so-called self. I come from the void and shall come to nothing. But taking my time. It is also said that in olden days you travelled so slowly that you were no longer the foreigner at your point of arrival . . .

The world I'm at home in is Africa. Is that true? Why? What if to be an Afriqua consisted of the denial of differences, if it weren't necessary to affirm your separateness in order to fix your identity? Now you say: but if you call yourself an Afriqua, is it not only because you want to identify with them? Isn't it because of your rejection of Europe? Listen, I own up to the discrepancies. I am of a people who are the mortification of Africa, a people of colonists without a metropolis, with whom nobody wants to share history. At present (to add insult to injury) I live among the *toubabs*, a flea in their blanket, just keeping my head down . . .

But to be African is not a choice, it is a condition. I look through the window and I see someone crossing that field of bare earth at a trot. You see, that's why I belong: I have the same fire in the backside to hurry purposefully to nowhere. To be an Afriqua is not through lack of being integrated in Europe (even though it is certain that Europe is no earth of integration); neither is it from regret of the crimes perpetrated by 'my people'. For three centuries 'my people' have been nothing other than Afriquas. No, it is simply the only opening I have for making use of all my senses and capabilities.

Besides, there are constants. The skin recalls, pain draws furrows and hollows and slits in the memory-field, the earth doesn't lie. Rather – a certain earth, a specific interaction of rhythm and space, grammatical annotations which spell a bond with the environment and the beings. This earth was the first to speak. I have been pronounced once and for all.

Which Africa? It is true that it is a staggering continent, apparently doomed to extinction. The figures, the percentages, the graphs already speak of death-tidings. Look it up for yourselves: ever more babies are born with Aids, like transparent and curly-eared visiting cards from the domain of the spirits; locusts stuff up the heavens; deserts devour and digest the earth; old circles are broken open; civic spaces shrink or wither; soldiers and politicians and apparatus people infest the State and produce corruption and waste and nepotism and clientelism; the intellectuals have wooden tongues and powdered arses; countries are governed by the diktats of the International Monetary Fund (IMF) and the World Bank.

The facts are headstrong, even when they're wrong. To the world, Africa is being gobbled up by the sands of silence, and for the second time. First there was the black silence of shame about slavery; now it is the indifferent silence of an unavowed *realpolitik*. And Africa has no card up its sleeve. Africa no longer has sleeves . . .

The more you travel, the less chance you have of arriving. That time, 1989, when we returned from our African journey and landed at Orly airport with the glass beads and baked clay bowls and imitation masks which we'd picked up for next to nothing, one of the French philosophers remarked: 'After all, we gave Africa back to them. It's only normal that we should recoup our lengths of cloth and our bracelets.'

Now, towards lunchtime, we arrive at Olifants camp. The buildings (with enormous tusks displayed behind glass), the restaurant facilities, huts and giant trees, perch on high ground overlooking the broad meandering Olifants River. Away upcountry it joins the Letaba before becoming the Rio das Elefantes on the other side of the border; to the right it flows past Balule and then branches into the Timbavati.

It is the hottest part of the day; we shan't be spotting many animals. Tame birds come bead-eyed to forage for crumbs on the tables of the terrace where we lunch. About half a mile upriver we notice a lone elephant standing among the bulrushes on the riverbank, with hindquarters like a bus for transporting prisoners. Probably a rogue bull. His ears are flapping to regulate his temperature.

Over the years the heftiest tusk-bearers in the reserve became known as the Big Seven: Mafunyane, Shingwedzi, Shawa, Kambaka, Dzombo, Joao and Ndlulamithi. Six of the original seven are dead, some of old age, others murdered or fatally injured by poachers. Their tusks are preserved at Olifants. Only Joao is still alive, but his defences have been broken off close to the lip, more than likely in the course of an epic battle for the covering rights of some cow; they now lie lost somewhere in the bush. Other corkers, thick in the tooth, still wander about: Tshokwane, Punda, Muzandzeni. It is calculated that a certain Phelwana perhaps lugged around the heaviest pair of horns of them all – one measured 260 centimetres and weighed 75 kilograms, the other of 55 kilograms was 230 centimetres long – but he too has long since entered the beatitude of the bone-world. The biggest surviving bull, Mandleve, is fifty-five years old and getting long in the tooth.

According to Dapper's writings, the Africans called the elephant *Elfil*. Marsh elephants, he reported, have hollow blue tusks which are bothersome to saw and not really worth the labour. Mountain elephants are dangerously cunning, with smaller tusks. Plain elephants are mild-mannered with big hookers as white and soft as snow which can be bent at will. Bush elephants are found in the Senega kingdom along the Gambia River; they cross the river in herds just like the wild pigs in Europe do. Elephants in Libya and the country of the Moors cannot abide the sound of their own voices. The King of Narzinga once saw a white one.

Dapper diligently collated the observations of his predecessors. Polybius, he wrote, recounts that tusks are used in Ethiopia as doorposts. According to Aristotle, their hindlegs have knees but the other Writers don't agree. Some submit that they have no articulations and are cast in one piece so that they cannot kneel and cannot get up when they fall over. The generative member is not all that impressive and looks like the horse's. Bxti swears that it can reach 1.5 metres but that only a measly 30 centimetres are ever used to put away in the lady's purse. The testicles are invisible and situated close to the kidneys – that's why intercourse takes so long. It would seem, however, that Ctesias misses the point when he affirms that their seed is as hard as firestone. Sometimes they eat soil and stones, but this doesn't accord with them (says Pliny), except when thoroughly masticated.

As concerns their copulation: Pliny says the bull will get lecherous at five years of age and the cow will be inveigled at the age of ten. Aristotle disagrees: to him they both get going at twenty. Usually they do it in the water, off to one side and on the sly. Some say it will take eighteen months for the calf to be born, others say three years, or eight, and yet others speak of ten. The cow gives birth with great pain and bent hindlegs. A few Writers say she bears only one calf at a time; others advance the figure of four.

On the way south we see ever more elephants. Here there are also giraffes, well camouflaged among the ochre-coloured trees with their spots like the shadows of birds. Every few kilometres the lilac-breasted roller waits for us. Perhaps it works for the security police. Even though the Mercedes is humming demurely, Yolande admonishes me to hold my tongue. I am too greedy a talker anyway. She says the animals take offence at the sound of human prattling.

We go whispering through the territory of deceased spirits. It is

77

customary for the Shangaans and the Zulus, when they come to crossroads or ford a river, to spit for luck on a pebble which they place by the roadside – one sometimes sees these piles of stones. I have already suggested that there ought to be a memorial site somewhere in this country for the victims of apartheid: let people bring their bleached stones to that place, perhaps with names painted on them or with holes like eye-sockets, and let us build pyramids.

In the late afternoon we fork off on a sandy track, the Muntshe detour. Coming from downwind over a slight rise, we suddenly confront a pair of pachyderms, enormous and sombre with ears like wings and trunks like prehistoric reptiles shaking down the air. We don't know who got the bigger fright, us or them.

Via the Mlondozi road we reach the Lower Sabie rest camp. The slewing sun is a golden crackling in the vegetation. Tonight the moon will be big and clear. Just on this side of the gates a small bus is parked at the side of the road. We stop. A man with a cricket hat points a finger and whispers about lions. In the gathering dusk we see two grey-tinted maned lions. One is lying flat among the grasses, twitching a tail. Perhaps they are stalking supper.

The Arabs call the lion *Aced* (thus Dapper wrote). They are courageous but cruel and will think nothing of attacking 200 Ethiopian horsemen. The fiercest lions in Africa are to be encountered between Bone and Tunis. Their tongues are rough and quick and burn like fire. (Bontzius says the rhinoceros's favourite method of killing a human is to lick him; the tongue is so coarse that it strips away skin and removes the flesh to the bone.) Lions live on cattle and camels but in times of famine they will deign to eat people and birds. The Writers disagree on whether they'd eat cadavers. Elien is affirmative, and to him they bury the rest under rubbish, or maybe even shit, from fear that other predators will come and score.

Lions indulge in coitus from behind and in all seasons, but more especially during spring. They tear each other apart and sometimes eight or ten males court the same female. With the sizzling heat of summer the exhausted males become impotent, so the lady will dally with leopards or hyenas – from such a slip of the tongue a *Crocute* will be born. They also sleep with dogs. Lion cubs are born with eyes open; this is unique in the animal kingdom. Although the cubs are born quite imperfect, the birth takes place barely six months after fertilization. Elien ascribes this to the claws of the little ones ill-treating the uterus, but for Aristotle it is because they don't get enough food.

Outside Lower Sabie's gates a troop of grey monkeys are gallivanting as if the road belongs to them. Later they set up a cry in the trees. It gets dark, travellers are frying meat on fires outside their huts. In the penumbra we stroll down to the perimeter fence to see if there's anything to be seen on the other side. A middle-aged man with a white moth for a face comes up to us and softly says: 'But surely, you must be Mr B!' I choke on a fit of coughing and decide it's time for supper. Yolande is making notes about the trees, although it is too dark for her to see the ink. The moon emerges swollen and warm from the soil, a Bushman-god in a land where the Bushmen have long since died out.

One wakes up early in the bush, carried from sleep by birdsong. Tonight – 22 February – we have to be in Swaziland. Under our door, while we were still asleep, somebody slipped a note. The sheet of paper is neatly folded. At first I imagine it must be the bill from the camp authorities. I read:

So you think South Africa must be saved from utter doom despite itself? And you, Mr B, believe you can set about the task by ordering your thoughts and impressions? We shall see what will happen. I have had my fill of prevarications. No one has dared put a knife to the abscess, perhaps because we are afraid to dirty the blade with pus and blood. I say time must spurt over our fingers. And the laying bare must happen vigorously because we have run out of time. I too used to be part of the South African people. That is, in an unquestioning fashion I shared the common myths and apprehensions and dreams. No longer. But I still know them from within. Now you say you won't rest until you have saved them from themselves. And what about me? Do you think one can just like that sweep one's past under the carpet? Sooner or later the score must be settled. I'm waiting.

Luckily my wife is busy in the bathroom; I wouldn't know how to explain such a mad letter to her. How did this person know where to locate us? Could it be moth-face of last night? Or some other vituperative outsider? Whoever it is, he pretends to know me. I go and look outside. Most people have already moved on. When I put our luggage in the boot Mr Ixele is lying there, grinning a wicked smile.

Next to the road we see a pride of lions, some quite skinny, and then a troop of baboons with a sentinel sitting a little removed from the others. Shall we tell him about the lions down the road? He has the stern look of a believer. Further along wildebeest congregate under shadowy trees, like old priests who, God knows, cannot remember where they forgot the prayerbooks.

Yesterday afternoon we drove past a cement trough where in earlier years 'Mafourteens' from Mozambique had to be disinfected against hoof-and-mouth disease. What does 'Mafourteens' mean? In prison 'fourteens' was slang for short-term detainees. Today we find a plinth which indicates where a certain De Kuyper and thirty foot-soldiers were attacked in 1725 by the warriors of a local king; they hastily had to beat a retreat (a journey of how many weeks?) for refuge in Fort Lijdzaamheid of the VOIC (Dutch East India Company) at Lourenço Marques. They must have fled through an invisible world, continually drawn into ambushes and harassed by beasts of prey.

Am I as estranged as that person who wrote the note? It's true, I think of myself as a cosmopolitan. Now I'm scratching for my Afrikaner roots again. The Afrikaners aren't such reprehensible bastards after all. If you leave them to their own devices they don't really bother other people. The problem is that their minds were warped by European exclusivism. At least they have a modicum of respect for nature and for animals. Well, a little. They look at trees and birds. They get excited about landscapes, they peer through portholes when the aeroplanes land. Is this a heightened sense of aesthetics or an alienation from nature? Would black South Africans also like to come and contemplate animals and plants in this way? Must one first become divorced from the earth to then want to return as if to something outside oneself?

For the last time we stop to look at *quaggas* – all those escaped prisoners. Yolande would dearly like to see a leopard, her favourite animal. But leopards (Dapper explained) have such an aversion to human beings that they'll even rip to pieces a drawing of one on paper. They are the foe of the cock, snakes and garlic. If you rub yourself with the blood of the cock you need not fear the leopard, and with a leopard skin around the shoulders you don't have to be afraid of snakes, and with a snakeskin around your head the cocks won't do anything to you. The leopard has much antipathy for the hyena – Pliny says if the skins of the two animals are hung together the leopard's will lose its hair.

There are many animals we will not be clapping eyes on here. The world is not what it used to be in Dapper's time. What kind of buck was the *Adim-nain*? And where can one find the *Dabuch* or *Jesef*? It was rumoured to be as big as a wolf but with the legs and feet of a man; it unearthed corpses to eat them. When hunters wanted to capture it they'd go into the bush with timbals; the animal was so charmed that it came forth from its lair to listen, and then one tied together its legs with rope. The *Dub* lived in the Libyan desert. It never drank water – if you threw water down its throat it would die. It laid eggs and its flesh tasted of frog. It was so strong that it still writhed three days after having been killed.

We leave the Kruger National Park by Crocodile Bridge. Yolande gets out of the car once more to converse with the trees and the plants, and to enumerate them. There was too much to say. This paradise offers a profuse richness. Buck and primate and feathered one and bug have a limitless menu of leaves and fruit and berries and bark and twigs and roots and sap and gum.

Perhaps the pioneers who entered this green labyrinth picked up the knowledge of those people who'd always been here. From some trees you can make soap, with others you fight fires, the fruits of the tassel-berry are used for stomach upsets, a brew of the wild fire-bush's roots will help with kidney problems, with the magic guarri (*Euclea divinorum*) you make beer, the living bark of the live-long is ideal for cordage, the marula's fruit contains a lot of vitamin C, the quinine tree provides medicine against malaria. Endless are the variations and the uses. Some will inebriate you and others will kill you. And so much of that know-how has been lost.

The fruits of the sausage tree are poisonous, Yolande explains to me; only baboons and bushpigs will eat them. The white stinkwood (*Celtis africana*) and the knobbly fig and the pigeonwood all have pale trunks. I can see that. The broom-cluster fig has nice edible fruit. Then there is the sycamore fig, the wonderboom fig, the rock fig, the mountain fig and the Lowveld fig which grows inside other trees. The leaves of the mopane are green butterflies; the tree provides food for mopane worms (*Gonimbrasia belina*), which we can eat. And the baobab (*Adansonia digitata*) is king, she insists. When its trunk reaches a circumference of 30 metres it is already more than 4,000 years old. The pods and the leaves are edible: you can make a porridge from the bulbs or a refreshing drink from the pulp of the fruit. This pulp will furthermore be rich in ascorbic acid, tartaric acid and citric acid.

The road takes us away to Komatipoort, a town of comfortable old houses with sumptuous gardens under huge trees. We stop for petrol. A farmer alights from his *bakkie* (open truck) and asks if I'm not by any chance Mr B. 'Are you coming in or going out?' he enquires. I don't quite know myself.

But here we don't want to linger. Just beyond the border is the first Mozambican town, Ressano Garcia. It is regularly attacked by Renamo, then the refugees huddle like maddened sheep against the border fence. The South African authorities open the gate and provide the hungry and wounded with a meal before sending them back the next day.

Many years ago, when the war was still only a Frelimo dream of liberation, we went camping in a holiday resort called Punta do Ouro. At that time the Transvaal farmers used to come and fish there. One morning over breakfast two big red-skinned blokes weighed me up and then the one asked the other (I could overhear them clearly): 'Tell me, is that not Butterbird Bitterbark over there?' 'By golly,' said the other. 'Now what is his problem again?' 'Oh, he's married to a Japanese,' the first speaker recalled. 'No man,' his mate objected, 'she's no Japanese, she's a Rhodesian.' 'Ah well,' number one concluded wisely, 'Japanese or Rhodesian, it's all the same.'

Lunch in Malelane. A bleached Indian lady is embarrassed when we express the desire to eat in her café – it is only for kaffirs. She directs us to a Portuguese restaurant. There we order sharp prawns fresh from the coast, and our fingers grow red from the oily sauce.

The eatery is part of a Portuguese shopping centre where one can also buy newspapers reflecting the Portuguese community's conservative views.

Now we head for the border post at Jeppe's Reef. The road runs through the mountains, over a plateau (Kaalrug) where sugar-cane plantations stretch to the horizons on both sides. The closer we get to the border, the smaller and tackier the homesteads become. At the crossing, South African soldiers in typical browns loll in the shade of a big tree. Now and then they search a vehicle, opening boot and bonnet, looking underneath the car with a mirror attached to a long pole. Women come by with enamel bowls of fruit or vegetables on their heads. On the other side the pot-holed road winds down, the fields are green. From time to time we notice clusters of huts and cattle herds.

During the late 1960s Yolande and I were in Swaziland at the time of the *Incwala* (the annual feast of the first fruits). South African exiles lived in the distant hills. The festivities went on for days. The *impis* of King Sobhuza gathered around the royal kraal. We visited the encampment of a regiment of elderly men of the same age-group. The ground was swept, the huts spartan, everything pain-fully neat and functional in typical military style. These old men would dance, put away huge quantities of meat and beer, and smoke *dagga*. One greybeard chanted the very long praise-song of his regi-ment, a kind of romanticized history of their feats. Another old gentleman wanted at all costs to buy my wife. Only when it had been explained to him that it would be impossible to deliver the bride's price of cattle to her parents overseas did he desist.

One night, when the moon was dark, the boys who were to be initiated, between the ages of nine and fourteen, trotted up the mountain to gather leaves and branches of a specific shrub, then ran back all those miles before daybreak because the branches had to be fresh upon reaching the kraal. A wilted one would signify that the bearer had broken a taboo by having intercourse with a married woman. We were present when they returned singing.

Afterwards a black bull which had never been touched by human hand was let loose; the boys were to kill him with their bare hands, but without drawing blood. A swarm descended upon the bull;

many were trampled, scratched or tossed in the air. Like grapes they clung to the horns and tail until the bull's legs gave way. One could hear the drumming of their fists.

Later in the day the oldest *induna* (councillor), blind and knotted like a mummy of brown parchment, was led from the enclosure on two sticks held by a youth who walked in front. He shuffled to a low rise, searched and called to the distance with a hand shielding his blind orbs. The last bird on earth. After a while the distance responded. A small group of warriors became visible afar, approaching the kraal at a slow run. They were soaked in perspiration, caked with dust. Days earlier they'd left the king's village at a jogging pace for somewhere on the Mozambican coast where they filled a bottle with sea-water. This water and parts of the bull were to be mixed with other components in a concoction with which the king was to be bathed in a shelter built from the boys' branches.

The king had been invisible for several days. He was dead. Naked he moved among his subjects and nobody was supposed to see him. He even copulated publicly with one of his wives, still invisible. Now he was going to be reborn.

The day was open and clean, not a cloud in sight. The king's clothes and his shields of the past year were piled up and put to the torch. Dancing started, regiment by regiment, an undulating, stomping and chanting mass of people, each *impi* with its distinct shields. Sun flashed on the assegais and the bobbing fighting sticks, plumes were as waves. King Sobhuza II, already an old man, his pale-yellow, lean body freshly clothed (monkey tails and leopard skins), with the black feathers of the widow bird, lourie and ostrich rippling on his head, stepped out with the regiment of his age-group. Among the milling throng was an envoy from the British royal house with white plumes crowning his helmet. One of the dancers was a white Swazi, burned sore like roast beef by the sun.

We witnessed the dance of the sea, row upon row, wave upon wave of warriors washing forward and withdrawing with the hissing of foam and the booming of breakers dying in a slow shaw-haw-haw-hoooo. The earth trembled, dust rose. Sometimes one or another of the warriors broke rank and came to sing the praise-odes of his group in the open area between facing lines. He'd buck and *giya* and swish his tails to challenge the whole world with a clattering of sticks on the cowhide shield. More dust obscured the heavens.

Then the queen mother made her entry carrying an umbrella. Women started rocking, all the king's spouses and daughters, hundreds of them, naked except for the clicking of small bead-aprons between their thighs, bangles and anklets, and a single feather in the hair. It became quiet, we all grew silent, the sky put on a coat, rain fell. The people cheered, the king smiled, the women ululated, the witchdoctors took big pinches of snuff: the queen mother (actually the king's first wife) had made rain once again; it was going to be a good year.

We stayed in the Mantenga Falls hotel. During the day the king's soldiers and comely young princesses came to drink. The women sow and plant and reap in Swaziland, men only do the ploughing. And somebody has to watch over the beerpots. One attractive princess beckoned me to her table. I was proud to have been chosen – maybe she needed to confide a cultural wisdom. But all she wanted was for me to buy a bottle of brandy for her and her *dagga*-dazed companions.

It was in that hotel that H. Rider Haggard wrote his African journal, *She*, the account of a mythical rain queen. Nearby was a high escarpment from where condemned subjects were thrown in earlier times. One morning, in the swimming pool, I trod upon an oblong slithery thing. I thought it was the garden hose; later a worker came with a rake and removed a black mamba nearly 12 feet long. The creature had been caught in the grounds the previous night and beheaded with a *panga*.

And so for supper to Boshimela, Jane Slabbert's parents' farm. Coral, the mother with the violet-coloured eyes and the laughing chest, employs twenty Swazi women to weave from local wool. Father Bob used to be King Sobhuza's Minister of Forestry. He had the hills planted with pine forests which enclose the farmhouse. Now he's old and deaf, with a mind as honed and unfettered as that of a Stoic. We have dinner outside under the moths and the gnats. The moon rustles. When she starts sinking over the nut trees and the giant magnolia we wend our way down towards the house which Slabbert and Jane had built. It is a roomy place of beams and poles with a thatched roof reaching down to the ground. Cows sometimes graze on the juicier roof-reeds. Slabbert fills the house with music. We listen to the chanting of Salif Keita, Mali's albino prince, to Mory Kante and Youssou N'dour. Somehow we're all woven into the rhythm of Africa. At our feet the dark valley. Slabbert wears a length of Swazi cloth wrapped around his traditional loins.

Next morning I jog past Bob's cowshed. Guinea-fowl flutter out of the way like frightened alarm clocks. The surrounding mountains are clear and still. The last time we were here Slabbert and Jane proposed late one Sunday morning to take us to the view from one of the mountain tops. The earth road wound through forest until we reached a naked ridge. An outlook fell away abruptly and snaked through canyons to the distant blue border. Right at the top, with only stillness and clean air all around, we abruptly came upon a big parasol, a table and four chairs. Slabbert laughed at our bewilderment. From behind an outcrop of rocks a white-jacketed waiter emerged as if by magic. His name was Rabbit Hood, he said. The table was laid, a bottle of white wine appeared in an ice-bucket. Closer to heaven we couldn't get. Like angels, temporarily relieved of the weight of our wings, we regaled ourselves with seafood and salads which, so it seemed to us, had descended straight from Unum's kitchen.

With the afternoon we drive back over the border. We turn off the highway between Hectorspruit and Nelspruit and return to where the Crocodile River borders the game park. Here we shall overnight in a hotel in the bush, the Malelane Lodge. The aged sun releases a smear of monk's-robe yellow against the evening sky. We go for a stroll along the high security fence. In the twilight on the other side we hear hippopotami oomphing in the pools.

During the night I dream the Lord is speaking to me. We have arrived in paradise. A grass-thatched roof full of Mozart music against the cheek of a hill. Below, unto the furthest farness, a valley. Up above the stars. I dream that we've come a long way to be here, through a sweltering day. Suddenly warriors step one by one out of the bushes by the side of the road with bodies daubed red, feather in the hair, bright-patterned cloths around waists, an assegai and a fight-stick in the hand. There's something the Lord wants to know from me, something he doesn't quite understand about this world. I can't imagine what it may be. I dream I wake up early, five o'clock. First light dawns over the mountains, green spurs of foothills rise from the darkened Hhohho Valley like a new land outlined by sea. I go outside. Small fires are burning here and there in front of a distant hut, as stars which have become too heavy and are now fallen. People are living down there, children preparing for school and women for the land, warriors folding and knotting red cloths around their hips. From the east a flame comes. A middle way. I turn my back on the grass-thatched house. The music is sleeping. I fold my hands together and talk to the Lord. Know then: form here is only emptiness, emptiness only form. Away, away, past away, completely away. Awake wa-ka! (Ga-te, ga-te / par-a-ga-te / par-a-sam-ga-te / bod-hi, sya-ha!)

8

PURPURA

It is certainly going to be another hot day. We spent the night in a suite with luxuries that we couldn't possibly have made use of at such short notice. Morning newspapers report the on-going Civil Co-operation Bureau (CCB) scandal. Magnus Malan, Minister of Defence, is covering for his death squads as best he can. They haven't really been disbanded: the operatives are still on Government payroll and sinister projects were approved of retroactively.

While my lady is putting on her eyes and mouth, I step outside, from the freshness of air-conditioning into the burn on the skin, to amble through the grounds of Malelane Lodge. A man emerges from the main building and walks towards a dusty red car parked some distance away. It is Walker of the indistinct face. We stop, facing one another, and he laughs. 'Twice in so many days!' he exclaims. 'What a small continent this is! If somebody was writing about us the readers would think, no, really, the narrative manipulation is too obvious!'

But he assures me that our running into one another is entirely coincidental. He's heading south, still in search of second-hand bones and nubile nymphs. He's been to the Lodge for an early meeting with a Chinese gentleman who, he says, may well be an ivory smuggler. We are so close here to the pachydermic grass-eaters with the petrified lightning bolts in their mouths, or the aphrodisiac outgrowths of prehistoric hairs on their snouts. The temptation! Not that he'd ever encourage poaching: he has too much respect for Africa. It's the circuit that interests him, not the merchandise.

He asks what we're doing here. I reply that we have an appointment with Enos Mabuza, Chief Minister of the homeland of Ka-

Ngwane. Walker laughs again. 'Watch out for the princes of this world,' he warns. 'It so happens that Enos Mabuza is a gentle man, a smiler. And he has nice eyebrows, you'll see. Not like the real monsters I've known elsewhere. Ah, this continent of ours. One day I must tell you about my experiences. But talking about eyebrows, have you heard the story about the assassin with the whiskers like the wings of a small bird?'

I have not. The sun is steadily burning its way into the sky. Soon Yolande and I will be fetched for breakfast. Walker tells me about a conflict between a Life President and His Prime Minister in a West African state. During an audience at the national palace they fell to arguing viciously. The country was bankrupt, the Swiss bank account obscenely swollen. The Prime Minister pulled a pistol from his pocket and fatally shot the President. The President's son and heir apparent – he was known as Baby President – heard the fracas and stormed into the hall of reception. In the ensuing shoot-out he killed the Prime Minister's private secretary, but the Prime Minister managed to get away.

This foxy politician, says Walker, was known for his bushy eyebrows, quite exceptional for an African. At home he shaved his eyebrows and used the hairs to fashion a moustache which he carefully pasted to the upper lip. He went straight to the airport and boarded the first flight out without being recognized.

Now, the dead President was as unpopular as his Prime Minister was beloved by the people. The son – out of fear that the population, catching wind of the Father of the Nation's demise, would stream from the shanty towns to sack the shops of the Lebanese, the Greeks, the Indians, the Syrians and the late President's clan – decided to camouflage the death. He seated the corpse in the state car and drove it through the streets of the capital, the way he used to do when his father was still alive.

This went on for several days. The late President was dressed in full gala uniform with all the customary tassels and bottle-tops. The windows of the car were kept closed. It was the hot and humid period of the year. Later the people remarked upon the fact that the President seemed to be lost in deep thought – he didn't wave at anybody, only his head nodded from time to time, and he never perspired even though the windows were rolled up and Baby

President's face was bathed in sweat. They also noticed that the President was getting bluer and more bloated by the day.

A thin man, aristocratic bearing, very smartly turned out, comes to fetch us in a small tourist bus. His name is Gija Frans Nyambi; he is the responsible liaison person of the KaNgwane Government. He drives us to the Chief Minister's offices at Louieville, the administrative seat of the 'homeland'.

KaNgwane consists of four regions, three of them – Mlondozi, Mswati and Nkomazi – strung in a narrow crescent around Swaziland's northern and north-western borders; the fourth, Nsikazi, lies separate a little further north. In fact, the same people live on both sides of the arbitrary frontier. Ms Rosemary, the Chief's secretary, takes us in to Enos Mabuza. We'd met him a few years ago in Paris for a meal just off the Champs-Elysées when a white PR woman, high-heeled and sharp-edged with efficiency, trotted him through Europe on a 'get-to-know-you' trip. He has the shadows of a moustache at the corners of his mouth, his hair is showing some cotton, his eyes are kind.

Breakfast is sumptuous. We review the present situation in South Africa. Enos Mabuza doesn't say much – he's a shy Christian – but we hear about some of his problems. His situation is unenviable. He stood firm all those years, refusing to be manipulated by Pretoria. It was known that his heart was with the ANC, and now that the ANC has been unbanned he is left twisting in the cold. Clearly the SACP did not intend to allow leaders like Mabuza – non-communist, incorruptible, with a strong regional base and real experience of administering poverty, moreover dealing humanely with the problem of Mozambican refugees flooding into his small territory – to achieve any influence within the ANC. He is too self-effacing, perhaps disabused, to say so himself.

He has his own political formation; indeed, he seems to have a truly democratic mandate to rule, but now ANC-inspired civics are fomenting unease in the rural areas. He is thinking of resigning, he says. Nelson Mandela came on holiday recently to one of KaNgwane's game reserves (before being ordered back to Johannesburg by Winnie) and scoffed at the idea of Mabuza, a much younger man than he, stepping down. What is he to do though? Pretoria is punishing him for his independence by financially discriminating against KaNgwane (central Government is not contributing to the cost of looking after the refugees, for instance); the comrades are intimidating the base, suggesting that he might have been a flunkey to the hated regime.

Awkwardly I try to express my sympathy and support. South Africa needs people of his integrity. But then South Africa doesn't know what it needs. On one hand we are too pusillanimous to make the Revolution, on the other we seem to be bent on going to the end of our self-induced Euro-centrist conditioning, to bring about our scorched-earth Utopia.

He accompanies us to the front door. In the entrance there's a framed photograph of him sharing a handclasp with Madiba. We embrace. He gives Yolande a shy smile as keepsake. Ms Rosemary walks us to the bus. She talks about the abiding influence Mabuza's mother had on him, a humble lady sitting flat on the beaten earth, about his scholastic bent of mind, his sensitivity and his deep Christian concerns. Would he be after a national destiny? No, no ways.

Gija Frans Nyambi guides us through KaNgwane, turning off on roads raising a swirl of yellow dust. 'Frans' was bestowed upon him when he started going to school: the white administrator insisted upon a 'converted' name. He speaks perfect Afrikaans as well as English, Zulu, Siswati, Sotho. He's been a journalist, then became an agriculturist. He is writing a book and helping some Stellenbosch anthropologists in their research into the deeper recesses of tribal wisdom. It is important that we should revitalize the idea that the land be transformed, he says; not everybody can be trained for an office job. Why walk around with empty briefcases under our elbows? We must become self-sufficient.

We seem to be crossing borders all the time – it is difficult to make out whether we're in South Africa or KaNgwane. In fact we are moving through the weird fantasies of an administrative mind fired by the engineering of mutilation. Gija laughs – the Boere moved people willy-nilly to justify demarcations, expropriations. It is called building nations. People are living with invented identities, with assumed lineages.

This plant (he points) serves for this and that, from the ashes of the other one over there a white powder is made; our healers can cure cancer. Yolande is all ears on the edge of her seat. He has seen with his own eyes how an *inyanga* grabbed the lightning-snake by the tail; a tree was split in two before going up in flames. People calling themselves comrades wanted to kill him because they said he was a witchdoctor. They summoned him to show what he was capable of, so he produced the thunderbolt and then they put a tyre filled with petrol around his neck and set him alight.

We arrive at a rural hospital. The director is a young man with prematurely grey hair. His blue eyes in a carefully still face never leave mine. It transpires that he is from Johannesburg, and a local ANC cadre. He runs a clean hospital. Most of the cases they have to deal with are stabbings, people being bashed and stoned. Alcoholism is a problem. Lots of hepatitis as well. Other tropical diseases more or less under control. Aids coming in. Many of their activities arise from social needs. The relationships with local whites? Hostile at first. Stand-offish. This is Far-Right Land, as you must know. He has had his differences of appreciation with the army, who came and wanted him to check on all the patients, turn in the suspects, turn away the refugees. Of course he'd refused: they're not here to be auxiliaries to repression.

There's an army base up there on Kaalrug. The farms all belong to one family. The farmers hire cheap refugee labour to plough; comes pay-day the army rounds up the lot and expels them to Mozambique. A new batch will be recruited to harvest and again they'll be packed off without pay. But matters are improving. They recently saved a farmer from death: he'd been bitten by a snake and could find no help in Nelspruit. Came here squirming, very much against his better white instincts, was well treated. Since then there've been meetings between staff and farmers to defuse residual tensions.

The young doctor guides us to the annexes. Here (he shows) we have the mothers staying with their new-born babies or with toddlers suffering from malnutrition (often the hair goes red), so that they may be taught basic caring skills. Malnutrition, partly through ignorance, is a scourge in Africa. There (he takes us) is a maternity ward. We enter. A huge naked lady, like a beached black whale, is lying on a table. A small white-coated doctor, French, but of Vietnamese origin, moves a stethoscope over her distended belly as if hearkening to the exotic songline of the submarine foetus. If that woman were to give birth now the child would certainly bite the obstetrician's hand.

Aloes grow like a regiment of baboon scouts in die-dark passes of the mountains. We drive by open-air schools in the shade of trees. Building is going on all over but they can't keep ahead of the influx. Already there are more refugee children at school than 'natives'. This demarcation is artificial, as is the line between Swaziland and KaNgwane. We are all one people, we speak shades of the same language. The authority of traditional chiefs reaches well beyond the borders. People share what they have – this is as ancient as life in Africa.

We pass long lines of schoolchildren returning home through the scrub, dressed in white and black. Some have reddish-tinted hair. KaNgwane, like other Bantustans, is becoming one big rural slum. In a village we observe the distribution of food to refugees from a flatbed truck. Women walk off with blue plastic bags of maize flour balanced on their heads. In a reception centre run by churches an impressive lady with body enough for three shows us the tarpaulins and blankets and buckets and eating utensils handed out to the fugitives.

Not far away we drive past the fenced-in metal scrapyard where lie the remains of the plane in which Mozambique's President Samora Machel and his entourage came to nought. It resembles some crumpled animal. He came down in the vicinity, crashing into a starlit hillside. Experts studied the wreck, but we shall never know the true story. There was evidence of false radio beacons to lead the aeroplane by the nose, drunken Russian pilots (one survived), defective navigation equipment, runway lights being mysteriously switched off.

We stop by the roadside where an old man is sitting under his tree of happiness sipping marula beer from a tin. To one side there's a pile of the brownish marula stones. The old man has milky eyes and a slightly tired tongue. Years ago he was employed in Pretoria, as a Government clerk, but he was sacked because he received through the mail a magazine considered 'subversive' – and it was an Inkatha publication! He lets us have a mouthful from his tin; the taste is slightly acid and fermented.

93

From a nearby hut two women, one very ancient, come to allow us to shake their limp hands. They will show Yolande how the hard marula stones must be crushed to extract the kernels, convoluted like small human brains. It is painstaking work. One has to use a rock. Stones have skins inside, like words. From this an oil can be made. My wife is given a plastic bag full of nuts to take along. The marulas, so it is said, will germinate only in the dung of elephants. Elephants dote on the fruit, which seems to pass intact through their digestive cathedrals and dungeons. In the Kruger Park we saw the pale morning eyes embedded in piles of light-green droppings.

On the way back Gija points at the low mountains where the electrified fence runs as a scar between South Africa and Mozambique. Among the refugees who've come across, he says, risking the fate of sparrows fried on the wire, are ex-Frelimo officers. These are now often the *passeurs* controlling the infiltration routes, charging up to R300 a head.

In the late afternoon we take the road back to Johannesburg. It leads us through a landscape of escarpments and valleys with lush orchards on either side of the Elands River, past Waterval-Boven and Machadodorp – where the Transvaal Republic Government fleetingly made a last stand during the Boer War of Liberation – Dalmanutha and Belfast and Wonderfontein. Towards Witbank we start climbing back up to the Highveld plateau. The world is after all endlessly flat around us. We see the burn-offs of mines and industrial areas. The dying sun dangling immediately in front of the car goes through all the permutations of red and orange and yellow, staining the sky, until it burns a hole in the night to release a spark-shower of stars.

In the dark my wife asks, and who was that man I saw you with this morning? She was looking through the window, not looking really, and there was a stranger with an unknown face pointing a finger at me as if it were a pistol. But you know him, I say, you saw him the other day in Venda, remember? Walker? Yes. What did he want? Oh, nothing, he was spinning a yarn. What about? Nothing to do with shooting, don't worry, he was imitating a musical instrument, just imagine, the sawn-off song of one wooden hand. Yes, yes, she says, but what about? Oh well, he explained how he managed to make his way to Africa. Went to Ethiopia pretending to be a touring clown, pretext of course – he just wanted to get to know the people and to find Rimbaud's bones . . . Also, he had a wound like a mask which had grown to the flesh, but this is really a secret: he was wild in his younger days, had wrestled too many women, he'd made a whorehouse of his heart. Outside he was smiling while crying inside.

Did he tell you all that? my wife asks. Sounds like Frank Sinatra to me. Well, maybe I'm inventing a bit, I say. In any event, Walker claims he could now no longer make love unless disguised as a clown with tears painted on his cheeks and a wing-like moustache glued to his upper lip, and with tassels and bottle-tops decorating his tunic. Sounds like a sick man to me, she says.

Near Djibouti he performed in the open air one night. It was dark and a wind with big cheeks was blowing, overturning the décor and howling wolf-sounds into his mike. He had this act where he played a violin very badly; the instrument would wail like a woman in labour, and then he'd pull a tiny violin from the belly of the bigger one. He couldn't judge the reaction of the crowd, didn't know who he was playing for; there seemed to be thousands of Issas and Afars out there in a sea of darkness, but they were very grim.

Maybe he couldn't see them because their faces were black, Yolande suggests. Maybe, I agree. Anyway, Walker said the wee violin nearly bit his hand off. After his number he slipped away behind the curtains but the impresario stopped him and sent him back on stage. 'If people didn't appreciate you they'd have pelted you with stones!' he said. 'They want more!' Meaning, they may not appreciate his leaving. So he sawed all five tunes of his repertoire slowly and rhythmically on his puny violin. People clapped their dark hands in time and wanted more and encore. So he repeated the same five tunes on his small saxophone. And then the same five tunes on his small concertina . . . 'And then?' 'Then you came out because Gija was there to fetch us,' I say. 'So now we'll never know the end of the story', Yolande says.

Tuesday, 26 February. I drive to town to check on my blocked funds. Again I enter the citadel of financial respectability. Upstairs, with a view over Jo'burg's skyscrapers, I am led into the sanctum of the unsmiling executive dame. She has to report, regrettably, that they will not be in a position to release the money. Reserve Bank may exceptionally let you draw R500 once; the balance they will decide about in God's own time, juggling with the wisdom and responsibility entrusted to them in the higher cause of protecting the Republic's interests.

I blow my top, rant and rave, make offensive remarks about bald-headed leaders of the State, threaten to have strings pulled, to say nothing about commandeering comrades with necklaces. I furthermore express the fervent desire that the New Order be realized soon so that these silly restrictions may be swept away. The dame thereupon produces something that could pass for a smile like an old razorblade which has seen much tougher beards than my pathetic growth, to inform me that, by her lights, the future may not be any better than the present. She was born and raised in Rhodesia and fled south before the rising tide of black chaos.

I ask to see her boss. She dials a number and from the next-door office a gentleman arrives, very affable and expansive. No, humpf and ho, let's have a go at these documents, um-mumm and joe doe oh, no, there's nothing one can do. I suggest that they send the money to the town where my father lies buried, that they make a hole in the concrete slab covering the grave and return it to him, the rightful owner. I'm even willing to buy the tools needed. Please tear the stuff in small snippets and pour honey over it. Ants will increase the investment.

The dame closes her lips over the blade; maybe she has a beard down her throat. The gentleman says they will keep looking into the matter, but he was wondering (big smile humpty-hoe) if I'd be willing to sign my books for him – he happens to have two copies in his drawer ho-ho.

With a weather-eye cocked for muggers I walk down to the Carlton Centre to buy a pipe and tobacco. A plump black girl – surely no pipe-smoker! – explains to me the secrets of properly raising a pipe to full flavoursomeness. She takes my name and address. I shall henceforth receive detailed and copious publications to be kept abreast of the evolution in taste and style, on a monthly basis. 'We shall put you safely in our computer, sir.' What kind of country did you think we have here then?

In Cape Town there's a small tobacconist just off Green Market Square where I used to satisfy my addiction during student days. The place is dark and oblong in shape, with glass jars of different cuts and colours and flavours in tobacco on the shelves behind the high wooden counter, and impregnated by the age-old smells of pirate ships and smoke-stained studies and twilight on the stoep and late-night stories around a fire.

Two brothers named Sturk run the store. They're both stocky and jug-eared and speak with throat-ripened accents that I took to be from Turkey. Their fingers are short, the scales on which they weigh their treasure are of red copper, they never age nor do they ever sit down. The one mixing the tobacco always laughs; his brother mans the till with thick-lensed glasses embracing the tip of his nose in such a way that he must leave the laughter to the mixer. They speak to one another as 'Mr Harry' and 'Mr Alf'; in my mind I had them down as Zog and Zob.

Thirty-odd years ago, it must have been 1958, Mr Alf, after questioning me closely and lengthily, prepared a mixture to help me over the threshold of a burning tongue and sore chest and watering eyes to the nonchalant puff. What a man I felt myself to be, with a good pipe and a private brand! Heaven beckoned. I swam in the sea, painted pictures, and went to District Six to listen to Dollar Brand tinkling jazz on his piano. I was even going to write a book.

Fifteen years later I was on the run in the country, the streets were wet and I desperate for something familiar to steady the nerves. I lacked oxygen. I sneaked in and bought a pipe and neither of the Sturk brothers batted an eyelid – well, maybe Mr Harry did, but his eyes behind the glasses were invisible. It must be said that I then had the smooth chin of a theology student.

Last year, 1990, I stepped inside in broad daylight with an old beard decorating my face and red shoes on my feet and a few dead books in memory, wrinkled like bottled elephant foetuses, and Zog said: 'Hello there. Haven't seen you around for a few weeks. Still take the same mix?' And he put his fist in a jar and came up with the same tobacco as if it had been only yesterday. I finally dared ask if they were of Turkish origin, given the name Sturk (and also because the mixture contains *latakia*), and Zog laughed: 'No, no, man, we're Free State Jews.'

On our 1987 swing through West Africa, Thomas Sankara had organized an open-air reception for the bedraggled 'passport-holders' from the beast's belly and the exiled (and estranged) ANC delegates. It took place in the grounds of the presidential palace of Ouagadougou, popularly believed to be cursed. The comrade President insisted upon living there to prove the superstitions groundless.

A jazz-band was decanting sharp rhythms – Comrade Tom himself was no mean hand with the electric guitar – singers succeeded one another; the only words we could catch were 'Soweto' and 'Nelson Mandela', perhaps because they recurred so often. Traditional dancers shuffled out like a human centipede; they wore skirts of grass and cowrie shells and flipped their hips so rapidly that we caught only a blurred whirring. Small goats were carried out on salvers, browned and stiffened by death and fire, naked tails sticking straight up. We milled around, drank, ate, licked our fingers, talked to the local big shots and the foreign diplomats. You could smell the pungent sweetness of sheabutter on the arms of the ladies.

The President was priest-like in his knee-length robe. He was also a fleet-footed dancer. After a while he led us to the front of the palace, had chairs brought out, invited us to sit down. We had an impromptu exchange of views, the stars slipped lower down the darkened dome. Somebody asked if he wasn't nervous with all the armed soldiers in the streets. Sankara answered that in Burkina the weapons were out in the open and not hidden in armouries, that the population was armed because it was *their* revolution, which is why he had nothing to fear. 'It is not because you've been bitten by a black dog that you need be afraid of a black sheep.'

Questions and answers came like fireflies. When one of our company dropped off from the exhaustion of intense concentration, Sankara would clap his hands. The ANC's Indian constitutional expert nevertheless fell off his chair. At one point the comrade President remarked that it seems to be further from Johannesburg to Soweto than from Johannesburg to Ouaga. Thabo Mbeki, the ANC-delegation leader with the vacuous but wily mind of a diplomat, tried to abridge the proceedings before we got to be too fraternal – 'the President must be tired' – but Sankara suggested that Mbeki could go to bed if he felt like it. The night was close around us. There was the odour of dust on the air, like an expelled breath of heat.

He wanted to hear us sing. We woke our meditating brethren; some were unsure on their legs from deep emotion. We stretched our lungs and sang: *'Hy lyk vir ons so baie na tant Koek se hoenderhaan . . .'* followed by *'Want hy's 'n lekker kêrel . . .'* ('For he's a jolly good fellow').

One of our company was the twin brother of General Constand Viljoen, then head of the South African Army; their very aged and bedridden mother had called him before he left for the black heart of Africa, put her hand on his head and prayed to the Almighty for his safe-keeping. She wept and said she didn't expect to see him ever again. Sankara wrote a letter of condolence to the old woman to say, dear madam, your son is in no danger and well looked after and we shall return him to you safe and sound.

Later, much later, I had to remember how Sankara once remarked that if his brother, Blaise Campaoré, ever came for him with a gun, 'He will have to shoot me, I shall not resist, because anyway, if that were to happen it would be too late.'

On Wednesday, the 27th, we drive to Pietersburg where I have a discussion with some lecturers at the University of the North. It becomes another moral outburst. Next day, heading back towards Johannesburg, we decide to stop off in Pretoria. We go deep into the city for lunch and a walk around its streets.

I had sworn never to put foot again in this enemy territory. May this earth be blighted! May locusts devour their jacaranda trees! May Loftus Versveld Stadium be used for political rallies by the ANC! May all the embassies wake up one morning and find that they're bereft of servants and political superiority and moral indifference! May the State Theatre be turned into a cattle market for wormy beasts from Botswana! May the married whores run out of hair lacquer and the accents of the society ladies be taped and played back publicly day and night at ear-splitting level! May the generals develop gangrene of the tongue! May the cocky students of its University be obliged to go and live in Mamelodi township! May its rugby clubs be beaten again and again by third-division black teams! May all the warders and the policemen and the security spooks and the government clerks – that is, the whole male white population of Pretoria, with their pig-thoughts and their fascist moustaches – wake up one morning and see themselves in the mirror and be struck down with the realization of who and what they really are!

But when liberation comes (well now, liberation . . . what liberation?), this town must be preserved intact as a place for the little ones to visit, to be made aware of the codes of total evil.

When I was captured in 1975, Jimmy Kruger, Minister of Justice, broke the news to Sitting Bull Vorster, then Prime Minister. (This was reported to me by Donald Woods, who later went to petition Kruger for Steve Biko's release, when Kruger told him the story.) The National Party was in congress in Pretoria. Vorster said to Kruger: 'Don't let anybody else know this just yet. Let me first go into the next room for a while and enjoy it all by myself.'

Sometime during my incarceration my father wrote to Vorster to ask for mercy, and he answered that nothing could be done, that it was an old phenomenon in Afrikaner families for one son to be a traitor while another is a hero, as happened with General Piet de Wet who defected to the British and General Christiaan de Wet who fought on to the bitter end; that my father had one son who was a traitor, namely the subject of his writing, but that he should be proud and happy to have another, Jan, who was a hero.

Steve Biko died not long after, slowly and systematically battered into unconsciousness by Vorster's henchmen, left naked like a dog to smother in his own blood and vomit and excrement. This was the murder that left Kruger cold.

In 1986 I came to Pretoria with Yolande to be given a literary award. The handing-over ceremony took place in the State Theatre. We were driven there from Johannesburg in a pounding rainstorm. No amount of rain can ever cleanse the cellars and the cells and the *waarkamers* ('truth rooms') of Pretoria from their stigma of death by torture, nor wash the minds and the hands of its securocrats. I'd made three demands: that the security police arrest me openly if they so wished, but I refused to be shadowed; that the Afrikaans Sunday newspaper – the weekly mash of tits and propaganda – should carry my public remarks *in extenso*; that I didn't want to put foot on the soil of Pretoria. Thus we were escorted into the underground garages of the theatre complex and taken upstairs in a lift. These ridiculous compromises!

During my speech of acceptance a man in the audience, a brother of Pik Botha, the Minister of Foreign Affairs and Clandestine Operations, thoroughly kicked to pieces the chair in front of him; when it was over he shouted in frustration at some young people present: 'And then you still cheer the bastard!'

Later during that stay I offered to read poetry to raise funds for the End Conscription Campaign (ECC; a movement of young war resisters), but the white comrades turned me down: I altogether smelled politically too unclean. Many of those Lefties are now pursuing their careers in London or Los Angeles, or consolidating daddy's corporate profits at home. Let them keep Pretoria!

Tonight, back at Meadowbrook Farm, Yolande prepares a meal for our friends. Present in the ornate dining room are Jonna Miles and his wife Elsa, Marti Green and his wife Hettie, Gerrit Olivefire, Coenie Goudini, Jennifer Friday. We eat and drink and smoke cigars, then we drink some more to rinse the taste of cigars from our mouths. Over after-dinner drinks Elsa explains that at least eight attempts have been made to steal her old beaten-up Peugeot. Everything ripped out, she has no ignition key any more and starts the car by connecting the wires. She now chains it to a tree in front of their house. Jonna is driving his third *bakkie* (a small open truck) – the two previous ones were stolen. Gerrit went to see a play in town with a friend; when they walked out of the theatre the car was gone. The primary school in Pretoria to which Marti and Hettie's children go has lately been enclosed by a security fence. *Bandiete* (prisoners) regularly come to repair the enclosure and to weed the grounds. From the fence they remove lengths of wire to make toys, small bicycles and motorcars, which they then swop with the pupils for pocket-knives.

We raise our glasses to liberation. Maybe we should get to our feet. Maybe it will be difficult. Marti confides that Joe Slovo is quite ill, have I heard? He has a small white dog which he calls Revolution.

9

MOON

It was Benoit Ngom and his African Jurist Association (AJA) who made it possible for me to visit Libya in 1985. (At a later stage he helped us get the Dakar adventure off the ground.) I was invited to Tripoli to attend a conference against apartheid. (Much money has been made, many careers built, a lot of political manipulations engendered in the name of the struggle against apartheid.) What a lot of bluff had been needed to bring the mad scheme off! No government or international agency had initiated the project (but Alex Boraine and Slabbert drummed up the financial support to make it conceivable, and the two of them had enough political credibility to entice the shakers and the movers to participate). We had no organizational infrastructure to rely upon (except for Chris de Broglio, our silver-haired travelling wizard and quartermaster). It was to be a scandalous infringement of Africa's ban on contacts with the white settlers from the South (although, as we half-knew, South African emissaries, all cloaked and daggered, had been sneaking through African corridors of power for years, corrupting and undermining as they went). We were trespassing on France's colonial sanctuaries (on purpose). We pretended to be complete idiots when it came to navigating through the saw-toothed reefs and choppy seas of Africa's political plots. Enough to scramble our images and metaphors!

We flew from Orly Airport. Our plane waited a long way from the terminal buildings, as if contaminated. The Libyans consider themselves in a state of siege; they are convinced that the West, especially through its agent Israel, will do anything to undo their revolution. (And if one compares present-day Libya to that of years ago it is clear that they are indeed going through a revolution.)

Benoit Ngom was at Tripoli airport to welcome us – a Doctor of Law, well over 6 feet tall, very dark, dressed according to the latest fashion; his bearing spoke of calm intellectual superiority.

The Libyans at the conference seemed to be all from the same family. In the congress hall I ceremoniously shook hands down the line and had no way of knowing whether these fingers belonged to a minister or his bodyguard or his chauffeur or an innocent gawker. Libya was a country of soldiers in civilian dress. We never saw a woman and all the men were between twenty and forty-five years old with identical black moustaches. (Only several days later did we encounter a detachment of female soldiers on our way to an outlying destination, beautifully wholesome girls with plaits and blushing cheeks. Wonderful what women can do to a landscape!) At first our black African brothers had some problems with our Arab brothers who tried to capture the conference and turn it into an all-out anti-Israel event. A pious Palestinian girl from a refugee camp, with *chador* down to the eyebrows, read a four-hour long tirade against Zionism into the record, but at such a speed that one only heard water lapping over pebbles.

There aren't all that many Libyans – a mere four million. Manual labour falls mostly to foreigners. The cleaners in our hotel were black. One assumed that they were migrant workers from neighbouring countries – Niger, Chad, perhaps Sudan – who shared the same religion, and I wanted to believe that the official policy against racism was indeed practised daily. But I also know that the history between Arab and black African is that of slave-dealer to slave; that richer Arab states give little aid to African countries (except to firm the faith), in some instances less than Israel; that slavery continues.

Driving through the city we had the impression of being on the set of a Hollywood production, *A Night in Casablanca* perhaps: fortresses with bulwarks and parapets, mosques, palm trees, blind white walls around buildings. We didn't notice poor people on the streets – actually, for a Third World city, there were few people about; nor did we see signs of opulence or privilege. We noted that people ate healthily: fresh meat, fresh fruit and vegetables, rice and bread and corn – and never too much. It was the drinking that posed a problem. All I could get hold of was syrupy, coloured, artificial juice. I heard say that there was some illicit distilling of alcohol, but where?

The hotel was spacious, probably built during the time of the Italians. Some taps didn't work. In the enormous foyer people with turbans and desert clothes, who'd just come in from the sizzling vacant spaces, sat conversing softly over small cups of black coffee or glasses of mint tea. When I switched on the television during the day there were hours of direct transmission from revolutionary people's committees: the manager of a power plant in a certain city had increased the electricity rates too abruptly and was now appearing before a people's court; a group of youngsters had come across camouflage clothes and Israeli weapons washed up on a beach: these had to be exhibited and endlessly commented upon. One evening very late a group of young people sat down in a circle in the semi-darkened reception hall and sang nostalgic folksongs accompanied by a guitar.

The blown-up photos, the posters and banners, the wall paintings, the quotations in pretty writing glorifying Muammar Al-Gaddafi feats and deep thoughts – these one could hardly miss. We were invited to a reception where piles of luxury publications were handed out: interesting works on the history, geography and development of the country, but also the 'green books' of the Leader (or Guide, or Helmsman), containing his undying wisdom and presented as the revolutionary religion laying down directions for Islam. Even coffee-table volumes were splattered with his likeness and aphorisms. One photo which caught my eye showed the Leader on stage, dressed up in his dandy's outfit of extravagant cape, heavily embroidered uniform clanging with more medals than the scales of a fish, and dark glasses; he was sacrificing his flashing smile to a crowd enthusiastically stretching out their hands to him, and I noticed that he was wearing boots with built-up heels. (Like Eugène Terre'Blanche, the AWB's half-aborted white *gauleiter* back in South Africa.)

It must be said that some of the 'green thoughts' made sense. He pleaded, for instance, for doing away with formal education, which, he said, only produced adapted idiots; it ought to be replaced by methods preparing people concretely and individually for the real world.

One comic-book supposedly depicted the hero's life – how he grew up in poverty, how he became aware of the injustices suffered by the people, how he has always had mystical tendencies, how he remained a desert man with strong faith, how he liked sitting alone under a tree to look emptiness in the eye, how his humble lifestyle is in contrast to the wallowing infidel oil princes of Arabia or bellboy potentates elsewhere in Africa.

It was senseless to expect him to play the international game according to rules of a Western-established world order. His attempts to trace affiliation from the French Revolution to his own social experiments were probably pathetic. I heard it said that he had a weakness for any comely female within jumping distance, that he was truly a playboy lover.

He liked Thomas Sankara, considered him a 'brother'. Later I discussed Gaddafi with Sankara, who had a lot of sympathy with the Libyan, but also criticism. Sankara felt that Gaddafi had achieved much, but that he failed to understand the fact that his advisers and ear-whisperers and major-domos often took him for a ride to keep him in the dark. They were still going to shoot him in the roots one day, Sankara said. Gaddafi often simply didn't know what was going on; he had the illusion that his directives were being carried out even when objective conditions showed they were not.

Sankara described how he went to visit the Leader's father: 'His mind is not so clear any more,' Gaddafi warned. And: 'The fellow is nuts,' the patriarch mumbled, referring to his illustrious son. Gaddafi sent a message to Sankara to say he was ridiculous in wanting to be President of his country. 'People like you and I aren't presidents, we are *leaders*; we are above politics.' Arbitrarily he promoted Sankara from captain to colonel. Sankara just laughed it off.

After a few days in Tripoli the mask of suspicion was suddenly removed. We had already been treated to a traditional meal by the Minister of Security and Justice in the barracks of trainee police-men. (I must admit to a few cold shivers.) We ate on mats on the floor from shared platters of couscous, goat's meat and vegetables. There were several hundred guests, the hall was big, and one could contemplate a sea of peacefully humming heads. With one excep-tion: our friend Tovarich, the Soviet ambassador, was too fat and too stiff to find his haunches; like an anachronistic rock of ages on a folding chair his massive sweat-blotched torso with the garish braces topped by a red face lorded it over us lesser mortals.

We also discovered the souk deep in the old city: narrow streets thronged with people in traditional garb, bartering and trading, drinking tea, watching the passers-by; through open doorways we saw craftsmen working.

Then, towards the end of our stay, we were unexpectedly taken by a bus to a holiday resort outside the city. The Libyans we'd met over the previous days were all waiting for us, dressed now in Arab finery and flanked by their gay wives and daughters. We were entertained on the old music of the land; youths with tambourines and flutes played, skimpily clad maidens did the belly-dance and black-veiled swordfighters bucked and slashed the air. Again we squatted, sat crosslegged or reclined around trays heaped with food. We were served scorchingly hot and very sweet mint tea poured from pots with long spouts held high in the air. There was laughter and the bird-sounds of conversation. We were introduced to care-free people cracking tall jokes.

The president of the Libyan Jurist Association presented me with an engraved medal and I stuttered a speech. People were disappointed. 'We'd heard it said that he's a poet,' someone complained, 'so why doesn't he give us a poem? Why is he going on about politics?'

At the far end of the hall a little old man jumped up waving a piece of paper. 'I too am a poet!' he shouted. 'And it so happens that I have here a poem.' In his socks he picked his way over the people on the floor to join me. His face was flushed with excitement, his glasses blinded by the vapours of enthusiasm. Silence. Shhh, please! He read, and the guttural Arabic sounded beautiful. Now one could gauge the impact of the spoken poetic word on such a gathering. People were hanging on to his lips and when he reached a passage of deft sound- and word-play their breaths were bated, to be released in a shared sob of appreciation rapidly rippling through the crowd. He was jubilantly cheered. 'Me too! Me too!' a second old gentleman, as diminutive as the first, piped up from somewhere to the left, and the whole performance was repeated. It became an evening of embraces, of pumping hands, of exchanging good wishes – a drunken joyfulness without any liquor.

That night, on the way back in the bus, I was about to chuck in the towel. (We went through several army road-blocks; later we'd hear that dissident officers had attempted a coup, were captured and executed while we had been feasting.) I pleaded with Benoit and his colleagues, with the result that we were taken along to their hotel, which was a lot smarter than ours. (Benoit and his mates always flew first class, stayed in the best lodgings, and had official cars at their beck and call.) In Benoit's suite, on a low glass-topped table, underneath a cardboard hood provided by the servant girl who prudishly wanted to protect her eyes from sin, there stood a lonely bottle of whisky. We knocked back the amber tots. I felt ready for a praise-poem to Unum God or Unum Allah (honour the Name) who'd had the benign wisdom of creating Scotch to console us sinners, and we put our heads together to draft the conference's resolutions.

Yolande and I had to return to Paris the next morning. It was a rush to get to the airport on time – to the end our passports were being retained by some Revolutionary Committee. They were suspicious of Yolande's French passport with its South African visas. The airport's security chief piloted us past the barriers and took us right into the plane. We had no way of knowing whether this was the right aircraft; all flights had been doused on the departures board. We were literally in the dark. Why all the secrecy? Only in the air did we know we were on our way to Rome.

It was as we waited for a connecting flight to Paris that we heard for the first time about a hijacked plane which had landed the night before in Malta. It was thought that Abou Nidal's terrorist group had carried out the operation with Libya's backing – it was known that Abou Nidal had a base in Tripoli. That explained our blacked-out departure of the morning.

In Paris we watched as President Hosni Mubarak of Egypt, his neck swollen with authority, announced during a television news-cast that Abou Nidal could be traced to suite so-and-so in the Whats-isname Hotel in Tripoli. We fell off our chairs: it was the selfsame room where we'd finally met up with Johnny Walker Whiskyman in living brown liquid flesh and blood the previous evening! Poor

Benoit! The Libyans promptly allowed American and British television crews into the country, and when Benoit left his room he walked smack into a firing squad of microphones and cameras. Awful confusion, big disappointment. (Abou Nidal may be faceless, but he's certainly not a tall black Doctor of Law!) Benoit immediately ducked back into his suite and the telephone started ringing: 'Hello? Mr Nidal?' They refused to take no for an answer.

This was an incident in the war of nerves between Egypt and Yamahiriya (as Libya is known officially). A few weeks earlier the Libyans had made fools of themselves when they claimed, with photos of a bloodied corpse as proof, that they'd tracked down and executed a former Prime Minister who'd fled to Egypt. Egypt's secret service had staged a false assassination – intercepting the death squad and then photographing an actor covered with tomato sauce in the dying-swan role of his life. Now it was the Libyans' turn publicly to turn the tables on Mubarak, and Benoit Ngom was the fall guy. That's how he got his nickname of Abou Ngom.

That night before our departure, in Abou Ngom's rooms, I submitted two proposals. One, to create a research institute attached to a West African university to which South African intellectuals would have access; and two, that African jurists should set up a special tribunal on the island of Gorée – rather like the Bertrand Russell Tribunal on war crimes in Vietnam – to judge the deeds and misdeeds of apartheid.

Unfortunately we left before the concluding session. Lo and behold, my AJA friends went and ruined it all in a fit of whisky-soaked, unrealistic greed. Instead of an institute they suggested the founding of a Steve Biko University. They also announced a yearly Nelson Mandela prize, consisting of a hefty sum, launched to recompense the most worthy combatants against racism. Where was the money supposed to come from? The world was to give funds to the AJA to administer. Thus the nest could be feathered with the misery of Nelson Mandela and his companion of misfortune.

Still, ideas never die; they just have to grow wings first. A year or two later, during the Dakar meeting, I had the chance of helping to draft President Abdou Diouf's opening speech, and we inserted a call for the establishment of a study centre breaking down the barriers between Gondwanaland and the rest of Africa – why not on

Gorée? (Daniëlle Mitterrand was present as patron of the meeting. I was lucky enough to help draft her answering speech, supporting the proposal.) In due time the idea was embodied in the endeavour to set up an Institute for Democracy in Africa. From there we could move on to the Gorée Institute.

Saturday, 2 March, late afternoon. Yolande and I drive to Pretoria to spend the evening with Judge K and his family. K is now a Supreme Court beak. He spends his weeks in Bloemfontein to review deaths and other condemnations. During 1977, when he was still Advocate K (Senior Counsel), he defended me when I was charged with terrorism a second time. He had prominent front teeth, a voice made husky by endless cigarettes sucked from a trembling hand, very sharp blue eyes.

Their house is in a leafy street on the outskirts of the city, on a ridge looking down upon the administrative Sodom. K is wearing shorts and sandals, his teeth are less outstanding, his eyes milder – particularly when he embraces Yolande for whom he has a soft heart, perhaps because he got to appreciate her mettle during the trial – he smokes a much slower pipe with steady hand, his laugh is as intelligent as ever. He takes us through to the back terrace – a platform over the precipice – where he is expertly preparing the evening *braaivleis* (barbecue). We drink to the past. We drink to the joy of meeting again. Things have fallen apart, in fact, the bottom has dropped out, but we have to live until we die. So we drink to the future.

Other guests arrive – a judge who is a boxing enthusiast, recently run over on his bicycle (it must have been an accident, even though he's at present leading an inquiry into possible atrocities committed by policemen during an exercise in crowd control), his wife, a couple of teachers from Venda, a Pretoria lady, Slabbert and Jane, and a big bloke in shorts who puts out a butcher's paw, introduces himself under an assumed name and says: 'So you are Mr B!'

The meat is excellent. Judge K takes me through to his treasury where he unlocks a bottle of Constantia dating from the year of my trial, 1977, 'kept alive for the reunion', and we raise a dark glass to the merry memory of Advocate Ernesto Wentzel who assisted K on the case, who has since upped and died and is now pleading the desperate cause of us sinners before Judge Unum. The night air is scented, the moon is out and surfing on its beams.

Back at the table K looks up at the moon and says: 'If there hadn't been a God we would have had to invent Him. How can one doubt when you see that?' This merits a drink. Musing on the lines between cause and effect, he is moved to tell us of an experience he had in the hunting field. A poor white had accompanied them on the trip. Each day, while K and the others were out tracking and hunting, this bum remained behind in camp, quaffing all the wine and emptying the coffee-pot. The excuse was that he couldn't rightly walk, suffering as he was from haemorrhoids. The hunters decided to teach him a lesson. One night they returned to find Lazybones as usual snoring a moon in his sleeping bag, so they stuffed a handful of springbok intestines down his pyjama-pants. Early the next morning he disappeared groaning behind a bush for his daily bowel movement. And stayed away and stayed away. The men started worrying that a lion might have caught him. Eventually he did stumble back into camp, his face an ashen hue. 'Look *mado-das*,' he said with a white voice, 'I think I'll head back to town for that operation on my piles. My foundations have just fallen out. I had to struggle for nearly two hours to get them back into my body again.'

This prompts Slabbert to remark that God doesn't sleep, even if the moon's a blind eye, and to remember a story about De Klerk's grandson. But the night has turned on its other side: we should go home, we shall hear that joke some other time. The car is wet with dew. I take Judge K in my arms and start dancing, lifting him off the ground and nearly dropping him over the edge on the den of iniquity below. I shout: 'I've got me a judge! I have a judge of my own and nobody can do me any harm now!' For a moment his eyes are like diamonds again.

K undoubtedly saved my neck. At Meadowbrook Farm under the black trees I dream I am on my knees next to the bath with my head over the edge. It is better to have the decapitation over the bath: it's bound to be a messy business, particularly because the woman is not all that handy with a sword. Nor does she have much strength in shoulders and arms. She has folded back the collar of my shirt – 'so as not to dirty it unnecessarily' – and is now rubbing Vaseline into the area where the blade must cleave, hopefully not by repetition. 'I'll never get it done in one stroke,' she complains. 'The sword isn't all that sharp either.' Her fingers are reassuring. 'The Vaseline helps, it will smooth the passage. It's about all that I can do for you.' I dream I see a red mirror.

We start our big trip south, destination Cape Town, on Sunday, 3 March. Jennifer Friday has helped us hire a car, a white Ford with a new-fangled safe-lock which makes it difficult to start. We pack the car with our belongings. Mr Ixele is in the boot in a nest of newspapers. Slabbert and Jane and Chisi and Timothy wish us a good journey. 'May God keep a protecting hand over you,' Slabbert says.

It is a typical Transvaal summer day, hot and blue; occasionally the vast land is swept by rapid thunder-showers. Signs indicate turn-offs to Voorspoed, Beginsel, Eden (Wellfare, Principle . . .). Yolande reproaches me for being too quiet. I say it is because a dark book is brushing against the edges of my vision, silting up the subconscious. 'I hope it won't be political,' she says. 'No, no – I call it *Utopia: the nightflights of a black tongue.*'

Outside Ventersburg we stop at a roadside café. Everything, so it seems, can be had here: meat pies, sausages, sweets, coffee, *magou* (a slightly sour drink made from maize), dog-eared comic-books, well-thumbed magazines with photos of half-naked lasses much breathed over, newspapers. Black-coated flies are health inspectors hovering over the food. Barefoot boys (both black and white) jostle around a machine where avengers on the screen are blasting one another with guns from outer space to an electronic hell. There's little traffic on the road. The day is an empty bowl of heat. Under a tree where the earth is red we stop to read the papers and to snooze. Somebody must have forgotten the moon up there in the blue sky – it is a white knuckle.

On down through the Free State the land changes, becomes flatter, more cultivated, in miles of maize fields. Hazily in the distance to our left Witteberg and Rooiberg, part of the Malutis throwing up a wall around the enclaved Lesotho. Sometimes we see swarms of small birds, hundreds of them, furiously fighting in tight swirling formations above the veld: huge bodies of punctuation marks without arguments. At one point we drive into an ominous cloud. I hear the pitter-patter of what I take to be raindrops as big as wings against the windscreen, roll down the window to sniff the fresh earth, and see to my astonishment that we have entered a veritable cloud of black butterflies.

We bypass Winburg, then Bloemfontein, then Kaffir River and Edenburg and Trompsburg. Towards Springfontein the day starts to die. Yolande has fallen asleep next to me, exhausted by the heat and limitless spaces. The land becomes more indented once more; we are approaching the Orange River, fed by the Caledon from Lesotho, which will meander through semi-arid land past evocative names – Grootdrink, Vioolsdrif (Big Drink, Violin Fording) – to clear its throat of diamonds at Oranjemund in the Atlantic Ocean far away.

Advised by Ukwezi Star, my wife insisted that we should spend the night at the Hendrik Verwoerd Dam, to wake up by the mirror of the man-made lake. I'm not sure whether I'd like to go to a resort named after the ideological Dutchman who engineered so massively the national-socialist nightmare of apartheid. The sun will go down right in front of us in the canyons near the river; already it is on fire, the sky enriched by tides of red and purple, and hills become humps of darkness. We are in the land of long shadows where distances grow and become inconceivable before they are enfolded in night's cloak; we are in the land of the evening sun.

At Donkerpoort (Darkness Passage) we leave the highway and drive through the dusk to Van Zylsvlei. To the right flocks of sheep are still grazing as if they want to trim the shadows. We stop at a hotel, in fact just a converted farm, ask for a room, and are shown to a thatched bungalow. Here we are on the border of the Cape Province, the northernmost rim of the Karoo. In the twilight peacocks shriek like demented dervishes. The water must come from a bore-hole. A pump with blades like the petals of a big metal sunflower creaks in the breeze. There's a small dam with croaking frogs. Tall bluegum trees are barely visible, then the elongated blob of a weeping willow. In front of the main building a few small palm trees, some low vegetation with, hidden among the grasses and branches, a miniature mock castle, probably of plaster, and painted garden gnomes. The moon comes out of a tree.

In the sitting room two old couples watch television and drink beer; the men wear shorts and socks pulled up to their knees. On the walls drawings of dogs, a reproduction of André Huguenet – a travelling actor of decades ago – as Hans die Skipper (Hans the Sea Captain, an emblem of Afrikaner popular culture) in red copper, above the door a small springbok also done in beaten copper. The evening meal in a hushed and empty dining room is, as ever, sad imitation English, the lamb overdone, the gravy an obligation, the waitresses dollied up with preposterous Victorian frilled bonnets.

In the bungalow there's a big bathtub standing on four paws, a water carafe under its crocheted doily, a radio rich in prayers and very localized weather forecasts. The moon is making a film of the farm and its desolation. From afar, from the direction of the workers' cottages with their plumes of smoke, the low murmur of human voices, a man curses, a baby yelps. Animals used to roam these plains, herds of buck, elephants, quaggas . . .

Before we didn't know of the existence of death, then we saw ducks copulating like the two hands of an old man trying to remember the art of forgetting, and we saw how the trees were black with fruit. The human being is destructive matter. The brief flame of knowing. *Homo detritus*. Carrion. My hands are rotting in Africa. The writer as destroyer of infinity.

From here on southwards through the Karoo the 'coloureds' have the traits of indigenous people who have disappeared – the Hottentots (Khoi) and the Bushmen (San; but 'San', I learned recently, was the Khoi word for 'robbers' and 'outlaws'): peach-coloured skins, prominent cheekbones and pleated eyelids giving them an Asiatic appearance, small ears like shells to the head, probably to hear the sea in the wind, and delicate bone-structures.

In the morning behind our bungalow five or six semi-naked children play with nothingness objects beneath a fig tree. A Khoi mother comes to settle the smallest one on her hip. I hear their chattering. Can it be that the lilt, the chirruping conversation, the sudden piercing cries, the sibilant laughter carry the echo – the 'master text' – of a long-lost language?

People from such vastly different backgrounds met in this land, forgot the words but remembered the tune. Each brought his own space and time. It is said that the Portuguese were surprised that dogs of the native nomads barked the same songs as those in

Portugal. They also noted that the smell of Hottentots was noticeable at a 'distance of twelve feet against the wind'. White people (the blacks say) give off a whiff of the corpse, at best the odour of sour milk. Words too smell. I know a newspaper editor in Johannesburg whose words carry such a stench that he must have a dead dog in the head.

People and animals moved over these expanses in quest of water and grazing, a measure of the seasons, leaving behind them mirages of life. Sometimes children here have no idea of rain until the age of four or five. In the old days, before there were fences and roads turning belongings into the notion of possession, dense herds of springbok (*Antidorcas marsupialis marsupialis*) would periodically flood the plains – nobody knows exactly why. In 1849 the good people of Beaufort West woke up one morning to the invasion of springbok accompanied by wildebeest, blesbok, quagga and eland. For three full days the *trekbokke* (as they were known) passed the village. Sometimes the buck would do their gracious leaps of 20 feet, arching their backs to flare the ridge of white hair, and then they would stampede. They moved in tides. 'They grazed hungrily but hastily and passed on leaving only torn earth.'

Garob (dry land) the tribes called the region we're about to enter. The only boundary will be the horizon. We have breakfast. I can't get the car started. The farmer has to come and help with jump-leads from his battery. And on we go, turning left to make our way over the Camdeboo, the eastern stretches of the Karoo. Hot already. In landscape the eye comes to rest. Landscape running through mind. ('Could those baboons we used to hunt remember me for old times' sake?') Low shrub, patches of prickly pears. Go to river to rub off prickly pears' needles with sand, wash them, bury them overnight, have them for breakfast, heavenly! Occasional shade tiny footprints of eternity.

Unexpected links tie this country to the outside world. J. R. R. Tolkien was born in Bloemfontein nearly a century ago – maybe hobbits still live under the arid crust of sun-soaked plains. A brother of Van Gogh, an engineer, lies buried in the Free State. Piet Mondrian had immediate family here who ended up in the dusty womb, and so did Richard Burton. Francis Bacon's mother lived not far off. In space of land the eye belongs.

Perhaps emptiness attracted people, going into their own minds to discover strange plants and fossils and unobtrusive forms of life where there seemed to be only barrenness and sun. The Karoo displays the most varied assortment of succulents in the world. Some are almost leafless: euphorbias and stapelias, leaf succulents with practically no stem, conophytums and lithops, and succulents disguised as stones. Also stones of iron and glass. Like rare specimens, botanists and zoologists ventured into an ageless world of vegetal stones and animal seas and magic cryptograms and small brown hunters.

They came across the wild granite which gives out brilliant yellow flowers when rain resuscitates the earth. The *kersbos* (candle-bush) burns steadily if lighted when green; as a torch it is used to burn off the prickly-pear thorns. The *rosyntjiebos*, or brandy-bush, with its star-like yellow flowers, gives small fruit which can be crushed and left to ferment in water before being distilled into *mampoer* (a potent alcohol); the Bushmen used this bush for their flutes and their bows – what more can one ask than to hunt, make music and get drunk? The camel-thorn, the biggest Karoo tree, is reputed to attract lightning, but the pods are nourishing. The *spekboom* (pork bush) is much sought after in times of drought. The *gannabos* supplies the ashes which go into the making of soap on the farms . . .

Moving along. Horizons flatten out under mid-morning glare. The magic of Africa is its rhythm of timelessness however urgently it may express itself. See it personified in the attitude of the man spending hours absorbed in the doing of nothing. See it reflected in the ritual of people talking to one another, the way bodies then move to positions of acceptance and of ease. The mystery of Africa is not in its darkness, nor in what the albinos consider its unexplored, dim past, nor even in its huge but untapped human potential, let alone its propensity for massive dying. No, the essence of Africa is in its clarity, its bareness, its horizons burned clean of history and of time. It is so clear, so *natural*, that it becomes incomprehensible. I had to come here to insert space, to make the inner construction a little more impervious to time. To blow the mind.

We leave the main road outside Middelburg, fork off into town to take petrol. At the crossroads a young black male squats on his heels with some articles for sale spread out before him; a middle-aged male, could be a white, in soiled light suit and red shoes, seems to be inspecting the wares. No vehicles in sight. Two nowhere citizens bargaining to exchange the useless for a little nothing.

At the service station our hired car stalls once again. The owner and a mechanic look under the hood. A young blond-haired onlooker remarks that people no longer stop for you when you have a breakdown in these parts – too selfish, life too fast, dangerous, breakdown may be a mugger's trick – 'only the browns will give you a helping hand.'

Outside town the black youngster is gone, the whitish man stands asking for a lift; he has an object cradled in his arms. We pick him up. He has bought a miniature windmill, emblem of the Karoo, made of tin. No wind to turn the sunflower-faced head, but then there's no water to be had. He puts it on the seat next to him. He says his name is Elixe ('close to the water of youth'). He is going our way. When he catches my eye in the rearview mirror he winks and smirks. Yolande has succumbed to the heat, her eyes close like petals to the touch. In the far distance I see sombre arguments of the Sneeuberge. Soon we shall start climbing, reach the pass, look down on the grey and purplish plains. As we turn the sun strikes a shimmering from the toy windmill's blades.

We ascend the Lootsberg Pass. Distances unfurl which we can neither read nor interpret. A vehicle far below on a track leading perhaps to a farm, raising a column of orange dust going on and on. At intervals homesteads, self-contained economic units – an oasis in the void, two three palm trees, tin roof of farmhouse mocking water to the sun, crouch of labourers' cottages with doorways smoked black, time-strangled symbiotic outfits as between white queen bee and workers, sharing poverty and backwardness and madness. But white poor is not the same as black poor. Elixe points to the right and we turn off into the hills, direction New Bethesda.

We arrive in a small settlement where time got lost. A police station with flag, a bottle store, aged inhabitants with woollen caps taking five years to shuffle 500 yards, horses in a fenced-in camp, dusty trees, houses with closed eyes digesting the weight of sunlight. (There used to be a Buddhist retreat here; now one can find overnight bed in the building, but all that's left of the teaching is that you have to take your shoes off before entering.) Off to one side a cemetery, Sneeuberg towering blue. Athol Fugard has a house somewhere in the village where he comes to collect silences.

We wish to visit the Owl House. We're directed to a modest construction on the outskirts of town. A stoep runs the length of the house, succulents grow along the high fence of a yard. I park the car under a tree, leaving the engine running. Our passenger decides to wait outside, muttering something about 'that mad old woman'. With Yolande I climb the steps. What a melancholic dwelling, and yet how wonderful!

A lady lived here all her life in solitude, creating from ground glass and coloured powder and cement a miracle court of light and shapes, dreaming of the Golden Road to Samarkand. The house is a poem of transformation – walls and ceilings glow and glitter with ruby-red and green and blue crushed glass, mirrors and lamps everywhere, and reproductions from illustrated magazines. She was called Helen Martins, but her real name was Mona Lisa.

People who knew her slightly – without ever comprehending – left descriptions. Potgieter: 'She smelt of ginger and had a slight stubbly moustache. She was strange but not intolerable.' John Moyle: 'She was tiny, thin and birdlike, in a faded cotton, little-girl dress.' The mothers must have told their children that she was a witch; at night, when owls hooted in the tall trees, they probably locked up their husbands. On certain nights she lit all the lamps and the incandescent schooner filled with a cargo of dreams and multi-coloured celestial orbs sailed through the darkness of the Karoo, reflected in a sea of stars.

'Ah Love! could Thou and I with Fate conspire / To grasp this sorry scheme of Things entire / Would not we shatter it to bits – and then / Re-mould it nearer to the Heart's Desire!'

How she sublimated poverty! Often she had nothing to eat. Cement owls stare an unsoundable sense at us. In the bathtub there's a mermaid. A young brown man shows us through the rooms. He wears a tie, on a table I notice his empty briefcase, his eyes are innocent, he wants to leave, go into the world, study, see television, taste hamburgers. In the fenced-in yard Miss Helen created all the world she would ever need – sculpted singers and maids and drinkers and birds and caves and temples and wishing wells and camels and pilgrims with pointed hoods and carpet-sellers 'taking a siesta beneath the burning sun'. A profusion of inventiveness, humour and sadness. Bottles became incorporated in walls, car headlamps serve as the unblinking eyes of owls.

On the chicken-wire of the enclosure she had arbitrarily decided upon an 'East' – the caravans all surge in that direction. In her notebook: 'Light ahead? The star was coming their way, and it was growing round like the sun, growing bigger every minute; so bright that it was a white blaze, the white centre of eternity, with time streaming from its spears. That was God, His face was going to show in that white light.' In this small 'camel yard' she established, as if by magic, mysterious migrations, taverns, a moon gate, the stable of Bethlehem, a fountain of eternal life, places of atonement and of healing, an eruption of wistful and exotic beauty.

In this garden of delights we meet an old man, slight in stature, with the broad face, slightly pleated eyelids and lithe limbs of 'the old people'. His name is Koos Malgas. He executed nearly all these works; Miss Helen had the visions, but Koos Malgas was the artist. He was with her when she died. Then he went to work for the Municipality in Worcester, proposed to make a sculpture for them in a public park. Boere with hairy faces and pig-thoughts laughed at him ('Who does this Hotnot think he is?'). Now he's back to look after the upkeep of the fragile dreams he shared with an elf. Maybe he'll make some more, but the Muse is dead . . .

Arthritis made old birds' claws of her hands; she could no longer turn the handle of the meat-grinder to crush the glass, she feared looking at the light of darkness. She wrote to a distant eye: 'The darkness is gathering around me – I am so depressed. I beg you, breathe it to no one . . . I have done nothing wrong. I have harmed no one . . .' In 1976 she killed herself, agonizingly, by drinking caustic soda. ('And the caravan moves north, O make haste . . .')

When she'd drawn up her will, she said: 'Come darling, what should we do with the ashes? I've often thought it would be nice to have Koos mix them with that beautiful, precious, red glass in the pantry, and then have them glued to my owl called Oswald. But the dominee would be upset. He is worried about me enough as it is!' The ashes are still in the house, in a small box on a shelf jostling jars of bottled fruit and containers of glass pebbles.

While Yolande continues taking photos and talking to the young guide and Koos Malgas, I walk back to the car. The boot is open, the unkempt hitchhiker gone! I look in the boot – Mr Ixele has also disappeared. A small brown child with spindly legs and wet nose points a finger in the direction of the cemetery. I bang the boot shut and drive the few hundred yards to the gate. Bluegum trees. The continuous chirr of cicadas.

There he is not very far from the arched entrance, on his knees, digging in the earth like a dog looking for a bone, with his back to me, impervious to my presence, panting hard . . . When I shout he swivels and snarls; the sun is in his eyes – it is as if he doesn't see me. I kick him in the ribs, hard, and he expels his breath in a grunt, turns, scurries away, still not getting up. I bend down and retrieve the head: the bastard's been trying to bury Mr Ixele!

Better get out of here fast. Red dust on my shirt. The head is heavy. When I reach the cemetery gate I look back: Elixe is hopping like a satanical goat and chucking stones, but not at me. A missile ricochets off a marble gravestone. *'Bly stil!'* he shouts. *'Gaan lê! Hou julle bekke!'* ('Be quiet! Lie down! Keep your mouths shut!')

Outside the Owl House I pick up Yolande and explain that I'd been to have a look at the graveyard – just morbid curiosity, Athol Fugard has reserved a plot there. I mumble something about the fellow who was with us having decided to stay on in New Bethesda, says he has family in the hills, must be a bit soft in the head, the heat perhaps. It is many miles later when she all of a sudden notices the windmill on the back seat. She's very upset. It's too late to turn back now, I say, the man must be gone.

I call my brother Jan to ask if we may spend the night at their house in Sedgefield. Most welcome, he says. On through Potjiesberg Pass, down through Speelmanskraal and Molenrivier. Mountains to the right, a hot wind, big ostrich farms with birds like soccer crowds, then through the spectacular Outeniqua Pass, vegetation denser and greener, higher pine trees, forests of ferns, down hair-bends to the town of George – rich, pensioners – and at Wilderness we hit the coast with its ridges of incoming waves washing up in spray and foam on white beaches.

We turn off to Sedgefield stretched around its freshwater lagoon and tucked into high dunes. From the wooden veranda around Jan's house one can see and hear the ocean. The shadows have caught up with us. There will be mosquitos and a heavy dew drenching everything outside.

A fork-tailed drongo, black from head to tail, flutters from a nearby tree to accept bread from my brother's hand. This is a nightly ritual. Rose, Jan's wife, prepares supper. Before eating Jan prays at table: 'Lord, for what we are about to receive, have mercy on us.' And then we start drinking seriously. We compare ideas and experiences, we skirt around issues so as not to argue, we get very drunk, the moon comes for a dip in the lagoon, the night is immense.

10

PEREGRINUS

Up early and run down to the beach. This thing, this watery beast shifting there, changing its colours from grey to emerald to night-blue, foaming copiously at the mouth, swishing and booming and regurgitating. I swim across the narrow low-tide water with its surging current feeding the lagoon. Not a soul on the beach. Run on firm sand where waves have withdrawn, all along the water's reach. Wind fills the chest.

In the night I shared stories with brother Jan. He'd pour a glass, I'd pour a glass, we'd drink. Maybe the atrocities which I and he witnessed or perpetrated ultimately constitute only a cloth of stories, of heroism and cowardice, despair and lies, fabulations and jokes. Gone, all gone, blown and decomposed.

He too experienced betrayal. Senior officers deployed strategies of nepotism and skulduggery and greed to organize networks of ivory smuggling. It was because he wanted to save elephants that the ferocious masters of murder (who, like General Magnus 'Mug' Malan, had never seen battle, or like Pik Botha would dress up in uniform – ah, the Nazoid fantasies! – and who would fall around disgracefully drunk around campfires) sent him away from the Border. He is now writing about it. If only he'd also talk of the people wasted, the blood on powder-blackened hands of Military Intelligence!

He did speak of torture in dug-outs, of underlings murdering an opponent and trying to cover up the evidence in a shallow grave with a hand sticking out. People were beheaded and death-grinning skulls brought home as souvenirs. Corpses were roped to Hippos and Buffaloes and other military vehicles as hunting trophies.

He was once responsible for training a hundred Barotses who

were to be ferried back home across the Okavango to destabilize the Zambian government. When the poor creatures were ready – it must have been near Kasane – Jan was withdrawn from the operational area on some fallacious pretext. A Greyshirt, a National Intelligence agent, took control. One of Jan's men witnessed the rest. The singing sacrifices were guided across and handed over to the Zambian army who lay in waiting, to be summarily executed. A few days later Kaunda and Sitting Bull Vorster had their 'historical' meeting in a train on the bridge spanning the two countries above Smoking Waters. Kaunda had been given this 'gesture of goodwill' and a new white handkerchief for his public weeping as well. Jan, when he learned of the slaughter, confronted the responsible South African general, who denied with dead-stone eyes. Much later he met the general at an official function; as they departed, the general turned and said: 'Yes, I just want to tell you that you were right about the killing.' A few months afterwards he was dead, self-inflicted by over-drinking.

The ferrying of corpses. When a *griot* (of the caste of storytellers and musicians) dies his body is laid away in a hollow baobab trunk. The young men carrying the corpse to the death-house fight among themselves to be the first to enter the cavity with the defunct singer, and thus be chosen to take over his role. What happened to Makatini's dead body?

I should take a few lines to dispose of the sorry story of my relationship with Johnny Makatini ... We met years ago in Paris when he was still young and keen, and renewed the acquaintance later when he was running the ANC office in Algiers from where he oversaw anti-apartheid activities in France – though the French brief used to be a bone of contention between London (and thus the SACP) and Algiers. At the time he pretended sympathy for the 'nationalists' or 'other Left' in the ANC: Kunene, Khokong, Matiwane, Tobe, the Makiwane brothers.

He started burrowing in underground activities, ineptly so – always late, often leaving incriminating clues lying about. Once his hotel room was burgled and his passport stolen; then he walked through immigration inadvertently showing my passport with its photo of a pale long-faced baboon, which he was taking back to

Algiers for renewal, instead of his own. Then he was nabbed at Heathrow because he'd changed passports in mid-air and I had to duck and dive not to be detained also (we had flown in on the same plane) and then he was deported. Then I prepared a double-bottomed suitcase with wads of South African money and Makatini managed to bumble the operation and have the mule (a fresh French damsel) arrested by customs at Calais – the thousands we squandered! All of the above in cahoots with a French-based clandestine organization supporting liberation movements.

Sometimes I had to find a safe house for Oliver Tambo, our powerless acting president, who'd go window-shopping with hat and stick and the pipe which he couldn't smoke in his mouth for decorative purposes only, dreaming of recomposing '*Nkosi sikelel' iAfrika*', every inch the Xhosa gentleman.

Makatini schemed. He was going to bypass the SACP which worked prick-in-arse with the French Communist Party (FCP), aided by the French underground structure which was in all likelihood controlled by the KGB. We travelled together. He was always an insomniac. In the dark orbit of sleeplessness he talked into tapes, sketching his ambitions, analysing and damning the SACP: he intended pulling a putsch inside the ANC to spring on the United Nations a new organization called the African National Command. These tapes he left in my safekeeping; many years later, after my release from the Whale, an SACP envoy tried to winkle the recordings from my possession.

Makatini had me organize an underground network. I and my outsider friends established Okhela, over which he had no control. Thus I left on a mission to the beloved bloody country – after informing him, arranging to meet afterwards – and thus I ended up in the dock, a plucked bird, unable even to claim publicly a mandate from the ANC. Not only did the ANC withhold assistance from my dependents, not only did they disavow me, but the London clique of bitter exiles intervened to stop any manifestation of international or local support for my cause. They blackballed and maligned me, abetted by well-meaning 'old friends' inside the country. Even Amnesty International was prevailed upon not to adopt me as a prisoner of conscience.

Never did Makatini so much as enquire about the well-being

of my wife – whom he used to call 'Makhoti' (Princess). Close comrades confronted him: he lowered his eyes and turned away. He'd been to Moscow, he was now (or always?) a member of the SACP; the priority was to expunge impure elements from the ANC; he was the diplomatic representative at the UN. The Revolution is supreme.

I returned to France. We met at a gathering in Leverkusen, West Germany. 'What are *you* doing here?' he asked, and I returned the question. Meanwhile I'd learned how he played a similar pivotal role (as go-between with the ANC, or as *agent provocateur?*) in the exposure and arrest of the non-communist leftist African Resistance Movement (ARM) in the early 1960s. In Leverkusen a South African MI agent, masquerading as a scenario fundi, tried to make me drunk and raised mischief by telling me that Makatini had objected to my presence at this meeting of Soviet Africanists, white home-grown progressives and the ANC. I confronted him: he pushed his glasses up on his forehead, assumed his expression of the sincerely injured dog, denied the imputation. 'We must talk, brother,' he said, and we never did. By then he was a sick man with an ashen face and dusty coals for eyes, suffering from diabetes.

The next time we saw one another was in Bamako. He had to leave that meeting in my care. And then, unexpectedly, one long night flying northwards from Africa to Europe, I saw him sitting alone in the aircraft. He was travelling business class, I tourist class, and he invited me to share his privileges. We talked and talked all through the night, as of old, of everything. Sadly, he still couldn't sleep, he was just a spent and shrunken operator. In Paris, cold dawn, another airport, another pilgrimage to nowhere, his luggage had got lost. He confessed that his marriage was on the rocks, child somewhere whom he never saw. A few weeks later he was dead, seemingly because he'd forgotten to take his dose of insulin. So close to return.

Before coming to South Africa this time I cleared out the loft, came across a box with some of his belongings: touching love-letters, never sent, all in the same words, to girls fleetingly encountered; a red-covered volume of *The National Question* by Stalin, with scribbles in the margins; a book of Zulu stories, for use at school; reports of meetings with ZAPU (Zimbabwe African People's

Union) representatives to cement the anti-ZANU (Zimbabwe African National Union) alliance; the tapes. I did away with the lot. I don't know where he's buried, except in my mind.

Moving the corpse. Tobe died in exile about eighteen months ago. He had been a leader in the 1976 Soweto uprising and fled the country together with a few comrades when the repression made immediate further action impossible. He was reputed to be a natural military genius. For a while he and his friends kept a semblance of insurrection going, moving with aplomb in and out of the country. In one incident three of their people burst into a bank on the Reef and held a group of people hostage in return for the release of a list of prisoners – I among them; but they perished in the ensuing firefight with military sharpshooters.

They hardly constituted a movement though. Better established outside organizations tried to rope them in. Tobe and two friends, Barnum and Siphiwe, surfaced in London, shepherded by the ANC. Asked at a press conference about ANC claims that it had been the moving force in the uprising, Tobe answered that he'd been born into it like his grandad and dad, but that the ANC was so deeply underground that it had become invisible.

The youngsters, clearly recalcitrant to the regimentation of opportunist tutors, found themselves cut off. For a time they were given succour by Nigeria, but Nigerians are by and large alienated gesticulators and of no help in a revolution. A few went on to hone skills in different African countries, in Cuba and in China. They tried launching some operations (I was approached to try to obtain arms from Gaddafi) but were soon stifled by older 'liberation movements' which had vested interests in the quest for power. (The trick is to mobilize fools for the Revolution, to abort it, then to use the corpses as stepping-stones to the masters' table of shared power.) My buddy, Chris de Broglio, kept them physically alive. Barnum ended up as a night-clerk in a seedy London hotel. Siphiwe was captured smuggling arms over the Botswana border and kept in jail by the Gaborone authorities after he'd done his time – he is still floundering from country to country for survival.

When I was expelled from prison and returned to France, Tobe was at the airport to meet us. The authorities put us up in the Hotel

Lutetia which had served as Gestapo headquarters during the Second World War – it was also the place to which surviving skeletons from the death camps were later taken to be identified by their families. After a few days Tobe went up the hill to our flat to see if it was safe for us to go home.

Eventually he washed up in Guinea, taken under the motherly wing of Miriam Makeba who was then married to Stokely Carmichael. There he started losing weight and his mind. I was asked to assist him, fatally ill and insane, into a European clinic. If only he could have been transported home to pass away on native soil. But he died alone like a fool.

And so the effort to have the body repatriated was initiated. Barnum could get no help from the Defence and Air Fund, which was jealously controlled by the ANC. The body started travelling, getting stuck for weeks on end in various African airports, decomposing. This continued for a long time and Tobe became a flying Sowetan. Eventually Barnum smuggled the relic over the Zimbabwe border, camouflaged God alone knows as what rotting Taiwanese spare part. A funeral was arranged in Soweto; factions fought over which flag ought to cover the coffin and people were killed. Barnum continues raising money in Johannesburg from flabby fat cats 'to help him bring the sick comrade home'. In New Sarth Efrica Tobe's name will figure on the ANC's roll of honour.

Carrying the corpse. The last time I saw Sankara was at a Pan-African meeting on apartheid in Ouagadougou. I'd written to him to suggest the creation of a council of African revolutionaries, people who wouldn't have personal power ambitions and who could assist one another; I never got an answer. Now I saw him in public but things didn't look right: there were armed soldiers in the hall, reports of tension and factions. His power-base had always been an uneasy coalition. His well-known advisers had disappeared to be replaced by scruffy men with puffed faces and scuffed shoes who dropped their pens and their empty briefcases. On stage Sankara studied the audience systematically row by row, as if taking stock. A young journalist asked him what advice he'd give to African peoples oppressed by their governments; he answered – with the foreign ambassadors present gagging on their ties – that the only way was for those populations to rise up and overthrow their leaders.

Blaise Campaoré did not attend the working sessions. We saw him together with Sankara one night during a social function. They sat isolated in the central enclosure of an outdoor venue, both spotlessly robed, purified for some ceremony, linked by inevitability; there was an emptiness and a silence around them.

Blaise was married to an ambitious lady of the family of Houphouet-Boigny, Ivory Coast's wizened President. The Ivory Coast (ruled by French business empires and multinationals) and other neighbouring conservative regimes, were worried about the spread of Sankara's influence, particularly among military officers thirsty for moral cleanliness. It was said that the flashy Madame Blaise mercilessly ragged her husband for being a perpetual number two, saving Sankara's skin on several occasions while living in his shadow.

After the meeting's final session, during which pompous resolutions were proposed and voted, a rumour sprang that I'd objected to the cause of the Palestinian people being linked to that of the South Africans. Infamy! I insisted on seeing the main organizer, Diallo, the man who'd originally introduced me to Sankara. (He was an estranged Fulani, or 'Peul', working for the CIA, but I didn't know it then.) Diallo was nowhere to be found. I did have a face-to-face explanation with the Palestinian delegation. Then we were summoned to the palace: Sankara wanted to talk to me. We waited downstairs in the empty reception hall with its bullet-scars of a previous coup, together with a few other visitors, maybe carpet-sellers or obscure soothsayers, dozing, fans curdling the air. Yolande went upstairs to chat to Mariam Sankara. I never saw the President.

Night passed and kisses were exchanged as cocks crowed. At six o'clock the Algerian ambassador phoned to present his regrets about the disconcerting story of the night before; they (the Arabs) realized that somebody was being mischievous. Diallo suddenly surfaced, took us to the airport, innocently enquired whether I'd seen the President, confirmed his esteem, pleaded absence and ignorance regarding the rumour, hinted that Sankara may wish us to come and stay in Burkina Faso. We left.

Two days later Sankara and his immediate entourage were lured into a trap by Campaoré's men: an encounter to resolve tensions between competing parties. The army had been convened in a building in the palace grounds. Campaoré, as military stalwart and shadow-brother to the President, controlled the regiment patrolling the capital (Sankara, too late, had had the intention of forming an independent presidential guard). The moment Sankara and his men entered the building soldiers in ambush opened fire. Sankara told his entourage to lie down on the floor – they were after him, not them – and stormed outside, laughing, with an empty pistol in the hand. His men were killed nevertheless.

It is said that Beau Blaise Campaoré, who'd arranged the meeting, was lying in his bed shivering and weeping during the carnage. Diallo held his hand. Later he'd appear on national television to say how shocked and saddened he was, to argue that the comrade brother President ('my bosom friend') was accidentally killed in self-defence – he, the new big brother President, and the lives of other comrades as well, had been threatened. In due time many more comrades and ordinary mortals were arrested, tortured and executed in self-defence.

Sankara's bullet-eaten body was left lying in the hot sun for hours, then chucked into a truck and taken to the outskirts for a shamefully shallow burial in heathen soil. One hand protruded from the grave. Students gathered and wept, soldiers chased them away. Diallo became an adviser to Campaoré.

A month afterwards the fratricidal President had the temerity to send an envoy to Paris to solicit support from Sankara's old friends. We said that we could go back only to pay homage at a decent sepulchre. Sankara used to remark: 'People won't point at me one day to say "There goes Thomas, erstwhile President of Burkina Faso", but "There is the grave of Thomas Sankara."' (This I put off writing, to keep the man alive in these pages for as long as possible. When we heard of his death Yolande cried and I went out to walk the streets.)

Maybe we were lucky that Campaoré didn't have a video-tape made of Sankara's agony, the way Prince Johnson of Liberia did when he had Sergeant Doe slowly tortured to death, offering him a cigarette along the way, scolding him for dirtying his pants, later to show the video for the delectation of foreign delegations who'd come to beg Johnson to take his seat in august and peace-loving Pan-African congregations.

Holding the corpse. On 29 March 1988 I heard that Dulcie September, an ANC representative, had been killed in Paris. I went to the ANC office in the rue des Petites-Ecuries, a working-class area where many Turkish and Kurdish immigrants work in the confection of clothes and the fur trade. People huddled together outside the street doors, policemen blocked the access.

Ms Dulcie had been threatened by letters and calls, provocateurs followed her on the street, troublemakers knocked on her door, her handbag with all her documents was ripped out of her grasp in a Métro station. That morning, just after nine, she climbed the stairs to her fourth-floor office as was her wont. With the post in one hand she put a key in the door and a shooter (or shooters) a few steps higher in the dark stairwell fired six shots into her body, two of them in the head. The murder weapon was a .22 pistol – unusual, because so light, but good for covering the tracks of a professional killer – probably fitted with a silencer, for no one heard the cracks.

At ten o'clock she was found on the landing by a neighbour, still clutching the mail. The detectives took in her staff for questioning, stripped the office of documents, address lists, archives, cash books and money. Twelve hours later they were still in custody and the spoils of the raid shared with American and South African 'colleagues': the murder gave the French an excuse to rip the ANC representation apart, probably in the name of 'effectively co-ordinating action against international terrorism'.

Before the corpse was cold, leftist organizations came to protest and to mourn and to fight over the political pickings. The sectarian and opportunist FCP accused President Mitterrand of complicity. A cortège with flags and torches marched on the South African Embassy, where the carapaced defenders of the bourgeois order far outnumbered the protesters. In the evening a group of mainly FCP demonstrators broke the windows of a South African tour company and tried to storm the embassy, and shots were fired at the Marseille consulate.

When I walked up the steps to the ANC office, the landing

carpet with its bloodstains had been removed and only tack-heads dotted the floor. The wood was discoloured. I touched it to feel for dampness. There were two bunches of flowers on the dusty thresh-'old and a card saying: '*Hamba kahle*, Dulcie. You have dropped your shield, but not in vain. The struggle continues.' Two black youths stood next to me to pay their respects with bowed faces; they were from Rwanda, they said.

Poor Ms Dulcie of the Cape with her slave name, perhaps with a secret yearning for snoek and *hanepoot* grapes, gunned down far from home by a valiant warrior against the Total Onslaught of communism, to become victim and symbol. Maybe she would have preferred staying alive to return one day to Woodstock . . .

I wrote an angry article in *Le Monde* asking for the diplomatic links between France and South Africa to be broken off. The South African Ministry of Foreign Affairs denied responsibility for the murder and suggested that it must be ascribed to internal ANC faction-fighting, and the French Minister of Police, a brute named Robert Pandraud, echoed the refrain! So did Charles Pasqua, Minister of the Interior, and Albert Chalandon, Justice Minister. A remarkable chorus of disinformation, to be read against the background of municipal elections which were about to take place, when rightist government parties tried to smear the leftist President for supposedly being soft on terrorists.

A modicum of research (as reported in *Libération*) showed that one of Pasqua's closest collaborators, a certain Jean Taousson, had already in 1985 been approached by the South Africans to enlist mercenary support for attacking ANC targets in Europe. Further information brought to light that the two killers were South Africans called Dirk Stofberg and Joe Klue of National Intelligence's 'Z-squads' . . . President Mitterrand called in the South African ambassador, who showed manicured white hands of innocence; he asked Prime Minister Chirac what he intended doing, and the answer was sweet blue-all. The case was buried.

The burial took place a week later. The body in its coffin lay in state in the Metal Workers' Union Hall. The FCP had hijacked the corpse, Ms Dulcie's family, who'd arrived from Cape Town, and the ANC mourners were whisked away from hotels paid for by the government to be put up in a communist suburb. The ANC representatives ate and drank downstairs from the wake. Wine flowed – the FCP had laid on waiters in white and bodyguards in ill-fitting jackets.

Upstairs the death area was penned in with red cord. Some delegations were refused permission to read out their messages of condolence: the Revolution is a closed shop. The Amandla Choir jumped to their feet periodically to pump their arms and sing a freedom song; one bow-tied boy, born in exile, sang with the conviction of someone who'd never left Soweto. Valiant militants stood as guards of honour around the coffin, swaying slightly in the breeze of history. People sobbed. There was a speech on behalf of the SACP. Messages were conveyed by representatives of the PLO, the Polisario Front . . .

And so we followed the hearse to the Père Lachaise cemetery where Ms Dulcie was going to be laid to rest not far from Colette and Edith Piaf. A grandstand had been erected, and a platform for the bier – we were going to have a heroic Stalinist-type burial. The black, yellow and green cloth of the ANC covered the coffin. The choir sang and swung and stomped. Speeches. Dulcie's existence was traced from early life in the Unity Movement, through prison and exile to this ignominious death here, now. In a foreign land. Red flags flapped in the wind, the sky became grey and cool. SWAPO's (South-West Africa People's Organization's) representative said Dulcie's death had been 'the most frightening day of my life'. Such is war. Georges Marchais, Secretary-General of the FCP, produced a prescribed harangue.

Then Mr Arendse from the Cape, Ms Dulcie's brother-in-law, spoke into the microphone. To everybody's surprise he produced a Bible and read in a strong Cape lilt about lambs being led to the place of slaughter. The interpreter, a female FCP comrade, nearly choked on these misplaced references to Unum and love. His wife, Dulcie's sister, was led to the coffin; she laid her yellow rose next to those of the other speakers, her shoulders in the poor dress were shaking. Mr Arendse bent his head and showed the palms of his hands to heaven and asked God to receive our sister – she'd earned it, she'd had a tough time. We sang a last 'Nkosi sikelele'.

Behind the choir we walked up the hill to the crematorium. Dulcie's father in Cape Town had requested that a pastor should lead a discreet service inside the dark ovens. Among the graves communist marshals fought viciously with chanting demonstrators from another leftist organization who also wished to lay a wreath.

It is possible to wash the memory of many stains; dreams, though, have a habit of retaining their bruises. Sea, the way it has always been, breaking on clean and empty beach, primordial smell of bamboo and seaweed, gulls climbing the wind and laughing. I am in the white foam of the waves, waiting for the back of a big one to speed me like a dolphin to the beach. Corpses floundering in the flush, tossing and bobbing like words which the watery throat cannot pronounce, these are shadows of my imagination.

We leave early the next morning. Where to? What does it matter? Africa is a ghost image – all surface, and yet it moves below; it is the underground eye of water in a world where people die from thirst. I bleed from the nose because I have danced too much. The surface of things coagulates to a dark mirror.

What is the writer doing in this war? One could say: looking for clarity. I used to think of myself as an optimist – that is, I believed man to be genetically programmed to move on from the purely animal, that clearness of purpose could lead to taking note, and consciousness to ethical positioning which could be fashioned to an aesthetical surface reflecting creative action. No, there is no dream. Revolution is a small white dog hunting a ghostly elephant. I am a gadfly. If one wants to sleep under the electric blanket of politicians with chalk-whitened bung-holes, one ought to refrain from pissing in bed.

Now I know the first and essential usefulness of the writer is to think up beautiful stories. I must try. One can teach a frog to forget that he's a frog, but by throwing him from the tower it is not certain that he will learn to fly. And now I am in the land of pregnant angels watching the grim and sore mating dance of the eunuchs. I remember seeing a wall-truth in Cape Town: 'WE HAVE MOVED FROM THE INTERREGNUM TO THE INTRARECTUM'. Somebody else had scribbled underneath: 'VICTORY HAS AIDS'.

The road to George, Groot Brak, Mossel Bay (behind a security fence a big new plant to treat gases extracted from the sea-bed), over the high bridge spanning the Gourits River, past Albertinia to Riversdale. Country of rolling hills, dark aloes, scudding clouds.

Turn off, drive through town, recognize general dealer's store (De Jager's) in whose courtyard, childhood days, we used to stable the horse that brought us to school. Find the way out to the farm, so much shorter than the one in my memory. Reach the farm, cross the Kafferkuils River (name now altered to politically correct Kuils River, new bridge, but the old narrow one where my father once crashed the Buick is still there, and the water has the same honey colour of my youth), up an incline so much less steep now (does time shorten perspectives and flatten the land?), riverbanks still overgrown with bulrushes. The old orchard with its walnut trees has been uprooted. Farmhouse façade shows small windows with green-painted frames, same thatched roof. The white-washed *ring-muur* (enclosing wall) has been dismantled though, the old drystone sheep-pen is gone, where the dam with its weeping willows used to be our inland sea an ugly steel barn has been erected. Stop. A wind shaking branches and flattening grass.

Do I hear voices? A jumble of memory shouts, groans, laughter. A singing silence in my ears. Beautiful horses grazing in a camp, white and orange-coloured. On. Go on. Other horses buried in the hills, dust of faithful dogs, children's clothes and footprints blown away, my mother used to laugh in the kitchen, the moon was caught in the branches of the cypress tree, an angry high-stepping cock patrolled the *werf* (farmyard), puff adders basked in the sun, winters my feet ached from the pre-dawn frost coating the world, there was the oily smell of freshly-shorn wool. Don't look back now.

On the other side of town I turn down the car window and catch a piercing whiff of the veld's dank and acrid smell, so peculiar to these parts. On the skyline the blue undulations of Langeberg. From one angle there's a formation of peaks and bumps known as Sleeping Beauty because it resembles the shape of a fat maiden waiting for her lover.

Heidelberg and Suurbraak. On the way we pass a clutch of rural labourers in a donkey cart, hats and a whip, then a farmer in his *bakkie*, one sunburned elbow in its rolled-up sleeve outside the window; unshaven cheeks and sunken gums give him the look of a Brueghel portrait; dog in back with snout in wind. We turn off towards Swellendam lying in the crook of well-dressed elderly mountains, somnolent town of old Dutch houses.

On a previous visit we spent a night here. I booked in at the Swellengrebel Hotel, gave our passports to the brown receptionist, conversed with him in Afrikaans. He found it remarkable that a 'foreigner' should speak his language, although, he said, he could detect the accent. I opined that the least one could do to show one's respect for the natives was to learn their language.

Now we stop for petrol. The attendant is a gnarled brown man treating me with deference because he takes me for a white, then he bends down and sees my wife in the car and immediately the tone of voice changes as he continues babbling a toothless smile, addressing us as '*my kjenners*' ('my children').

The day is hot and blue, clouds have evaporated. There seem to be no other travellers about. Before hitting Riviersonderend we cross a small black car creeping over the hills from the opposite direction, an old roofless Morris. We recognize the two occupants with their hair streaming in the wind, make a U-turn and give chase. When we draw abreast I force their car off the road. The driver glances sideways and says: 'O God!' They stop in a shout of dust. Then they see us clearly, and we all get out to embrace and to laugh. (They are relieved, must have thought we were highway robbers.)

It is Jan Biltong Rabie, the man who inspired me to write when I was still wet behind the ears, and his wife, Jabbery, the painter. Jan is seventy-two years old and lean like a Bushman hunter, his hair tousled; he wears shorts and rubber slip-ons on dirty feet. Jabbery has the blue eyes of her native Scotland. She is trying to keep her hair in a bun with two chopsticks and cavorting like a sailor on one good leg. They're on their way to Robertson where Jan is to open Jabbery's exhibition.

Yes, we shall visit them at Onrus, we promise. In two minutes Jabbery manages to ask five indiscreet questions, and then we must part to proceed towards our respective destinations. ('We thought you must be in the country,' Jan says. 'A man phoned to ask if we'd seen you, by the name of Elixe – says he knows you from Paris.' 'Balderdash,' I say. 'I must be a figment of his imagination.')

The vastness around Caledon and on to the Hottentots Holland

Mountains is known as the Overberg – the Southern Cape's granary, limitless expanses curving and dipping, blond, faded yellow, khaki, a hint of green in places. The earth is rich and brown like that around Siena. If the mountain ribbons were thinner, and had there been the smoky fingers of cypresses, one could have imagined oneself in Tuscany. The harvest must have been taken in. In the distance a farmer on his tractor raises a chapter of dust.

From Grabouw we climb the mountain range. Farms hereabouts are renowned for their apples. Mountain-flanks covered in forests of pine and fir, unseemly and ugly, reminding one of Austria or Switzerland. Production of paper in this country is controlled by a monopoly – and its importation from abroad is subject to a stiff duty – so that books are far too expensive and small publishers are dying. A roadsign asks to refrain from feeding baboons. We see a clan of the animals showing off their bald backsides to motorists, as trophies of intellectualism.

Then, abruptly, from the top of the pass, the silver glistening of False Bay at our feet. Down we go. Far in front the massive flat-topped Table Mountain. A haze over the city. To the right, soaring blue, the one more dramatically beautiful than the next, Helderberg, the peaks of Stellenbosch . . .

Always ahead the Table, the Big One. Even when giants still roamed Urd it must have been an enigma, a reference to times long before human consciousness. One can see it, but one is blind to its sense. Approaching it down the west coast at nightfall, it is cut off against the firmament, monstrous and majestic. It is as big as the ocean lapping at its feet. Sometimes it wears a scarf, or covers itself with a blanket, or an enormous wave of cloud so white it pains the eyes, washing over its crest and fixed as if suspended. It can be black or blue or green or grey or golden or rose-coloured. Looked at from the southern suburbs it is not flat at all, but jagged and ominous, reaching higher than the sky, folded in ravines and bleeding white waterfalls; then, when it is already dark, shoots of light will fan through its gaps as if the dying sun were fingering it in blind wonder.

Of little consolation to the multitudes squatting in tin shacks and plastic shelters among the Port Jackson growths on the Cape Flats, the shanty towns crawling inexorably over hot white dunes. There a war splutters and flares with the mocking mountain as backdrop, feuds erupt nightly, shadowy figures with hoods shoot and fire-bomb the camps to leave old people and children and goats dying in the flames. From a distance, as one speeds down the highway, one sees the tall pylons of concrete, steel-topped by powerful projectors, just like those in concentration camps all over the world, the only State concession to security. Somehow they remind me of visions in Bosch paintings.

Closer to the mountain exquisite white suburbs are laid out, cool houses with luxuriant gardens behind security walls topped with broken glass or electrified wire, flanking the streets which are shaded by trees and have dainty flowerbeds decorating the side-walks. Blacks walk the streets for survival, begging for work or hand-outs, pilfering and burgling whenever they can. Behind the walls, trapped by gates and automatic doors and red-eyed alarms, whites live out their suburban fantasies of glossy magazines – but their hearts cringe with fear of the rising tide of barbarism, and sometimes they are torn to bloody strips by their own mad dogs.

We reach Newlands, the home of the Foxes. In this haven of good taste we shall spend the night. Suzanne, Yolande's friend, welcomes us, cool and lovely as ever. On the walls are warm paint-ings and drawings of her brother François, the flames of an intelli-gent heart against the eternal void of a gathering darkness. The Foxes' son, Master Justin, fine-boned and blond like a naval officer, pours the wine. Food is brought to the table. Revel, the lord of the house, arrives back from work. We eat and we talk. This is the house where Yolande and I spent our first night after prison, and from here we departed with clothes borrowed from Revel. I was a jailbird who had to learn how to walk, and she led me by the hand.

Thursday, 7 March. Revel left early for the airport to fetch Lady Barbara Bee, who has flown down from Johannesburg. They are in time for breakfast. We have it outside under the vine and bougain-villaea-shaded pergola. It never gets hot in this garden. Lady Bee used to be responsible for the ANC's Culture and Arts Depart-ment. I've seen her hold forth forcefully in international confer-ences – Dakar, Marly-le-Roi, Victoria Falls – with a broad Ameri-can twang (she taught for years in the States). Now she is a personal assistant to Nelson Mandela and she clearly dotes on the old man. Recently she accompanied him on a trip to Japan. His hosts, wanting him to relax, offered the services of a masseuse: he was horrified at the prospect and acquiesced only once it was presented as a democratic decision by the whole delegation, and then Lady Bee had to be present.

It is not easy for her to be back in the country, she says. Her son wasn't brought up with a sense of inferiority because of his blackness: he's at a loss in this new world. He still sometimes hides in the cupboard, terror-stricken at the sight of a white policeman or soldier – the people who came on raids to Lusaka where the ANC was exiled. And then the horror, Lady Bee explains, of driving to work in the morning, past those new extensions with all modern comforts being built for whites, and a little further along the cardboard slums for blacks. Of course her child can now go to a 'white' school, but the exclusion is *de facto* – blacks just don't have the money to keep up with the whites.

It's so difficult here. So drab. There's such a parochial cultural poverty, no big-city life at all. Why the cultural boycott should be maintained? Because we will be swamped by mediocre foreigners flooding in if we open the gates; we don't even have the infrastructure to handle the aid we get from abroad. (I couldn't help laughing at the specious reasoning.)

The hell here, what are we going to do? She grabs hold of my wrist. 'Those people out there, they are going to kill us all! Children are burning down classrooms!'

11

NIGHT

I never cease to be astounded by the variety of people one meets in this country: it is a privilege to listen to them, to be allowed into the mind of the Other, to walk around there, to note the changes, to come across familiar features, to pull up the weeds in order to read the inscriptions on the graves, to be moving upon silence like a long-legged fly upon the stream, to learn the complexities of everything and its opposite being true.

South Africa is the favoured terrain of double-think, double-talk, double-do, of hidden agendas, where birds sit in the trees like severed hands and fly up to scribble inscrutable truths. Drops of blood on the leaves.

The only way to see South Africa is to close the eyes. But whenever you look away the past creeps up on you.

Ancestor worship can be expressed in unexpected ways. Some months before visiting South Africa Yolande and I came to a worker city in the north of Spain where we stopped for an evening meal in a run-down establishment. With us we had a family of friends from Gondwanaland with whom I spoke our 'corrupted creole version of Dutch'. After a while the waitress came over and asked if we were from Sarth Efrica. We said yes. And she? She too, she admitted. A long time ago. How strange. (She was no longer young, with artificial yellow hair and rather extravagant buttocks.) When most of the diners had left she brought a chair and a glass over to our table and sat down. Her name is Saartje Beard, she said. Did odd jobs after leaving school early, married, divorced, grown-up daughter with a fur coat somewhere, left home and country to knock about Africa, then 'overseas', and finally here (with a baleful sideways glance at a man with brilliantine on his hair wiping glasses behind the counter).

Africa? We were interested. She laughed bitterly. 'Africa BC', she called it. Beggar Continent. 'Africa believes in symmetry – the higher the population growth rate, the lower the rate of food production. One can say excessive addiction to symmetry leads to cannibalism,' and she laughed. Had we noticed how nobody cared any more? A few years ago all those drug artists were still falling over each other to invest in charity. And now? 'Dear Africa, we may not be able to send you any food this year, but we do have a stock of records and cassettes of "We Are the World" and other immortal hits that we can let you have for dirt-cheap prices.' People she knew in Perpignan wanted to do something about the neglect, had T-shirts made: unfortunately they got it slightly wrong – the T-shirts read 'Remember Arfica?' She laughed some more.

But what was she doing in this place where hardly an Afriqua ever passed, surely, let alone a South African Afriqua? She was quiet for a while, went to the bar to pour herself another drink, returned. 'Yes,' she said, 'this story goes back a long way. When I was small I was very happy. My parents weren't rich but I went to a good school. Until one day, I was about ten years old, when they came to take me away. We left Upington for Woodstock in the Cape, a "mixed" area, you know. When I was bigger my parents told me it was because we were coloured. People – neighbours! – had started a whispering campaign against us in Upington. Of course I couldn't believe it. Don't you think I'm white? I became obsessed with the need to know the truth. Every child has a root, don't you think so? I don't know what I was looking for, but I didn't find it.

'After school I returned to Upington and got a job in the magistrate's office, under another name. I started going through the records. It took me a long time – it wasn't easy. The fault – if you can call it that – lay in my mother's family. I had to be careful not to be found out. Early this century a Khoi escaped from the local prison. It was thought that he'd made his way to Bechuanaland. His native name was Kaggen, but the farmers called him Kamiljoen. He was a good tracker. He'd been accused of raping a white Boer girl. Must have been a cultural misunderstanding. A child was born, a

139

little girl. The mother committed suicide, the grandparents didn't want to know; she was brought up as a ward of the church. This was my maternal ancestor. Ever since then her descendants tried to marry, or at least breed, white.

'I couldn't stop there. I left Upington and drifted through Africa. Many years later I picked up the trace again in London, in documents of the old Bechuanaland Protectorate. Not for nothing was my forefather a tracker. A Spanish adventurer had spent time in the desert there, gathering plant and animal specimens, and he returned to Europe with his favourite hunter. The Spaniard's name was Darder, his hunter was known as Caméleon. There the spoor ended.

'Then, two years ago, I was in Barcelona, and quite by chance I read something in the paper about a Museu Darder in Banyoles. I went there with my heart in my throat . . . It's silly, really, but all I had left from Africa was this necklace of ostrich-shell . . .' (She put her hand in her blouse and pulled out the double string of beads cut from the whitish egg.) 'I put it on. He was there, Kaggen Kamiljoen . . .

'There was nothing for me to do in Banyoles. I looked for work in the region, met this man . . .' (She looked at the *chico* behind the bar.) 'He treats me well. You should go to Banyoles, it's pretty by the lake . . .' Her voice trailed off. We were all silent.

The next day we found the Banyoles museum in a small building. Darder had been a medical doctor and explorer from Barcelona and for some reason his plunder was bequeathed to this balneary resort. The rooms contained the most eclectic jumble of exotic animals and freaks stuffed and mounted in glass cases.

In one room, pegged out behind glass panes on the wall, two human skins, of a male and a female, white subjects blackened with age (we all grow black in death), the hair of the scalps still curly, with the awkward flayed shapes of orang-utans.

All by himself in a glass-walled enclosure in the middle of the room there was a stuffed human being. He was frail, below average height, of an indeterminate age. He wore an orange-coloured loin-cloth of leather, on his left arm he carried a small shield also made of leather, his right hand held a spear; attached to a beaded neck-lace he had what must have been a headdress of dried rushes. The ears were small and perfectly shaped like seashells, the lips had been painted red, the cheekbones were salient, the cheeks sunken, the hair on his head grew in small tufts, the eyes – though certainly of glass – looked as if they were staring into the distance. He still had his toenails; his skin was very dark and leathery – perhaps it had been varnished.

We walked away silently. ('There is silence where a song would ring. / There is nothing now, where it once sounded.') In the foyer we bought postcards. The lady on duty told us they were hoping to modernize – they had a lot of visitors in summer. Some people returned. 'There's a woman, for instance, comes here quite often, seems a bit mad though harmless. She sits in there for hours talking softly to the hunter and then she always leaves food behind. Stupid, of course, as if the African would eat Catalan fare! Blonde woman. Must be a foreigner. We don't show her away, we just remove the food afterwards.'

It was my sister Rachel who first informed me about Uys Krige's death. I'd called her to talk about Oubaas, our father. 'Uys just passed away,' she said, and I thought to myself that his lifeboat had finally found a white flag to hoist in order to sail away from Onrus Bay and disappear in a blue oblivion.

I got to know him in Cape Town where he lived with fellow writer Jack Cope in a beach house against a Clifton slope. How alive the Mother City used to be before fascist political engineers and other black-shoed Broederbond planners destroyed it! I used to think of it as an Alexandria in the southern Atlantic. Odd characters washed up against the mountain-flank, extraordinary destinies were played out in the tavern of the seas. The cosmopolitan make-up of the city facilitated its sparkling artistic and political life – the Muslim Malay community with their *kramats* (holy burial tombs) of noble forebears dotted around the Peninsula; emancipated slave descendants from many parts of the world, with quicksilver wit; eccentric scions of old Afrikaner families of mixed origin; refugees from Central Europe; deserters from dim foreign pasts; black labourers and trade unionists and intellectuals; effete Britishers looking for sun and a tax-haven; brown families from St Helena; dispossessed barons and shady war criminals; painters with little goatees and doe eyes and funny accents walking like ducks; Portuguese greengrocers and Indian tailors and Chinese launderers; long-legged, barefoot beauties from upcountry farms; *dagga*-smokers and antique dealers and Trotskyites and mad versifiers and nudist nature lovers and magicians and textile workers and jazz musicians and degenerates and creators and ascetics and foreign sailors who came to District Six and missed their boats and hedonists and doom prophets and charlatans and black-suited fundamentalists and suicide artists and crayfish fanatics and gamblers and crazy middle-aged students from the Congo and *samoosa*-eaters.

There used to be jazz dives and night-clubs and theatres and art galleries serving sherry and wild parties and ferocious discussions and red-mouthed harbour whores without teeth and vendors blowing bugles to sell their snoek and amateur political saboteurs and single-minded mountaineers and a symphony orchestra and subversive publications and journalists with fleas and bars burning down and naked midnight swimming and crammed double-decker buses and a carnival lasting a week and cinemas showing American musicals and fat mammies with flowery *kopdoeke* (kerchiefs) selling flowers on the Parade and prim office-girls with tight squiggly bums walking on stiletto heels and sad deep-voiced choirs wearing red fezzes and blazers and pocket-picking *skollies* (hooligans) and bearded bums called *bergies* sleeping on the mountain with the baboons and boat-builders and cheeky newspaper-vendors and soap-box orators and ageless nymphs playing Shakespeare in the open air and proletarians breeding budgies in Afrikaner suburbs and ancient polished motorcars and tattoo parlours and yogis and academics wearing medieval gowns and cabbalists and boxers and tea-party addicts and down-and-outers and star-gazers and visiting gurus and kite-makers and oriental weddings and real bookshops and experts in anemometry and poets who contracted tuberculosis after producing one slim volume of eternity.

Then came the time of the bacon-arsed politicians with the hairy faces and the pig-thoughts, the short-back-and-sides bureaucrats, the policemen with dogs, the bulldozers, the entrepreneurs, the murder squads, the death laws, the grand schemes, the blood and the blight . . .

It is only now, more than thirty years on – after the expulsions, displacements, imprisonments, censorship, repression, destruction, corruption, riots and resistance of the intervening years – that the first timid signs of a cosmopolitan cultural life are resurfacing in Cape Town.

Some of the exiles have returned; access to the harbour has been established with the opening of clubs, restaurants and theatres on the waterfront; surviving buskers make old music on the pavements; the National Gallery has re-opened; a sharp new weekly, *South*, is published; State culture is finally on the retreat; new voices have emerged.

We met Uys Krige again in Paris. After Cape Town he'd gone to live in Onrus, the village where my parents retired, and they became friends. Together they waited for death to find them by the sea. But most of all I was attached to Uys because, as a poetic precursor, he turned his back upon the pretentious Pan-Germanic canon of his epoch (to say nothing of a 'racially pure' world of ideas), and created an access to the lighter, more lyrical and surrealist Mediterranean climate. In his life, also, he was involved in the struggle against fascism during a period of fraternal fighting among Afrikaners. Maybe the options indicated by him have faded: today the young writers sit with their ears pressed against Anglo American doors.

Uys was a vibrant, loquacious, curious person. This is the way I remember him: Uys on the stairs outside our Paris flat with a hot-water bottle cradled in his arms. It had been a cold night and his son Taillefer was sent to their hotel for the bottle so that we could fill it with boiling water; now he was torn between the need to get back before the water cooled and his desire to ring up a few last words. Three steps down, two steps up, 'Breytie, now just tell me again . . .' (He was the only person who ever called me by that name.)

Uys, scarf around the neck, quacking all by himself at the counter of our local bistro. It was a national holiday, the streets were empty except for a layer of snow. We'd been away and we found him there upon our return. His thin shoes were soaked, the cardboard soles peeling off, his only protection against the cold the scarf and an outsize jersey, and he was blowing the mind of our bleary-eyed Auvergnat café-owner with a fulsome report of his prostate and stomach ailments. In three marathon instalments Uys had succeeded in passing over to the *bistrotier* his total life with all its ills. Monsieur Jean was now partly responsible for Uys; already some of his 'medicines' were stocked under the bar counter.

Uys, after their departure from Paris, writing a letter to my wife whom he called 'Skapie' (lamb). It was a miracle the missive ever arrived: after closing the envelope with its single sheet blackened on both sides he must have had an afterthought because the envelope also was entirely covered in scribbles like weeds smothering the flower of an address.

Uys at home with us. André Brink was lodging in a room one floor down. There was a phone-call for him from his London girlfriend. Uys, after a while: 'Who is it? Who is it?' André: 'Shhttt, no wait, man. You don't know her.' Uys impatient, grabbing hold of the extension, listening with, chipping in with comments, just wanted to say 'good evening', and pretty soon he was in sole possession of the line and embarked upon a lengthy conversation with the unknown dolly, a sheepish André standing by.

But Uys with the distant gaze, his melancholic nostalgia, his ear finely tuned for nuances, his treasure of world literature (once he had added on to the original in his translation of a Shakespeare play out of sheer love for the characters), his big heart, his extended family of friends. I'm convinced he must be up there in heaven joking with Lorca, Neruda, Cortazar, Borges, Roy Campbell . . . (for political differences will no longer matter). The stories they'll be telling one another! Maybe a few Afrikaner poets will also wander across from their 'own' residential area to shake his hand.

After Dakar, Uys's niece Grethe and her husband Moons spent time with us in Spain. We often talked of Uys, who'd written one of his best books, *Sol y sombra* (*Sun and Shadow*), about his Spanish experiences before and during the civil war. Grethe has the family's quick mouth, broad forehead, blue eyes set deep in their sockets, flattish nose, inquisitive spirit, easy way of slipping from Afrikaans into English and back again. She said Uys was not well, his teeth were bothering him; her mother had gone to Onrus to be there, the end was probably at hand.

We last saw Uys alive during our 1986 visit to South Africa. Jakes Gerwel (my lost but brave communist friend from Western Cape

University) drove us out to Onrus for the day, to the house of Jan Biltong and Jabbery. A second car transported Sog Serfyn and two technicians – they were filming our return to the country. (That very morning we'd had a blazing row because Sog wanted to shoot my first visit to my mother's resting place: I refused to be trapped in the sentimental situation of 'Boer boy returns from exile to weep on his mother's tomb'. Yolande would not even speak to the man. Jakes, in his inimitable calm fashion, just listened without commenting.)

Accompanied by Jakes and Jan Biltong we proceeded to the cemetery at Hermanus, the next town up the coast. My mother lay against a slope under a polished granite stone with an unexpectedly stern inscription: '*My genade is vir julle genoeg*' ('My pardon – or mercy, or grace – is enough for you'). It was a double grave; Oubaas's bed was ready for him.

What could I say? 'Look, it's me, Ounooi. I'm so sorry I couldn't be here to say goodbye. And I'm eaten up by the thought that you died of a heart broken by the sadness I caused you.' But she was beyond such considerations. We arranged a small bunch of wild flowers in the vase and then went for a stroll through a plantation of young bluegums so that Yolande Mariposa could dry her eyes.

A small cloud of black butterflies hovered over the site. What brought them there? The fragrant veld? I never knew before that there were black butterflies. It was restful in the sunlight among the hills. On quiet days with the wind coming the right way one probably heard the sea. I thought that my mother must be happy, surrounded by neighbours and acquaintances, and now and then a retired bowls-playing general. It was good soil in which to become dust, and many a memory, recipe and remedy must have been exchanged there.

After my mother's burial the prison authorities had allowed me to receive an album of photos taken during the ceremony. Regularly, when the cell was 'ramped' (searched), the Boere would leaf through the album with pathological curiosity. (Oh God, what a pleasure to finger another's pain!) On one of the photos Uys could be seen in the background: bewildered, black suit, black tie, black glasses, slippers. Were his feet after all impaired by that cold tramp through Paris years before? Oubaas also wore dark glasses where he stood assisted by his children. The two of them looked like Mafia godfathers.

But that afternoon we considered that it would be better to have Uys brought to Jan Biltong's house rather than us go to disturb his retreat. It was already late when Sog Serfyn went to fetch him. I got a fright when he hesitantly climbed the few steps to Jan's garden in the afternoon glow. The man looked uncared-for, his collar and sleeves were frayed. Is that a death-mask? The eyes were sunken, the cheeks had lost their flesh, and with the sun coming low through the branches one could see the glint of white stubble on his chin. He had the bird-claw nails of an old man living alone. But when he flashed the best porcelain any shop could provide in a smile of youthful insouciance, then all the old charm was back.

We sat around a table outside, drinking tea (Uys was niggling, but Jabbery knew exactly how he liked his), and conversed in fits and starts. His thoughts, I'd been warned, no longer progressed in a linear way, were wont to graze further afield. *He did not want to disappear.* Four times he repeated himself: 'Tell me now, Breytie, who of our friends still live in Paris? There must be, there was, *ag man*, what was the name again? . . .' And then he fished up somebody dead these forty years, or who'd never resided in France.

Still, when Sog Serfyn's camera started rolling he was immediately as image-conscious as he'd always been (one wasn't going to let disintegration get a grip after all!): off came the glasses, the hair was patted down, the best smile suspended from the lips, and he didn't even want to turn his head in my direction to continue the conversation because the profile had to be just right.

Shortly afterwards, in a hurry for no apparent reason, fretful all of a sudden, Uys got up to go. No, no, he didn't want us to accompany him.

A last photograph showed him in bed at home, bearded, his eyes big and dark. He only ate sweets towards the end – still waiting for a line that would lead to a new poem. A line guiding him to darkness.

12

PROTYLE

We have been back in this country for long enough now to start feeling 'at home'. The days are longer, lazier. Less seems to happen. We cannot run away from the past – indeed, our past is the actual running. It is good to sit down and sort out the thoughts. Much is not clear yet and it is too early to propose a coherent vision (it is always too early), but some impressions are setting.

Vrye Weekblad reports a case of assault. An aged black man, William Mashiya, who has five goats, lives as a worker on a farm bordering on that of Eugène Nuy Terre'Blanche, the 'God-quoting' leader of the AWB. On a Saturday afternoon Terre'Blanche, accompanied by one of his 'soldiers' in khaki, both armed with revolvers, came to Mashiya's house and accused him of having stolen a sheep. Mashiya: 'I was at home with my five children. He [Terre'Blanche] said: "You bladdy kaffirs. You pigs. Today we kill you all." I know Terre'Blanche. Did not this child grow up before my eyes? And our children played together. He ordered me and the children out of the house and told us to put our hands against the wall. Then he hit me. He cursed me all the time. He hit me in the face and I fell on the ground. Thereafter he kicked me in the ribs and stomach. I tried fending with my hands. So he choked me.' The other man looked on and beat a child who'd started crying. The children ran into the house and Terre'Blanche followed them and clobbered them, breaking two chairs in the fracas. All the while he screamed: 'Today I must finish the kaffirs here.' Mashiya says maybe Terre'Blanche was drunk. Terre'Blanche warned: 'Tonight you mustn't sleep because I'm coming back.' Thereupon he assaulted another farm labourer, Ismael Lentsho, aged seventy, who died two days later of 'pneumonia'. The district surgeon of

Ventersdorp, Dr Justus Roscher, refused to make an autopsy. To the newspaper he declared: 'I can't remember that I treated the man. I see too many of these people every day and I don't know the surname. Their surnames all sound the same and it is confusing.' Mashiya tried laying a charge at the police station in Ventersdorp. 'The police there told me they will not open a docket. They told me to go away.' Two days later he went to a lawyer in Krugersdorp.

Sowetan runs a story on the disbanding of the security police to become part of Crime Combating and Investigation (CCI). (In fact the head of the security police was appointed over-all commander.) It also reports that forty-eight principals at schools in Mamelodi, Pretoria, were this week chased out of their schools by pupils.

Die Burger publishes a denial by Dr Robbie Robinson, director of the National Parks Board, that the unseasonal and artificial opening of the Touw River estuary into the sea at Wilderness had anything to do with a phone-call made by Crocodile Botha, who lives in that resort. Dr Robinson says the mouth had to be bulldozed to allow big fish which are ocean-breeders to swim through. Some other inhabitants of Wilderness are most unhappy that this should have happened because of 'a single phone-call'. Crocodile Botha says he has nothing to do with rivers and lakes.

We are staying in Paradise House, the summer cottage of the Fox family out at Simon's Town. '*Simons Baay in de Baay Falso*' (Simon's Bay in False Bay) was visited in 1687 by the Dutch Governor at the Cape of Good Hope, Simon van der Stel. He recognized its excellent moorage, protected from the worst winds, and ordered it settled. In 1743 Baron van Imhof surveyed the town and it probably hasn't changed all that much since. It is said that this safe natural harbour was one of the main reasons why the British attacked and occupied the Cape. Over centuries it became the most important naval base in the southern Atlantic. Harbour and town now constitute the South African Navy's headquarters; from here the oceans are scanned. A big part of the base is buried in mountain bunkers behind the town.

Paradise House lies against the slope, screened off by tall trees and fragrant bushes, a humble but magical dwelling, flat and white-washed. The front stoep overlooks the bay: first, the way a bird would see it falling down the mountain wind (as they often do), the railway line and its station below from where we sometimes hear a clickety-clack. Then, to the right, the town stacked in terraces of Victorian and Georgian buildings and the harbour with piers and grey frigates; and to the left, hugging the coast at the foot of the range, the road heading for Cape Town via Fish Hoek and Muizenberg, white settlements sparkling in the sun. In the lee of the harbour wall a host of yachts with, wallowing at anchor like a swan among ducklings, the antiquated vessel used for laying and repairing submarine cables (called *SA Cable Restorer*). Sometimes the ominous black shape of a submarine surfaces on its way into base.

The water changes in humour and hue depending on the hour and the winds – from metallic grey to indigo to white-flecked emerald to the evening's silver and rust when the sun starts bleeding, and on to the liquid unsoundable black of night, sometimes crusted over by a glassiness of moonlight.

Clouds in the sky by day, an infinity of stars at night. Across the vast body of water, on a crisp day, one can see the white hem of sand running around to the Strand with above that again distant jagged peaks like the backs of a school of mythical dragons. At night loops of lights string jewels around the sea's throat.

Other people come with the house – a family of Xhosa squatters. Suzanne 'inherited' Bruman from a neighbour. In return for once a week raking the leaves and cutting the grass and looking out for the cobra who has taken up residence in the garden, Suzanne and Revel had a wooden hut built for Bruman on the terrain. His wife, Alice, arrived from the Transkei to see him right, and with her the children. Alice sometimes has a clay-whitened face. She is rumoured to be a *sangoma*.

I sit on my heels next to Bruman, who is cutting the lawn with a pair of shears. He wants to know where we come from. I explain about distant places, air travel over stretches of water, but he doesn't believe me. 'London?' he asks, and I give up and say 'Yes.' 'Factories?' he asks, and I agree, elaborating on cold reaches and foreign languages, but there are blacks there too. He shakes his head in disbelief. No, this man with the red shoes is a liar.

The rattling wind and the slanted land come into the bedroom, enter behind the closed eyelids. Night-thought becomes dream. As so often, I again find myself in captivity. I dream the ground of the camp is covered with many small stones which shift and slide under the boots when you run. He comes running all down the wire fence from the top area where his quarters are, Nelson Mandela, clumsily sliding over loose shoal, excitedly waving a sheet of paper. It is the order for his release. Now I no longer care about the dangers of my associating with him. The warders will be watching us closely and they will come to conclusions. So be it. I hug him fiercely. He is tall but his body is surprisingly soft. He has a long black beard and a young face. 'Mandela! Mandela!' my heart chants. 'Free at last!' He returns the way he came with a shambling gait, to get his gear together for the departure. The warders hold me back by firmly gripping my arms. Soon they will be going through my poor pockets again, the insatiable jackals, and putting a plastic-coated finger up my rectum, and flipping over the sleeping mat in my cell. They will intimate that I have destroyed my own salvation. So be it. At the last moment Nelson Mandela comes loping down the incline once more with a gift for me. This he'd like to leave in my care as a keepsake – an AK-47 assault rifle crudely carved from yellow wood. I clutch the precious treasure to my chest. Worms have perforated the butt and parts of the barrel. It is worn smooth by patient hands. Then he goes. I think he is quite lost. Outside the gate he is trying to scramble into a prison van. I squeeze my voice through the tight grid of the camp's perimeter to warn him off: I say he should walk up the road to where he will surely find a taxi rank. 'Home!' my heart exults. He turns to wave; his face is soft and innocent above the beekeeper's beard, and then he ambles out of sight. The land falls away here. We are on the heights. But a haze of red dust permanently masks the sun.

I first and finally met Mandela when he came on a state visit to France during 1990. It was a cool day, rain had started falling at intervals, everyone was worried about the proceedings, which were to take place partly in the open air. At a sale I bought a white suit for the occasion – it was much too roomy for my frame. I returned to the shop for a smaller-size jacket. The young vendor was reluctant to change the item. I explained how important it was, that I was going to dine with Mandela. He was most unimpressed and continued chewing his gum. With this I wore my red shoes of exile.

Daniëlle Mitterrand invited me to accompany her to the airport and we drove there with stabbing lights and whooping sirens. He stepped off the plane which the French had sent to London to fetch him and his entourage. Someone held an umbrella over his head. He walked towards the arrivals hall in his slightly stiff but determined way. I was waiting on the steps; he saw me from a distance and I noticed his lips pronounce my name. He approached, we embraced, he said: 'I've come to take you home.' I also cheek-buzzed his consort, Winnie, who left a lipstick flower on my shoulder (and I had trouble explaining this later to Mariposa). He was gracious and dignified, assuring Madame Mitterrand: 'If it hadn't been for Dakar I would not be here today.'

The 'official arrival' took place that evening on the Parvis des Droits de l'Homme (Rights of Man Square) of the Place du Trocadéro. The pompous ceremony was organized by the Ministry of Culture. The area had been blocked off, heavily armed police patrolled the streets, the public couldn't get beyond shouting proximity – even so FCP militants and other leftists close to the Socialist Party managed to come to blows, punching, kicking and thwacking one another over the head with slogan boards and banner sticks. Ah, for a real hammer and sickle!

Nelson and Winnie Mandela advanced dramatically over the empty and glistening square to be met halfway by François and Daniëlle Mitterrand. Rain came down in ropes. Grace Bumbry sang from a heaving bosom, a hundred violins sawed away, billowing yellow and red and blue smoke engulfed the esplanade, Madiba (under an umbrella) read a wet speech, I got soaked to the skin, we went up to the offices of the Fondation France-Libertés for dinner.

A striped tent had been pitched on the terrace overlooking the Seine and the light-sugared Eiffel Tower. Eleven of us sat down for the meal – the Mitterrands and the Mandelas, Wole Soyinka, the Nobel laureate who'd flown in from Nigeria (whenever a head of state beckons he will comply), Grace Bumbry, Barbara (an anorexic French cabaret crooner with big dark glasses), Peter Brook (an English theatre director), Thomas Nkobi (my bald friend from Bamako, the ANC bagman), Renaud (a rebellious young French troubadour). Mitterrand took pity on my wet shoulders and had a red shawl fetched. He wore a black one to accentuate his clerical disposition, his wife's was white.

Mandela charmed everybody, but in fact he was seducing Mitterrand by subtly playing up to his nobler instincts, assuming him to be in solidarity with the struggle for justice. Over the fish we had a slight difference about the origins and the nature of Afrikaans (and started speaking the *taal* to one another with Mitterrand asking: 'What? What? What are they saying?' to his helpless interpreter). For me Afrikaans is a creole language fashioned in the mouths of slaves, and not some bastardized derivative of Dutch. Wole Soyinka guffawed. The wine was too good. Tom Nkobi found the fancy French fare insipid. Winnie acted demure. Mitterrand ate his food rapidly, masticating thoroughly like a French peasant, and sucked his teeth.

I watched for differences and similarities between the two old codgers. What did they share? Resoluteness, perseverance, longevity, commitment to a course (if not a cause)? One sensed that they were checking each other out. They are both ladies' men, with a connoisseur's eye for curves and lithesomeness.

Mitterrand is a power-artist. The art of the master of politics is to make it look as if the unfolding of events, the repositioning of forces, the evolution of old structures and the creation of new ones – the deployment of reality in other words – are part of his plan or vision. Riding the tide of history is presented as the creation thereof. It is partly the astuteness of being able to profit from whatever happens, partly a breadth of comprehension and a richness of experience, partly the gift of anticipation, partly even a certain sagacity – but mostly it is a manipulation of perceptions.

Mandela has a moral dimension, he rings true, he engenders sentiments of goodwill and brotherhood and justice. Mitterrand is adept at political survival, the Florentine prince, the regal fox with a socialist coat.

These differences also reflect historical evolutions. France is an old state – centralized, baroque, byzantine, feudal and sophisticated. The people serving it form the caste of professional lackeys – arbitrary in their contempt for inferiors or 'outsiders' or 'the public', obsequious to superiors or to the nether parts of the powerful (be they dealers or favourites) at court with all the flourishes and curt-sies and silvery-tonguedness of those who live by the light in the eye of the lord, and with a dagger up the sleeve waiting for the stumble or the turned back to avenge the self-imposed humiliations of having been flunkeys. Mitterrand, maybe contrary to his own better intentions, must assume the role of the sphinx sitting in the gilded chair.

Mandela, on the other hand, gives the impression of being an architect of events, still expressing the cresting wave of liberation. He is the repository and the embodiment of a movement of profound expectations and aspirations, of a break with the past. He also has his keepers, of course. Those surrounding (and guarding?) him – the Rottweilers – are to some extent ideologues and militants, but progressively they are revealed as common commissars, garden politicos and members of the apparat or the nomenklatura. He too lives dunked in a power-struggle even if he tries to rise above it. His danger is not the intimate betrayal of a sharpened bicycle-spoke in the back, the transmitted disease or the hollowing out of corruption, but the bazooka shells coming through the bedroom window.

The following days were marked by a rigmarole of receptions, official dinners and diplomatic visits. People bowed and scraped and elbowed themselves into photos. Mandela didn't seem to be fazed by the adulation. His public and private discourses were the same, his commitment never wavered and his analyses (of De Klerk's character and motives and function, for example) firm and transparent. Everywhere he went he was the gentleman. At Prime Minister Rocard's table he was witty, and when he'd had enough he got up in dignified fashion, whispered in his host's ear and left the party. Apparently he never tired. Only once, going downstairs from Madame Mitterrand's office, did he lean rather heavily on my hand.

Madiba, who actually only travels abroad to ask for money, was candid about his own problems, explaining that hot-heads in his organization restricted his actions. In reality he gave the impression of being the perfect, accomplished prisoner, going where people led him ('I'm in your hands') to do what he was told. There was about him an aura of lack of will. And yet, too, a constant alertness. The eyes, though kind, were observant. His right cheek has a coin of discoloured skin, perhaps a splotch of old age. His mind seemed totally unshackled, freed from fear and small considerations, so that he could speak it directly (in contrast to Mitterrand's which is infinitely devious, or that of De Klerk – maimed by apartheid – which has to juggle with the unsaid and the need to emit double messages). His fingers were square-tipped with strong fingernails cut short. He seemed to be oblivious to contradictions – in that he may be like a small boy bluffing, trying to string impossibles together. He spoke with old-fashioned turns of phrase which revealed the British-type education of a previous age. He was cool and schoolmasterish, though, nearly neutral, and didn't initiate strong emotional reactions. Only the lips in repose betrayed him – severe, dark, aloof, bitter. It is the mouth which sometimes says more, and more eloquently, than the voice can; lips close over the unsayable: *This cannot be spoken about, so why bother?*

When darkness comes I remember Lagos and its secrets. I'd gone there for a meeting of African writers. Monsieur Thibault, the French ambassador, received us in his residence, where we drank a lot. Life is a battle, he said; only the strong will survive. For instance: a rich Lebanese businessman had been kidnapped. His captors asked for a hefty ransom; when it was not forthcoming they had a chopped-off hand delivered to his home. The horrified family promptly paid up and the abducted man was released on the beach – with both hands still intact! It was rumoured that a certain Walker, 'a white African', had been involved in the crime, but he was never caught. Here robbers were tied to empty oildrums on the beach and publicly executed. The taxi trade is in the hands of people from Benin; they all wear cloth caps.

That night the First Secretary drove me to my hotel. The car went with a thump over some object on the asphalt. The First Secretary had a word with the chauffeur, then sat back and said not to worry, it was only a corpse, must be somebody who'd fallen off a bus earlier in the day – these things do happen. The moon was so clear that I could see a build-up of thunderclouds. Still later there were lightning snakes and a deep rumbling and then the rain came down – 'Tomorrow everything will be washed clean and you will see how beautiful Lagos really is,' the First Secretary said.

One was ceaselessly accosted by exquisite young whores, female and male and in-between or polyvalent, in and around the hotel. They'd come up close, shake their tits and wriggle their arses and whisper urgently: 'What room number?' Never had I invented so many numbers.

Every time we move between Simon's Town and Cape Town we pass Pollsmoor Prison in the distance. Don't look – and yet I cannot help seeing it out of the corner of my eye; it accompanies me like some dark peripheral image. Maybe I should just check quickly, find bearings – and I get a glimpse of the brown-brick buildings with their barred apertures, the slant-roofed workshops, the water towers and the watchtowers.

Place seems to have grown. Still prison though: shithouse where I defecated my years. I've often thought of going back for a visit. Will they allow me in? Must be *bangais* (prisoners) I know there, still doing their time, or who've returned for a new stretch. Does a man carry off his country on the soles of his feet? Whatever happened to Flame the methylated-spirits drinker with the red beard, to Radamanthos the gangster judge, to Nefesj, to Whisper Van Deventer with his throat cancer, to Bosvark, to O'Kennedy the shy 'female', to El Ziryab of the eyes like black wings, to Jan Blom, to Dampies, to Lofty the toothless murderer, to Bat the ex-soldier, to Spirenis, to Rudi the diamond-cutter with the kidney stones, to Kapoen the eunuch, to Yard Crud, to Bob Hope, to Flatus Perrectum, to Black Camel with the pliant lips, to Mongool, to Thekwane, to Landsvullis . . . ?

People were killing themselves out of lassitude, nausea, imitation, *braggadocio* or plain curiosity. Would Mugu still be there? His one hand had been sliced off at the wrist by a spade. He used to say the missing hand could feel bad weather coming – it would be as if he had a fist full of rain. He claimed he was still a dab hand at playing the saw or the guitar. I thought of returning and offering to rent a film for the birds. But I turn my head away, afraid to go near. The imperceptible odour of a mass grave drifts over the place.

Driving along the Ou Kaapse Weg (Old Cape Road) to traverse the mountains I remember lying in a cell in the valley and hearing cars going up this pass, and thinking how free those people must be! Look back from the ridge: peaceful scene really, like a factory farm with vineyards not far off, a swerve in the skyline and then continuing mountains. In the cell next to mine there was a cynical fellow, Don Espejuelo, a deft plagiarist. His defence was that he rejected the notion of property – the whole world with all its riches should be at our disposal, particularly since 'our profession is dreadful, writing corrupts the soul.'

I thought of him as my mentor. Sometimes he'd come up with a wacky saying like: 'There's no music in politics'; or 'The problem for the Empire of Utopia will be how to move from communism to socialism' – I never knew whether these were his own conclusions or a borrowed bit of nonsense. Nearly always he'd be tinkering with political concepts, yet he also said (quoted?): 'Artists in politics are like the whore's child at the wedding; we remember things out of season, and get the stick.' For he pretended to think of himself as the essential writer. He was working on a manuscript which he wanted to call *The Contaminated Heart*.

On the morning of 12 March, while Yolande is picking up the threads of her network of friends and observing the world with unprejudiced eyes, I visit Alex Boraine at IDASA in Plumstead. His right hand, Ms Clark, arranges for me to exchange our capricious car for a flaming red one. I request Alex to intervene with the Governor of the Reserve Bank, his friend, to have my miserable money released to me by United.

That evening we have supper at Kalk Bay with Alex and his guests – André du Toit and Maretha, and three visiting friends from the Soviet Union: Vasili Solodovnikov, Samander Kalandarov and Vyatcheslow Tetiokin ('Slava'), all of whom work in Moscow's Soviet Afro-Asian Solidarity Committee.

I encountered Ambassador Solodovnikov and Slava in 1988 in Leverkusen, West Germany. At that time Solodovnikov, who had been the Soviet Union's man in Lusaka, and thus the front-line link to the ANC, strenuously denied having played any role in defining the strategies of the 'armed struggle'. He talked wistfully of Africa, of how Tsarist Russia used to have a voluntary spy working the banks of the Great African Lakes and how they seriously considered intervening to grab a colony; later a fleet was sent to scout out the possibilities of snatching Madagascar. Nothing came of these Russian attempts to penetrate the southern hemisphere. In fact, nothing came of all their efforts to win influence in Africa. Gigantic earth-movers and ice-breakers are rusting in Ghana and in Egypt; even the Congo no longer wants their ideological guidance. Their example of industrialization and communalization turned out to be disastrous. What has happened to the Revolution?

They all love South Africa We eat *perlemoen* (Venus-ear or abalone) and toast one another. I say: 'Why did you ever give up on your expansionist revolution? All of this [waving at the candle-lit tables, the hornet-waisted waitresses, the wine, the lapping sea outside] could have been yours!' Solodovnikov laughs and shows people's silver teeth. At the other end of the table André, Maretha and the third comrade with the sombre countenance (he's the intellectual from an Islamic republic) have a silent, glum conversation, like Trappists with toothache.

Shall we solve Afriqua's problems once again? Many Russians have been arriving in the country, prospective immigrants singing sad songs in Johannesburg restaurants. It is the done thing for some Afrikaners to have a tow-headed Russian speaking borscht Afrikaans as protégé.

On Wednesday, 13 March, the wind is blowing hard. We meet for lunch at Suzanne's Newlands house with John Maxwell Coetzee and Stephen Watson. The writer and the poet both teach at the University of Cape Town. John Coetzee we met many years ago in New York during a PEN congress; this is the first time we have had the rare privilege of seeing him on 'home ground' – indeed, he is the bird living in dense undergrowth: one hears his allegorical song during certain seasons, but never sees him. In spite of shyness he does articulate, or rather, he engages in low conversation, sipping a glass of water. He is slender, fleck-eyed, with a short grey beard, the high forehead of the insomniac and the reserved bearing of a quail-hunter. Stephen Watson is as demure as his colleague, but younger – also not as sad as John. His smile is crooked, his laughter frank. He's not as vulnerable as he looks though: of late he took on the fashionable leftist intellectual establishment, arguing for poetry against the voracious appetite of politics. In a South Africa of bleating fellow travellers this is indeed going against the stream. (And against the dry dream.)

13

FIREKNOW

I wake up with a subconscious phrase groping for definition. 'Fighting for the middle ground cannot be a matter of compromise, it must be a question of justice . . .' Today, Thursday, 14 March, we drive to Stellenbosch where we have a lunch appointment with Johan Degenaar. Then we shall spend the night in the home of Toetsie Star (Ukwezi's sister) and her husband, Bill Louw. The wind, always the South-easter, tears around the peninsula to shake the mountain.

Johan Degenaar (together with Martin Versfeld) is one of our foremost philosophers, nimble in his analyses, de-boning a given slab of perception fibre by fibre, finding jubilation in shades of signifying. Both Degenaar and Versfeld are humanists. This country's thinkers are often humanists; public political life, nevertheless, used to be pre-humanist before collapsing into post-humanism.

We drive along the highway past D. F. Malan airport, with turn-offs to Langa and Nyanga (Sun and Moon), 'old' black townships by now; then to more chaotic squatter zones – Crossroads and Khayelitsha. Dense Port Jackson bushes border the four-lane speedway, camouflaging to some extent the sandy wastes. Through the green wall we perceive extended 'settlements' of tin and ply-wood and sack and cardboard shacks, like a flattened rubbish heap.

Along the road we pass an elderly black man, apparently miles from any habitation, pushing a supermarket trolley loaded with stakes – as if he's been chopping down telephone poles. We see the incredibly tall pylons with their powerful lights lording it over the townships; surely no stone can smash those suns. We pass a herd of goats grazing within metres of whizzing vehicles. We come across three African hunters armed with sticks and accompanied by at least thirty lean dogs. On an open stretch in the scrub there are a number of huts built of plastic sheets and reeds by Xhosa adolescents sitting out the isolation of their initiation period; a few, clad in skins or loose robes, their faces and bodies daubed white, loll close to the huts or stand forlornly leaning on long sticks. They're called *amakwethu*. This period before circumcision is known as 'going to the mountain'; when it is over the purifying white clay will be replaced by red.

Suddenly our car runs with a shudder over a huge wriggling object. In the rearview mirror I get a glimpse of the slashing coils of a snake, dark and unexpected – it must be rare for such a big specimen to be found so near Cape Town – ominous, like a submarine surfacing in False Bay.

The road into Stellenbosch forks off the highway, sharp blue mountains peak as backdrop, vineyards on both sides, alleys of oaks or palm trees lead to whitewashed, thatch-roofed wine estates. A 'Southern' slave community living in a time warp. The town is a museum to 'old money': all the houses seem to be historical, hoarse oaks embrace across the streets and furrows of running water bring a tinkle and glitter of coolness; shrubs sporting purple and red and pink and yellow flowers protrude from behind white garden walls.

In 1986 I came to this white citadel to make a speech to a hall of young people who stood listening silently. I tried telling them to become involved in the struggle for decency, that they could and should so do as Afrikaners – it would be the only way to exorcise paralysing fears, it was *normal* to opt out of apartheid. In the front row a handful of National Union of South African Students (NUSAS) members sat, bravely braying a *'Viva!'* The hall was grim. In fact, it was garlanded with darkness. I might as well have been from Mars.

During question time a young girl wept and asked me when the Revolution was due: she was having trouble sleeping at night. ('Hush, girl – if ever there were to be a revolution it would come inadvertently.')

I returned during August 1990, again opening my foolhardy mouth. The stage was shared with Patrick 'Terror' Lekota from the ANC. Now, with new winds of fashion blowing, NUSAS adherents were far more numerous. There were also a number of black students noisily shouting ANC slogans. I waded in making very clear my disdain for starry-eyed recent converts in general and Stellenbosch political yuppies in particular. I said it would be disastrous to leave the past with hands poking out above ground; I warned against the new hegemony; I pleaded for vigorous independence of mind; I even held up Buddha to their incredulous eyes (ah, you fool!).

Patrick Lekota told them in Afrikaans exactly what they wanted to hear ('We shall always need thee, oh white élite'). Sighs and smiles of relief lit up the faces. André Brink was in the audience clapping perplexed hands; so was Albie Sachs who said to me when it was over: 'But aren't you *ever* happy? Now that we've won, can't you *rejoice*?'

It was rough to be both clown and fool. I'm glad Yolande Sonrisa was there to comfort me, to cool my fevered imagination and the narcissistic deathwish, to bring a modicum of equilibrium.

Then people came to ask for autographs. A man in his thirties, short hair and dead eyes, edged up to the table and just stood there with a thick tongue. Eventually he handed me a slip of paper. I unfolded it: it was the photocopy of a small poem in the Chinese fashion which I'd written to my fellow convict Don Espejuelo on the day of his release; the ancient man was now dying of smoker's disease in a hospice for derelicts in Somerset West. Dead Eyes leaned forward and whispered that he too was an ex-con, and had I heard of Sergeant Arselow's death? Arselow was a vicious, cold-blooded warder working in Pretoria's hanging jail; he always wore red shoes. Seems he died with wife and child in a car crash. I felt nothing.

Among the journalists in the hall was Sog Serfyn of the *Vrye Weekblad*. I remembered him from when he was a documentary film-maker. He managed to bully the text of my contribution out of me and faxed it to his boss in Johannesburg. Sog Serfyn wrote a further article describing me as 'a rebel without a cause', an angry middle-aged man, a disgrace to victory and to hope.

Johan Degenaar lives across the road from the house where we shall spend the night. Mrs Degenaar is preparing a talk on the painter Vuillard for a group of art enthusiasts later tonight. Johan takes us to lunch in an Italian restaurant. As ever, he promptly initiates a seriously playful conversation. Like other local thought-tinkers he explored the notion of nation-building now that the iron grip of apartheid repression is relaxing, but unlike most he instantly realized this to be a false route, that it was more important to identify the sinews and the reflexes of democracy: 'The middle ground we struggle for is lucid consciousness.' He grants the oppressed majority their 'moment of revolution', but doesn't intend lying down accommodatingly to give up on any part of his intellectual heritage. He is for ever rubbing his mind against whatever ideas he may encounter.

A doll in black serves us at table; she is a student earning pocket money. She recognizes us and comes to ask if I could please copy for her on a sheet of paper her favourite poem from the volume *Lotus*. She only remembers the first line: '*as die asem 'n skip is . . .* ' I don't recall the rest either, and must try to make it a lead to a new effort:

> *For Tracy, in 'Mamma Roma'*
>
>   if breath were a ship
>   the lips would be a coast
>   where the heart washes ashore;
>   with time, only at times
>   a tongue-tied fire of happiness
>   flares upon the beach: voice then
>   falls silent in a spherical vowel,
>   the keel is ash
>   and a hand stalks on stilts
>   to chart the phantom sails'
>   love-cry

After lunch Johan takes us to the house of Jan Duiwel. Jan Duiwel bludgeons students with Political Science. The two, Jan and Johan, are like water and fire: Johan – mild, with tie and quizzical expression; Jan – wild, foul-mouthed, his hair and beard standing on end, a torn shirt, a bottle of wine in the hand – but they obviously share a profound mutual appreciation.

Jan Duiwel, bosom-buddy to Slabbert, was also on the Dakar expedition. We laughed all the way. He must have the largest fund of baroquely filthy tales in the country. He takes care to keep his inborn crap-detector clean. Hailing from a modest family in the northern badlands of the Cape Province, he criss-crossed the country on his battered motorbike and came to academic life relatively late. His intellect knocks about in weird spaces (as a free jazz fanatic), but suddenly becomes hard and pointed when he pushes an argument.

Jan curses the cork from a third bottle, lowers his bull-like head with the bulging eyes and starts wrestling again with a pet subject, the State. To him the State must be Satan. He is devoid of sentimentality, uncluttered by attachments to language or cultural and ethnic grouping, yet totally loyal to his friends and fierce on their behalf. It is my delight to realize that we're probably both anarchists at heart.

Leaf through a volume on South African genealogy (the 'white' part, obviously – this is ersatz Europe): a certain Jacob Johann Breytenbach emigrated from Würtzburg some time during the eighteenth century; the first Cloete (mother's tree) already came in 1652, from Keulen (Cologne). Sadness. 'Give me back to myself!'

Why did I come back? Nostalgia, unfinished business, loose ends, to complete the incomplete, for annihilation, deathwish. Why will I not return to stay? Too late now. Foreigner here. Painted monkey. Bitter dreams. No roots. Attachment too painful. Deathwish . . .

14

OASIS

We leave for Paarl. This is the beginning of the Boland where I grew up and went to school: mountains, valleys with a river, vineyards, orchards, heat, wind. Yolande has an appointment there with an expert on hearing, someone who will explain to her the nuances of birdsong. On the veranda of the house where she is to meet the person, recommended to us by our friend Eva Landman, a large number of birds flutter and flit.

I while away the waiting by visiting the Taalmonument, a grey structure erected in honour of the Afrikaans language, visible from a distance against a flank of Paarlberg. It is an obscenity of ethno-cultural arrogance. The grouping of various shapes purports the symbolization of different values: thus the soaring penis is the clarity of Western heritage, some miserable hut-like blobs at its base (the testicles?) illustrate dark indigenous cultures, and an insignificant box-like slab commemorates the Malay contribution. The insult must be destroyed! At the very least I must go and piss against it. I park the car.

Halfway to the structure a man steps out from behind a tree, adjusting his pants, and hails me. 'Mr B, I presume? The poet come to pay homage?' He must be about my age, a little stooped; his white suit is tired from having been slept in, his red shoes have white laces, the beard he let grow came out dirty. He is carrying a plastic shopping bag.

South Africa is rich in illuminated hermits living in the hills, prophesying to baboons and to birds. The man shouts at me. I turn back and walk fast to where I left the car. He's still shouting. I look around and see him silhouetted against the sky. He's got his hand in the bag. Now he's pulling out fistfuls of bloody torn-off birdwings which he throws in the air. I start running. He's hollering: 'Hey! Hey, you gods! Look at this! Do you see? You are all d-e-a-d!' And from the valley the faint echo comes floating – *dead . . . dead . . . dead.*

Yolande is waiting on the pavement outside the house where I left her. She's angry. What took you so long, she wants to know, and what happened – you're trembling. The heat, I say. And that bloody monument on the mountain. Really upsetting. Went for a look but there was a wedding party, people strewing confetti; they must be marrying Death if they want to be photographed against that . . . that gravestone. She says she didn't have much luck either: Eva Landman's friend, who looked very disturbed, speaks only Afrikaans.

We continue in the direction of Wellington. This time we shall not go by the house where the parents used to live. Of what use will it be? They're gone. From outside it will look the same, but the insides have been ripped out. Recently a literary sleuth contacted me to say she's been to the house. The town clerk took her to a warehouse where some rubble removed during alterations was kept (the house was bought by the Municipality). He showed her a beam from the room where Yolande and I were supposed to have slept during our 1973 sojourn, with carved on it '*Gueule de bois*' and the date. 'What might it mean?' she wanted to know. 'Hangover', of course. Sounds genuine. Was there no rope attached? The lines only dangle in beautiful places after all. 'Grevilleas', the dwelling was called, after tall silky oaks across the street.

In town we stop and buy newspapers, a comic book and a shoot-and-sob novel of the 'station literature' variety. Yolande is looking for dried fruit. An old gentleman walks in to accost me: 'You must be Mr B.' He saw us enter the café. I won't remember him – he used to teach literature at school. Shamefacedly I try to hide the acquisitions behind my back.

Our destination, Montagu, is the town where my brother Cloete with the short hair and the even shorter fuse lives, the one who growls from the side of his mouth. I remember coming here on an outing with my parents and their friends when still very small; the men wore white pullovers and cream-coloured trousers and my uncle Koos played the accordion; my mother danced. Cloete's house perches against a hill on the edge of Ou-Dam, the 'other' part of Montagu laid out by a previous administration to provide cheap housing for war veterans and railway pensioners, and in fact largely inhabited by 'other-coloureds'. My brother built his own home – a square white-washed dwelling with a flat roof of corrugated iron and green-painted doors, shutters and roof-gutters, all of it protected by a low white wall: an outside and inside of simple, exquisite taste.

White doves wheel over the town. Baboons sometimes saunter down the hill to bark at my brother; he snarls back. He wages a war of attrition against moles which dig up his flower bulbs and gnaw at the roots of his vine and his guava trees. Ants carry off his sugar. Cloete sits on his stoep to look out over the pattern of flat roofs (Montagu with its palm trees and bougainvillaea is an oasis in the mountain) and curses the world for its decay and its deviousness. 'Let them go to hell – I'm going to play golf,' he says. Or: 'Thank Unum, I only have another ten years of life left.'

Behind Cloete's property, where the hill folds away into a ravine, we see the tips of some neglected almond trees. It is called Amandelhoek, he says. Towards the end of the previous century the Jouberts were the most influential family in town. One of the sons was musically talented (his grand piano can be seen in the local museum). He left the country and spent eight years in France; nobody knows what he did there. Upon his return he 'took a brown woman unto himself' and became the black sheep of the clan, and so he built a house near a fountain in the mouth of the *kloof* (canyon) and he planted almond trees there. He was dirt-poor and survived by doing menial tasks for one brother who had a shop, and another who had a farm. There was bad blood because he'd help himself from the shelves of the shop, and instead of looking properly after the pigs of the second brother he'd be sitting under a tree to compose a song. When he was reproached for allowing the pigs to destroy the beanfield, he said: 'You hired me to look after the pigs, not the beans.' He died leaving one daughter, Mignon Joubert, who taught music in Robertson.

(Early last century a European took a Hottentot woman, Saartje Baartman, to Britain. She was paraded through Europe and made to appear naked in the side-shows of village festivals where good white people paid to gape and gasp at her anatomy, particularly the famous 'Hottentot apron', a fold of flesh overlapping her sex. When she died of miserableness and madness her sexual parts were cut out and autopsied by scientists keen to extend the limits of glorious light-bringing objective knowledge. Her corpse was embalmed. A cast made of her body can still be inspected in the Musée de l'Homme in Paris – the building bordering on the Parvis des Droits de l'Homme where the Mitterrands entertained the Mandelas.)

In the evening the wind rises, warm and enveloping. In the darkness Cloete takes us down to the hot baths. We put on bathing costumes and enter a pool. It is so warm that one soon starts perspiring. Wind ruffles the water surface and wassails in a palm-tree top with rustling sound; it brings the fragrance of warmed aromatic herbs from the canyon. There are more stars here than anywhere else in the world: they come because it's quieter and because of the labyrinth of ravines in which to hide by day. Cloete says two black eagles nest up in the rocks of the dimly outlined peaks which we see from here; they live off rock-rabbits. In the next pool a couple are calmly having intercourse; the water hardly moves. My brother describes how a German very nearly drowned – fell asleep and gently disappeared; took nearly a minute before another bather noticed bubbles and something amiss; they had to pump the warm liquid from his lungs.

Supper is fish and cool white wine. Followed by brandy and sighs. We are both getting a bit thick in the word. Speak about the mechanics of reality control. This government is weakening, their capacity to rule eaten away. My brother is an Inkatha apologist, I am of the ANC. This we do not talk about. He pours more brandy. The town is cloaked in silence, with stars pinned to the cloak, except for a lonely dog in the distance reciting his dog alphabet in an attempt to spell 'cloak'. Then I show Cloete the comics I bought and the soft-cover *Die Wit Tier (The White Tiger)*, which describes the brave deeds of a bushfighter. Cloete has spent time as a reporter in the bush wars of Angola and Namibia.

New Nation says the causes of the weekend carnage in Mzimhlophe on the Reef in which twenty-four people died after an attack by vigilantes are still unclear. In renewed internecine violence in

Tembisa on the East Rand, five people, including a six-year-old girl, Nkele Basi, were shot dead and set alight on Monday by a group of men with AK-47 and Scorpion rifles. An eye-witness, Godfrey Machima, said the shooting started at about 11.30 p.m. when armed men surrounded the shack-dwellers. 'I witnessed a policeman toyi-toying in front of one of the bodies lying on the ground. I tried to take photographs, but the police took the camera from me. They didn't give me a receipt.'

Paarl Post reports the release, for lack of evidence, of two white policemen accused of having killed a black farmworker. In another incident a trap was laid on a farm for a suspected diamond-smuggler. A car without headlamps drove up in the dark and stopped; the diamond detectives drew their guns and surrounded the car only to find a uniformed colleague making love to a young lady inside. There's the story of a prominent ear specialist, Professor Ollewagen, returning to Paarl two days ago to find his aviary of exotic birds totally sacked; the bodies were found scattered in the backyard cages with all the wings systematically torn off. Police are looking for a 'foreigner' who was last seen walking on the road to Wellington.

Early in the morning I go running through Keisieskloof winding its way through two nearly vertical walls of yellow and greenish rock. At the entrance a sign points towards another canyon called Donkerkloof (Dark Ravine). Burbling stream of brown mountain water, in places overgrown with bulrushes and reeds, early morning scents of the myriad medicinal herbs and sweet-smelling grasses bedecking the slopes, fat brown rock-rabbits scatter out of the way and stop a few yards further to look back inquisitively, birds like stones from a catapult whirr from the reeds to rise in piercing song against the sheer rockface, blue sunlight lights up the higher reaches but down here it is still cool. On to where the ravine mouths on the baths complex and back the way I came, running by a mountain tortoise as big as a hunchbacked six-year-old child on all fours.

Cloete says it is dangerous these days to have workers climb on your lorry: in Robertson there's the case of a farmer who drove his lot of hired grape-pickers to the station to pack them off to their native Transkei; they weren't working enough to his taste. The workers refuse to get off the lorry until they've been recompensed properly; the police will not intervene. This has been going on for three days. Now the farmer intends getting a court order against 'the illegal occupation of his work-tool'.

Relations between farmers and their labourers have been soured by ANC 'agitators' coming from elsewhere. Brown and black people expect the country with its milk and honey and new houses to fall in their laps just like that. This is Boesak country, with Allan's younger brother as local dominee leading the brown community. Government has no idea what's happening in rural areas, my brother growls; the tissue is tearing, essential services have deteriorated, with the privatization of hospitals no sick person can afford an ambulance into town.

The 20th. On my morning run I come across my own tracks in the *kloof*, and next to one (where I crossed the river yesterday, hopping from stone to stone) the perfect imprint of a little buck's hoof.

We leave for Ashton, with a bag of lemons which Yolande picked from Cloete's tree. A little further we turn left in the direction of Bonnievale. Vineyards, with at the end of each row a rosebush, each of a different colour. Another hot day. No signs of last night's rain. A few puffy clouds. Near Bonnievale the road follows a wide irrigation canal taking water from the Breërivier in the valley to more inaccessible parts. When I was born my father was employed as a labourer building this ditch, my mother followed him, we lived in a tent. I tell Yolande the story and her eyes light up.

This is my world, my voice fits precisely in these patterns of speech, my eyes see the same aloes the ancestors did. Do I think the same thoughts? What is a thought but a conjunction of position and posture? A hairline crack of awareness repeated and repented infinitely? A bird flying out of the head?

We enter the town and after some searching find the house where my paternal grandparents, Oupa Jan and Ouma Anna, lived. Almond trees at the back. No dog anywhere in sight. The cemetery lies the short distance of a cock's crow away. All life is a conspiracy against death. (And death a summary of life.)

The warm fragrance of sun and pine-needles, the chortling of doves and the shrilling of cicadas. Ants everywhere. I should write a letter to Oubaas, to report this visit to the dead. Peaceful here. We wander through the alleys separating the graves, some headstones are lopsided with lettering effaced by time, some have moss and lichen splotching the granite, the poorer ones are covered with sun-sucked periwinkle shells. In one corner the tiny plots where children lie buried ('Angel factories').

We come upon their resting places, simple and grey: Jan Dirk – 7.12.1855/25.10.1948; Anna Maria (*née* Olivier) – 10.8.1867/ 5.7.1948. It took him all of three months to fade after his lady died. On Oupa's grave there's a bunch of wilted wildflowers. Would his hands be as big in death as they were in life?

In town we stop for meat pies and cool drinks. A vehicle draws up and heavily armed men alight and walk into the café to reappear with satchels of money. They transport funds in rural areas. High-way robberies do occur. A young tousle-haired fellow comes to our car. 'Excuse me, you wouldn't be Mr B by any chance?' My mouth is stuffed with food and he takes my mumble for affirmation. 'Thought so,' he says. He points at a clothes store. 'Did you know this is your cousin Matty's shop? I work there. She's done well, has four shops in this region.' Her parents, Uncle Nick and Aunt Joey, lived just below that hill in a house surrounded by fruit trees; we saw their graves this morning.

Out of town past the cheese factory, over the river, up hill and down dale, flocks of ochre-coloured sheep feeding in the ochre-coloured veld. The time of year when stubble from the wheatfields is burned off and a blue haze fills the air.

Over Stormsrivier, Langverwacht (Long-awaited) and Wakker-stroom (Stream of Wakefulness), Caledon, out the other side where the tarred road turns to dust, crossing mountains towards the coast, along evocative names describing these valleys where lepers with grey flesh lived isolated in olden days: Hemel-en-Aarde (Heaven and Earth), Solitaire, Diepgat (Deep Hole), Suiderkruis (Southern Cross). One theory has it that the river flowing from the last ridge to the sea was called Onrus (Unease) because people living downriver worried about contamination from lepers in the mountain.

At Onrus we find Jabbery at work in her loft studio. She swings down the outside staircase, tacks towards the house and calls: 'Jan! Jan!' No answer. I peep through the window. Jan Biltong is lying on his stretcher, eyes resolutely fixed on the ceiling, his two gigantic dogs draped at his feet. When I walk in he shouts: '*O God, dis jy!*' ('It's you!') and jumps up.

First he must show Yolande his vegetable garden. She is close to his heart, he wants to share his enthusiasm. I produce two bottles of Roodeberg from the car (Mr Ixele is lying grinning in the boot), which we share with the unselfish help of M. C. Botha, a next-door writer. On the wall there's a portrait Jabbery painted of Uys Krige, his hair all yellow and his forehead wide.

When evening light starts lengthening the shadows and the thrashing sea becomes more audible, we go to pay our respects to Oom Beyers Naudé and his wife, Tannie Ilse. They spend their annual holidays here in a cottage with a view of black rocks and spume. Ilse, frail but happy to have her warrior prophet of a husband to herself this once a year, is recovering from a car crash that broke her legs; Bey is relaxed in shorts and sandals.

The last light skimming off the sea finds us in a clearing on the village's outskirts in the small graveyard where Uys is buried. Mattheus Uys Krige – 4.2.1910/10.8.1987 ('to the source of/everything the sun/one fragrant urge/one golden desire'). The dusty poet's grave is heaped high with periwinkle shells worn silver by winds and rain and now capturing the final glimmering of this day. Yolande picks up one with nacreous tints, hands it to me, 'to bring the hollow rhythms of the sea to your ear'. In the dark we shall drive back to Simon's Town.

This road, with sea as its destination, evokes other memories. I landed at Lomé early in November 1989 on my way to Accra, whose airport was closed down, ostensibly for repairs. (In Ghana however I heard talk of uncommon military movement.) The young consular official waiting at the exit spoke a quaint French: 'Are you going to *last* a long time?' he asked (meaning, 'Are you staying long?'); and : 'The cold is *touching*' (perceptible), 'I've never *experimented* it before.'

He drove me to the border where an embassy car from Accra was due to pick me up. In front of a store called Mon Pied (My Foot) we witnessed a woman being run over by a taxi, the impact a dull thud. Small goats were feeding along the road, the pavements were of brown sand. Hooters blared, the air was dense with exhaust fumes. Suckling pigs were snorting their way through heaps of rubbish dumped on the beach. The canoes looked as if they'd been hewed from palm logs, muscular fishermen were dragging them above the high-tide mark. The sea showed a long, slow swell of a turbid green hue, the sky was overcast, the air humid but cool.

My official handed me over to immigration in Aflao, the border town, and I started waiting. What struck me was the *familiarity* of the frontier post, just like a South African Railways waiting room or one-man police station. (British influence left a similar smear wherever they went.) There was brown linoleum on the floor, brown chairs and a brown desk with a white stencilled inventory number, a file cabinet of grey metal, a pen-holder, an almanac, a coat-of-arms on the wall – the wall painted a creamy yellow – a refrigerator in the corner, a noisy air-conditioner, curtains hanging from a pelmet. The touch of difference was a reproduction of Christ on the wall, pulling away his upper garment to point at his sacred heart bound by a wreath of thorns and crowned by flames.

I waited and the expected embassy car never turned up. Immigration officers came and left, clicking their heels, saying 'Sah!' and submitting reports to the man trying to look busy behind the desk. This desk officer made a few phone calls (mostly to his wife, judging by the drift of the conversation and the forefinger in his nostril), then left and returned with a deal: a Lebanese lady and her chauffeur were on their way back to Accra – they were willing to give me a lift. Some money passed hands.

We drove by establishments called My Good God Hotel, Low-cost Kindergarten, Spider Mechanical Workshop, Drinking Bar (where we stopped), Psalm 66 Secondary School, Tarzan Enterprises Ltd, Bread of Life Canteen. I saw a bus named Don't Blame The Children, another I Never Knew, and one advised: Do Not Give up. Your Miracle Is On The Way.

The conference of African writers to which I'd been invited was an absolute shambles. Poor Marcelino dos Santos, now that the dream of a Mozambican revolution had been reduced to acrimonious squabbles and blown-away lives, was inveigled into becoming a vice-president of an intended Pan-African Writers Association. Together with the Angolans we caucused, being from the same region. The self-appointed president was a tall Ghanaian with a brave beard – let's call him Kofi to avoid slander. He must be one of the most shameless thieves operating in West Africa. He had his whole extended family (from town) put up in the delegates' luxury hotel for the duration of the conference, handed out autographed photos of himself with the Pope, recited embarrassing praise-songs composed for every head of state, and swindled thousands of dollars – Ka'afir, being from those parts, put me wise to the deal – by obtaining foreign aid for the air fares of people who never got invited and then cashing the tickets. Flight-Lieutenant Jerry Rawlings's wife came to inaugurate one evening event, and Kofi, surpassing himself in lyricism, solemnly thanked her, hand on heart: 'Madam, all I can say is – you're a woman!'

I never did get to deliver a paper at the Accra conference. Maybe just as well – it would have been a virulent reflection on our continent's decay, arguing that it's all our own fault. One night I went for a walk outside. It wasn't entirely dark. A hand had pegged a chunk of moon on the night sky, like a silver altarpiece, and a scattering of luminous clouds showed that some ancestral spirit had been whiling away time by blowing smoke-rings. I was filled with awe at the eternal beauty of it, diminishing our human concerns, or at least putting all in a bigger perspective. There was a temptation – call it the tug of death or oblivion – just to 'let it flow,' to get drunk on the beauty of Africa, to block out the pain and the sorrow, but also the small excitements inherent to our existence, the symptoms of our urge to do something about ourselves and our environment . . . The more I paced up and down, the more anguished I became, my thoughts flooded by the bitter blood of anger. I sat down, blackening page after page – all of it utterly useless to either the conference or me. What sense could my contribution have? I wondered what *right* I had to utter a discordant note.

Of course I failed to talk any sense into myself. The theme of our being here, I would have reminded my colleagues, is to work towards the liberation of the mind. Have we integrated the failures of our continental history? . . . But the conference was bogged down in the sharing of loot among thieves. In the end I stopped going altogether and took to walking the streets.

*

Yolande, with a smile like a butterfly, says: 'If you keep on making notes all the time you won't *see* anything.' I say: 'But it is in the writing that I see.' She: 'You miss so much. All the odours and the savours which you never experience. All this writing, writing – it's the drug of politics – it deforms the mind and narrows the spirit!' I: 'It is the fault of my hand.' She: 'Your hand will wither and fall off. And then you will be blind.'

15

GUIDE

This is the way we came. From where the Phophonyane Falls thunder above the Hhohho Valley, in the distance the purple Lebombe and closer Kobolondo or Gatoorkopberg (Arse-over-Kettle). Through Mhlambanyatsi and Bhunya to the Nerston border crossing. Then Amsterdam, Piet Retief (Hondkop to the left), Kwamandlangampisi, Wag-' n-bietjie (oh, Wait-a-while), Wakkerstroom and Volksrust with the glorious battle-hill of Majuba on the horizon. On to Vrede (Peace). Not for long. Jakkalskop, Leeukop, Roadside, Kaalkop (Bald Hill), Pramkop (Udder Head), Skuins-hoogte, Warden (hard by Kafferstad), via Kruispad (Crossroads) to Bethlehem. Slabberts, far in the distance Mount Horeb, Fouriesburg, Appelkooskop (Apricot Hill) and Wonderkop, Kommando-nek, Ficksburg, glancing right to the killing fields of Spioenkop and Vegkop, Eerstekamp, Modderpoort (Mud Gate), Gethsemane lies over the mountain frontier in Lesotho. Marseilles, Faust, Thaba Phatswa, Kommissiepoort, Hobhouse, Jammerdrif (Sorry Passage) and off to the right Skiethoek, Wildehondekop, Kafferskop. Wepener. Elandsberg. Zastron. Aasvoëlberg (Mount Vulture). Genade-berg (Mount Mercy). Dansters and Winnaars (Dancers and Winners) are railway sidings. Houtkop, Rouxville, Beestekraalnek, Aliwal North, Jamestown with away to either side Swempoort and Predikantskop (Preachers Hill). Laggende Water (Laughing Water), across Stormberg direction Molteno to Syfergat (Seep-hole), Carrickmore, Boesmanshoekpas, Malabarsberg, Sterkstroom to Queenstown. Over the Black Kei. Goshen left. Katberg, Outyd (Old Times), Fort Beaufort, Koonapshoogte, Grahamstown.

Father, it was your winter of 1989 and it was cold. We drove the whole day long, Slabbert and I, in his white Mercedes. We had to. This was the only way it could be done.

Yolande and I had been to the writers' conference at Victoria Falls, then spent some time in Harare before flying on to Swaziland where we arrived without visas. We had applied for permission to be allowed to visit you in Grahamstown. We hadn't seen you since that one fleeting afternoon in 1986 when we carried you outside on the lawn under the trees of Rachel's garden.

How cruel these Boere are! Why the petty hatred, the harshness, the vindictiveness? I thought about it a lot as we drove down the country over a map of names marking the dreams and sorrows of pioneers and settlers. I could read the land, the resting-places of the tongue, the intimate symbiosis between shape and sound encapsulating a vision or a battle fought or a vantage-point or a narrow gap in the cliffs or a hole sunk for water. Could people have been so close to beauty and death under storms of sun and winds of stars – and produce degenerate descendants crossing off lives with a stroke of the pen behind their desks of State? This was not what you'd taught me.

Were they punishing me, and us, for the uncomfortable things I said in Pretoria's State Theatre in 1986 when they allowed me back into the country together with my 'non-white' wife for a few weeks? Was it in retaliation for the enthusiastic reception we received during the same trip, one rainy evening at the 'coloured' University of Western Cape? But it was not, is not, *their* country. The State may be theirs – this carnivorous cyst of moral malady, this abortion of infamy and greed; the country was always *ours*. And they knew only too well that I was no longer involved in any subversive activities. Or is the cause of justice always a threat to tyrants?

Rachel had written that you were growing old, weakening. I applied for permission to come and see you. For so long our lives had been torn apart. How I wished to sit at your feet once more, to comfort you. It was 1987. The Interior Minister of the time who handled the request was reputed for his manly drinking from Natal, Slopmouth Botha. This is what then happened (my sister only told me this much later): two security dogs were sent to the hospital where you lay, an old exhausted man in his eighties, to interrogate you. And when they could elicit no statement from you – how could they? you could no longer speak; did they twist your paralysed arm? – they rummaged through your bed-locker and those of the other old men in the ward as well. And Slopmouth made a statement to the press to say my application had been turned down because your condition did not justify it (although he cynically expressed 'compassion'). and because I was a security threat.

I wrote him an open letter:

You know well enough, and the paranoid monsters with the short hair and the chewing-gum thoughts who whisper in your ear ought to know, that my wife and I only intended a family visit to my father . . . Keep your drooling 'sympathy' to yourself. There used to be a time when Afrikaners respected the aged and the weak; there was a time, despite the planned injustice perpetrated against the majority of our compatriots, then already, when the Afrikaner could still walk upright and look his neighbour in the eye without too much shame. It has long since passed. What do we care about the tear on your cheek and the trembling of your finger when you pull the trigger again and again? . . . My own case is of minute importance, I'm only one among thousands in a similar or worse situation. We are the dwarfs. But we are the immense majority. We see what we see, even if your sophists try to cover up reality. We count the deads. We know who make the power decisions: your police counsellors and your military experts. We observe how you pretend to be holding free elections under a state of emergency, whilst eavesdropping on one another and stabbing each other in the back; we know of your occupation troops in the black townships, of the children in your jails, of your murderous expeditions across the borders. You have degraded into implements of murder. You may pull the wool over God's eyes, but the people will not be fooled . . . You stand in the dock of history with blood-besmirched hands, and some of the blood comes from your own people. I wonder, if ever you were to find yourself in hospital one day, old and lame, whether your son will want to come and visit you?

Outrageous words, Father. I was bitter. In 1988 the Western Cape University conferred an honorary degree upon me. Again I tried to enter. Again I was rebuffed.

This time Slabbert interceded with Foreign Affairs; I believe the matter was discussed at Cabinet level. We were offered a deal: allowed into the country for four days; we would have to enter and leave via Swaziland and make our way by air from Swaziland to Johannesburg for the connecting flight out; not make use of internal flights but stay on the roads; and it was to be a 'private family visit' only, with no contact with anybody else. I threatened to go public with these impossible restrictions. Slabbert, tireless and loyal, negotiated some more on our behalf – I shall always be grateful to him for the kindness and the time he gave – and it was granted that we could drive back to Johannesburg and leave from there. We'd have to report at a given door and time to be received and shipped out by someone from Foreign Affairs. We finally obtained our visas, stipulating clearly the purpose of our visit, in a fortified 'consulate' in Manzini, and had to trace the route we intended taking on a map. We'd decided that it would be too tiring for Yolande to make the trip. Too saddening as well. She and Jane were to go directly to Johannesburg and wait for Slabbert and me there.

It's a long way from Swaziland to Grahamstown. We took turns driving. The country was heartbreakingly beautiful. How much it eats me when I'm not here! It is the heritage you left me, an inner presence, the sliding distances to which I belong, the reverberations etching my dreams.

From Jamestown on we were driving in the snow – the windmills, the dams, the roofs, the hedges and the trees were all coated white, substance drained from the land with the fading of ink. White sheep stood huddled and still in virgin fields. This was a rare sight. The pass over the Stormberge was closed to traffic by a red-nosed policeman and we had to turn right and descend towards Molteno. We entered, or crossed, the Ciskei at some stage and the rural poverty was evident, the veld browsed bare, cattle bunching against the road-fences for a nibble of grass through the wire. 'And this used to be fertile land,' Slabbert explained. 'It's the arbitrary concentration of people which destroys the environment and dislocates the communities.' Tiny dwellings were scattered over the hills; they were often painted green as if with some leftover suburban swimming-pool coating.

We snaked along the contours and over the ancient mountain

shapes of the Katberg Pass, a good gravel road through a bare but impressive pattern of untouched territory, not a soul in sight. There was no snow now, just a cold wind. We switchbacked down the more wooded southern slopes to stop for lunch in a hotel at the mountain's foot. A fire crackled in the fireplace and we allowed ourselves a good bottle of wine. It was late afternoon by the time we reached Grahamstown.

Rachel took me to the hospital to see you. I think she'd prepared you beforehand. You smiled your crooked smile, your eyes were as dark as ever, your dead hand was covered by the jersey over your shoulders. You tried to speak your non-language, asked after Butterfly Smile, wanted to know how I got here, wanted to know and say so many things. I took out and showed you the warm presents she'd sent along. I held your good hand. What could I tell you about France or Berlin or Zimbabwe? You listened like somebody who would never judge again.

André Brink and his wife Marésa came for supper at Rachel's house. A cold mist swirled outside. We drank and talked late into the night. Rachel took me shopping the next morning. I bought a pair of red shoes with white laces,

Then it was time. It was time to say goodbye, Father. You were sitting upright in your bed when we arrived. You knew. Your eyes clung to my face. Was it rue? Did you want to go home? Were you afraid of the door? There is no home any more. I tried to explain, to smile and laugh, I promised that I'd be back soon-soon. We were going to take you out of there, remember? We were going to return to the farm, Father. You still had to show me how to milk cows.

You took my hand with your good one, this one which I'm using now, and laid it flat next to yours on the blanket. You looked at our two hands for the long moment of a lifetime, as if comparing, and you shook your head sadly. What were you saying? That it's been so long since you felt the sun on your skin? That you would never work again? That your hand has let you down? I have your hands, Father.

Then it was time. I kissed your lips and walked away. I couldn't take it. Rachel stayed behind for a while. Outside the door of the ward I stopped and looked back. You were weeping in total abandon. I remember the greyness of the tears, the wetness of your cheeks. I'd never seen you cry like that.

Adelaide, Bedford, Daggaboersnek (far off the Winterberg), Cradock, Rooiberg, Doringberg, Hofmeyr, Teebus and Koffiebus (Tea-cosy and Coffee-pot), Venterstad, Norvalspont, Donkerpoort, Springfontein, Vanzylrivier, the battle of Boomplaats buried in time off to our left, Pompie, Kafferrivier, Kaalspruit, Bloemfontein. We spent the night in Bloemfontein. Darkness. Lumsden's Horse, Keeromsberg, Brandfort, Houtenbeck (Shut-your-mouth), Mosuwane, Vetrivier, Theunissen, Maribakop, Rebelkop, Ventersburg, Geneva, Holfontein, Beginsel (Principle) and far to one side Koppie Alleen (Solitary Hill). In the distance Mirage, Gunhill, Kroonstad, Jordaan, the False River, Amerika (to the right), then Verbetering (Improvement), Rooiwal (Red Wall), Greenlands, Passie, Kristalkop, Wonderheuwel, Vredefort, Parys, Vaal, Sebokeng and Johannesburg.

Our four days were up. Yolande and I were now illegally in the country. In the evening we made a fire in Slabbert and Jane's house and watched television. A newsreader announced that the Minister of the Interior, Slopmouth Botha, had decided to grant us visas 'on humanitarian grounds' and that we were due soon in the country. On the late-night news another journalist corrected the bulletin by saying that we'd already been and left.

Slabbert took us to Jan Smuts Airport. A well-mannered, French-speaking gentleman took us in his charge; he pretended hard not to be from National Intelligence. We were offered coffee or beer in a secluded part of the airport building with no other passengers in sight. We sat back on the luxury sofa and chatted. Somebody came to fetch our passports. Another person took care of our luggage. National Intelligence shook our hands and gave us over to the care of an elderly body who escorted us discreetly on to the plane.

Then it came to pass. My sister called early one morning, December 1989. Hoar frost on the balcony outside. Yolande was remarking that the sparrows had been to eat all the crumbs. You had died, Father. When it was too cold for me to stay awake. In what mirror did I lose my face? I went walking through the park, crystals on the leaves, people's faces like small steam-engines.

When I was small, before Mother ladled out the soup in the evening, you taught us about folding our hands and closing our eyes. I remember the rhythm but not the words. Your one leg had become gangrenous – we call it 'coldfire' in Afrikaans – the doctor decided to amputate. Yesterday. You woke up when it was still dark. They'd taken away your glasses and your teeth, ah Father, and you saw that the leg was gone. And you turned your head to the wall and sighed. White is the wall. Warm with sun. Suddenly there will be no new yesterdays. Death is when one has used up all one's yesterdays. Thoughts hurt my head. There's the story of the trout caught with the neck-hair of a cock twisted into a fly. A fly is knowledge. Ah, Father. You have moved. You are swimming like a trout in the dark grave without walls. I thought: death must be like sleeping as fast as a fishing line without a hook. The raven in my chest was spreading its wings, pecking at my throat.

Rachel called to say they'd taken you to Port Elizabeth for cremation. I flew down from cold, white Europe. Cloete waited for me at the airport. We drove to Hermanus, golden summer morning, breeze off the sea. We were early, went for tea, the café-owner told us the story of how he was out at sea on a boat once to help scatter the ashes of a deceased friend on the waters, and then the wind had turned.

When we arrived at the church the others were there – Jan and wife, Rachel and daughter, one of Cloete's wives and his children, Jan Biltong and Jabbery . . . Rachel carried a small casket of beautiful brown wood. She handed it to me. 'Now you can hold Father for a while,' she said. Your ashes. I was holding you in my hands. So light, like burned-out fire. I wondered about the leg . . . Rachel told of how brother Jan talked until late last night, all his memories of you poured out . . . And today in the car he sang all the way here.

At the last moment our youngest brother walked in, Basjan Beer, the one you loved the most. He moved into the bench next to me, smelling of liquor. His hands trembled, he was wearing dark glasses, he didn't want us to see him crying. Christo Alheit led the service, my old buddy from schooldays in Wellington. How many times we used to roam the streets at night to steal fruit from the neighbours' trees, to start all the dogs barking, to run with the stars. He spoke of you as 'Oom Hannes'. Christo's old man was the dominee of our congregation when we were young. He was in the back of the church now, bent and grey. He finished the service with a moving prayer to some deity up there where the mind cannot reach. I went to shake his hand. 'And so, you haven't lost the faith?' he asked. It would have been too long a story . . .

We drove to the cemetery and walked up to where Ounooi lies buried under the fluttering of butterflies and the twittering of birds. Jan was holding the casket awkwardly, the wind lifted the hair off his forehead. Somebody had to say something. Jan cleared his throat, said: 'At least now Oubaas and Ounooi are together again.' Broke off. Looked away. Silence. Sun. But the crust over the grave was too solid. Somebody was going to have to return later to make a hole.

And in the evening we all gathered in an Italian restaurant in Cape Town for a meal around a long table, all your descendants of difficult sons and daughter and grandchildren. I missed Yolande's quiet hand in mine. Jan expounded his beliefs for the preservation of elephants in Africa; they're landscape gardeners, he said, breaking down the dense vegetation to make it possible for other species to live. Afterwards I walked down towards Cloete's flat in town where I was to sleep.

Wind was curling white over the mountain. You'd been my guide, Oubaas Father. My initiator. My elephant. My deepest yesterdays had been coloured by you. When I was very small – do you remember? – and we walked home at night, you carried me on your shoulders. Your shoulders were a ship. I felt your rough cheeks under my palms, I could reach up and pluck the swinging stars.

This I wanted to write to you tonight, now that we've been to visit the fragrant places where your footprints may still linger for all we know. Ash is the memory of fire, the slow and separated wings. But the flame never dies. It moves on to become a guiding star.

16

PHAKATHI!

We picnic with John Coetzee and friends in the Silvermine Nature Reserve on the mountain overlooking Pollsmoor and Retreat and Lakeside below. The aroma of heather, wildflowers, plants and herbs, making of the peninsula a botanical haven, meets us. In John's party are Dorothy Driver, an academic, the writer Ingrid de Kok and friend, John's daughter and beau, and a brown woman who has returned to teach at Western Cape after spending many years in Britain.

John Coetzee's eyelids crinkle at the corners. We gently tease and prod him until he thaws and starts relating in a soft voice the strange reflections he gets from people approaching him about his work. Since many of his characters have mangled speech organs, people are surprised that he actually talks. Ingrid de Kok has stories about the quarrelsome dialogue between writers and hit-people of the People's Culture Syndicate. Maybe we are all exiles. From a copse birds fly with a flurry of wings.

I ask if anything more is known about the Richard Rive story. Knew him years ago when he was a young writer in the company of Uys Krige and Jack Cope. He was found savagely battered to death in his own house last year, after a ferocious struggle. Police later arrested two suspects in Upington with Richard's car and video-scope and watch. Their defence was that they'd been sexually assaulted. Ingrid quotes something from Stephen Watson: 'If everything was political, what would be left to enable us to evaluate politics itself?'

In town I go to talk to the Dutch branch manager of United Bank. A penny must have dropped somewhere in the maniacal system! He's willing to release my money! Withdraw the lot, stuff it

182

in my pockets, close the account down, and make my way to the car all the while watching over the shoulder for *skollies* with naked blades. On the way out of the city I notice painted in big red letters on a wall: 'SO BOTHA HOW MANY OXEN HAVE DIED NOW?'

Tuesday, 26 March. At the airport before sunrise. Wet and windy. While Yolande sorts out the tickets I nip into the shop to buy a newspaper. Bump into Jay Naidoo of the Congress of South African Trade Unions (COSATU). In public he can be flinty and arrogantly dogmatic – at the Marly-le-Roi conference outside Paris, that bitterly cold December week in 1989, the two of us clashed, I can't remember what about; there was an apology later – but in private he will charm the bloomers off an elephant. He's been to Cape Town for an encounter on economics between bosses and workers. His big black eyes are apologetic. Asks if I'm back for good now, says it ought to happen. It is a standard remark. Asks if I too go hither and thither for *meetings*. The political person doesn't easily comprehend the notion of drifting.

The Marly-le-Roi get-together was one of the last of its kind outside before banned organizations and people returned home to face and dictate the music of dying. 'Home' is where the footprints of the ancestors cannot be effaced. (Of the high-level talks between leaders that then started in the country, Jan Duiwel remarked later: 'Warlords meet: the people die.') I'd helped organize the event under the auspices of the Fondation France-Libertés. Another organizer turned out to be an agent of French counter-espionage; when this came to light he was promptly sent packing by Madame Mitterrand. Several of the people attending had just been released from prison.

In the evenings a bus whisked us into Paris for official dinners, with police outriders separating the waters with wailing sirens. At the Prime Minister's residence the then occupant, Michel Rocard, a short man, welcomed us in the foyer; my compatriots mistook him for the doorman and handed him their coats and scarves. Inside, Henry Fazzie, a venerable grey-bearded trade-union leader from the Eastern Cape, recently from Robben Island, sat down in a high-backed chair with gilded legs – what luxury for an old jailbird who had only one borrowed suit – put his hat on his knees, and promptly fell asleep.

The dark hours were spent discussing, drinking, discussing. On the night before we met with French parliamentarians in their august sanctum, some of us gathered to masticate the hard *biltong* of the South African Problem. Present were Judge Ackermann (respectable human-rights crusader in buttoned-up waistcoat), Murray Hofmeyr (hardbitten captain of industry), Franklin Sonn (the proverbially pious political survivor), Brigid M (an ANC lawyer, proposing toast upon unsteady toast), Thabo Mbeki, Trevor Manuel (with woollen cap over his ears), Chris Louw, Slabbert . . . Also a journalist called Ghapzella who, as a camp-follower, had been diligently servicing the ANC delegation's needs the whole week long. Some also serve who just bump and grind.

Thabo and Murray heatedly argued the merits of conflicting economic systems. Judge Ackermann was called upon to arbitrate. He rose, legs well apart, to speak with a glass of authority in fist. Ghapzella was sitting behind him and grabbed hold of his appendages of masculinity – maybe she wanted to evaluate the weight of judicial opinion – and 'Amandla!' the judge shouted with popping eyes . . .

Murray Hofmeyr was at his post the next morning in the big hall of Parliament, red-faced and sweating, looking neither to left nor to right, but at least not falling off his chair. Thabo Mbeki was to address the assembly as ANC delegation leader, but had had all the stuffing taken out of him and was nowhere to be found. After an embarrassed roll-call one of the comrades weakly offered: 'He's sick in bed.' One could understand why South African capitalists are such tough nuts to crack. Pallo Jordan was called upon to stand in for the leader. He asked to speak last, and while the others delivered their perorations he wrote out a lecture on the French Revolution. (Before sinking into politics he'd been a historian.) As it is said: somebody has to teach the grandmothers how to suck eggs.

We are off to East London on a visit organized by IDASA. Gradually we climb above the clouds, the cover dissipates and we catch glimpses of rugged coast, lakes holding light high in the mountains,

184

stretches of sand-dunes. Hermien Carolus, IDASA's Eastern Cape representative, waits for us at East London's airport (probably called Verwoerd or Strijdom), tall, a thatch of blond straw, big mouth with cigarette, chic. We hire a Mercedes. Hermien Carolus precedes us in her car to the Protea Hotel (big and empty and sad) where we are to stay. The streets are inordinately broad, uphill and down. There's a dimness over the sea.

The place looks dead. It used to be a humming industrial area, now there's nearly nobody about. The port is left to decay. For lunch we are taken to a seaside resort higher up the coast. Hermien is full of excuses for her car's quirks: it was blown up outside the offices of the End Conscription Campaign – two landmines nearly wrecked it entirely; she just had to have it repaired though; now every time she turns to the right the hooter starts blaring.

Change clothes, on to the restaurant where I am to read poems. A private house that's been restored, the blue ceiling has a pink ledge. I know none of the people except Hermien, Thin Dominee and wife (with whom we lunched). Yolande, beautiful and shy, hides under my elbow. This was Hermien's idea. IDASA is into culture as well. Take whisky, thank you. Look at list of expected 'guests.' See the name of Jan Walker. Shock. Here? Thin Dominee ('Please call me Olfert,' he says) explains this Jan Walker has been in and out of East London these last few years; recently started an organization in town called 'Comrades for Christ'. Very active. Hands out soup and political tracts to those who doss outside. Heard you were coming, insisted on being present, says he knows you from years ago before you got to be all full of shit. (Olfert is not above a mild expletive). Another whisky? Thanks. Need it.

Yolande straightens my jacket, whispers instructions for me to speak slowly, pronounce properly, put away my pipe, have some more salad, not drink so much. A knife tinkles against a glass and I am introduced. Only one or two black faces, a small family of other-coloureds, an Indian couple. The rest all palefaces, men with rugby hands and aftershaved cheeks, their ladyfolk with black-painted eyes and preened hair-dos and demure breasts in shiny dresses. Cultural legs. Walker doesn't turn up after all. Never did like this kind of nonsense. People embarrassed to listen to poetry, trying to look into the near distance without seeing. I embarrassed too.

185

Mumble. Yolande Sonrisa frowning. Waiters and cooks laugh and clatter in the kitchen. Lucky sods! Afterwards Olfert admits a whisper into my ear confiding that he's been writing poetry too. He's wearing a cool tuxedo and a bow-tie of the latest fashion.

On to Grahamstown where we spend the night in Rachel's house, every day more like Ounooi's. (Yesterday, on our way through the Ciskei, we visited Steve Biko's grave outside King William's Town, then spent time with teachers and students at Fort Hare University.) Family photos on the wall. One or two of my very early paintings. Another country, another life. Father's hat on peg behind the kitchen door. An old sighing dog sleeping in a basket. Rachel's daughter, Anna-Kind, is getting to be a long-legged lass. Breakfast.

Then visit to Rhodes University, Afrikaans Department. Orphaned since André Brink left. Big portrait of the departed master as stern academic deity looking down upon drones from staff-room wall. 'Can there be a second coming?' they ask. Tim Paleisamen, one elephantine leg in plaster, presides over the bereaved faithful. All fit around one table. Tea and biscuits from a tin. Senior students allowed in to swell the ranks. Ding-dong of concerns. Afrikaans dying. Surely work of quality is a prerequisite for survival, but cannot guarantee it. They now have four third-year students, but only two second-year ones. More lecturers than students. In Stellenbosch too there are more teachers than honours candidates. Soon a senior Afrikaans student will be like someone going to a brothel to have his pick of pouting lubricators touting their shop-soiled attributes with the silicone implants. Tim asks whether it is ever permitted to analyse a poem. I agree to say 'yes' if I can have some more biscuits. What will become of Afrikaans departments? Will they merge with institutions of African Studies? 'We can bring them the theories.' 'Yes, but we are bargaining as beggars, and isn't "theory" a European concept?'

Lunch in town. Next to a design poster purporting to depict Montmartre another promises rewards for weapons found – from R6,000 for an AK-47 to R3,000 for a limpet mine. A cockeyed economic principle is at work here – what's to prevent you buying guns for peanuts on the Mozambique border and flogging them to the police? And the police are the ones freely putting the weapons back in circulation!

Buy newspapers. The *Daily Dispatch* reports that the taxi war has shifted to East London's main streets. The ANC branch in King William's Town deplores 'the senseless killings' of people. Violence among taxi-men poses a danger to the general public. The organization appeals to taxi-men to develop a culture of resolving their differences peacefully. The Border branch of the SACP calls on taxi-men to demonstrate that they value human life. Gangs of thugs are also hijacking minibus taxis. 'The Afrikaans poet and author, Mr B, accompanied by his wife, visited East London yesterday. Mr B, who spent seven years in jail after a Terrorism Act conviction in 1975, said last year he may never settle permanently in South Africa, but he would like to spend time here and take part in the debate on the future.' Editorial on health spending in the Cape Province: 'Increasingly, it is clear, those who can pay will receive First World health care, while the poor may have to settle for less.'

Sowetan shows horrific pictures of a massacre in Alexandra. One image has relatives holding blood-soaked clothing inside the house where fourteen people were killed while holding a vigil for victims of a previous spate of bloodletting. The latest killing brings to more than eighty the number of people who have died since violence erupted in the area three weeks ago. Comment on front page: 'The violence is, also quite clearly, out of control of any political leaders . . . It is time for good men and women to help themselves for nobody else is going to do it. Things just cannot go on like this.'

On Good Friday, the 29th, we leave with Rachel and Anna-Kind for brother Jan's house at Sedgefield. My little brother, Basjan Beer, will also be staying there. Jan and Rose themselves are away but will join us on Monday. Hot but quiet day. Listen to a tape of African Jazz Pioneers. Turn off for quick visit to a hamlet named Salem. Settler church with caved-in churchyard, next to it the presbytery dated 1834, then Salem Trading Post, cricket pitch, tearoom, and that's it. Sitting in the shade of a tree a Xhosa witch-doctor with a tame baboon on a chain. In the road a cheeky wagtail. Rhinoceroses have been released recently in a nearby reserve.

Bloukrans, Grootrivier, Bobbejaansrivier, forests and ravines.

Plettenberg Bay where rich and powerful come to bronze and booze discreetly. Hard by 'coloured' extensions called New Horizons, Garden of Eden. Along comes an accident – car with dented trailer, minibus lying on its side, shreds of a burst tyre, people milling about, drunken passenger in the middle of the road trying to divert traffic with generous gestures, in the lee of the taxi-bus (which must have carried an overload of brown travellers) a motionless figure reclines, blood has seeped away in the sandy soil. Another Easter statistic.

I remember seeing a group of men silently struggling in the road outside Jonna's house. The one whose arms were being pinned had a flashing knife. When I looked again they were all gone as if nothing had ever happened.

17

AORIST

It is better to write one's memoirs when still young, when one can yet strike resonances from the unknown. Passing time brings only shrivelled yesterdays and a bitterness to the tongue. For me it is too late. Phantoms break from my dreams and want to share my tobacco, they read the newspaper over my shoulder and deposit the soot of their experiences on the white sheet of paper on my workbench. My journeys have become embarrassing confessions. I have grown a life and that life is now threatening me with death, like a gangrenous Siamese-twin brother. The more I eliminate, the more images arise to cloud the vision.

We have a misty morning. Sky and earth merge in a grey haze. Run. The beach is an endlessly wet mirror at low tide. When you look closer you see small hermit-crabs scuttling, leaving tracks the way the child I once was did when I pushed my Dinky toy motorcar through the sand. Waves come towards the land as white measuring lines of evanescence. An old fisherman and his grandson are drawing lines in the empty mirror. In places they've dug holes with spoons. What are they looking for, I ask. The old man takes a watery squint. 'White mussels,' he answers, gesturing towards the plastic bag held by the boy. 'As bait, but there's not much.'

Images and shards of impressions come and go. Words can be bait. I remember many things. A small white dog runs down the beach looking for its master. I remember that the Revolution washed away. As late as 1987 there were up to 25,000 people in detention without trial.

The ashes of Bram Fischer, the advocate who became an underground hero and communist leader and who died of cancer in jail, are still in the possession of the Prisons Department. He's been dead these fifteen years. 'Bram had the gift of love,' says his daughter Ruth. 'He had the bluest eyes. He always wore a hat, like Vorster or Gorbachev. He never went out the front door without a hat.' I remember how proud I was when Marius Schoon, who spent time in the same prison as Bram, told me that the two of them discussed my case. Marius Schoon's wife and daughter were barbarically assassinated by a South African explosive device.

Knife Owen, editor of the *Sunday Times*, writes: 'Twice in recent months, secretaries on their way to work have had to step fastidiously around corpses left lying for hours in the streets near my office. This, I suppose, is a small precursor of the "ungovernability" which, according to both the Finance Minister and the Governor of the Reserve Bank, will befall us by 1995, unless foreigners come to invest money here.'

The day passes. In the afternoon we all go down to the beach for a swim. The water's swell is slow and blue. Exhilarating to dive in through the foam, paddle while waiting for the right wave, cut in fast across its run just at the point of breaking and tumbling and to ride its crest (the crashing suspended) until it leaves you floundering in the shallows. We used to amuse ourselves thus for hours on end when we were small, Basjan and I. We're dolphins again, even if we now look more like walruses . . . Then to roll in the hot sand, to feel the tingle of sun on the skin and salt on the lips . . .

Evening paints the dunes an orange tint, then blackens the sand. Mosquitos drive us indoors from the veranda. Tonight Angel, brother Jan's daughter, tells us stories about flowers and plants – she's a horticulturist; a bee stung her on the ear and now there's a buzzing in her head – and Basjan Beer explains his melancholic philosophy until Rachel gets annoyed and tells him to go to bed.

On Monday Rachel and Anna-Kind leave for Grahamstown with a friend going up the coast. Towards nightfall I drive with Basjan to Crocodile Botha Airport near George where our eldest brother and his wife will arrive back from their gathering of ex-paratroopers in Bloemfontein. Jan steps off the plane with a fleamarket of medals clanging on his chest. He's been seduced into active service again, this time to go to train black commandos in the Ciskei. Gone are his dreams of preserving elephants. Clearly it is more exciting to shape people for killing. We open a bottle of wine, and another, and hearken to the tragic mumbling of the broken waves at night.

Oblivion thoughts. When I fall asleep I'm trying to kill the pig, a huge boar. But it's not that easy. The stones in the enclosure are slippery with blood. The pig screams a steady vomit of furious sounds. I'm sitting on his back. He shakes me off. His neck and withers are slashed, the meat open and raw. The axe is embedded in his back. Now I must take on the beast again, grab hold of the axe and administer the death-blow. I look deep into his unfathomable black eyes with the long Greta Garbo lashes. He belches his voice in my face: we are one.

18

SNAKES

We travel back to Paradise House with ever-changing light stroking the land. Along the road we stop at a café to buy the bloody papers. Yolande sighs and says: 'Again?'

South reports that released political prisoners are angry and bitter at the preferential treatment given to exiles to integrate them into society while their needs are being ignored. Almost 70 per cent of their membership have not been able to secure employment since their release and most are reliant on financial assistance to survive . . . Highly trained policemen, military servicemen, ex-servicemen and paramilitary personnel are among thousands recruited to join the Wenkommando (Victory Commando) of the AWB. Training camps are 'preparing the Boers for the coming revolution . . . Boers must be militarily prepared for the chaos of a system of one person, one vote.' One does not have to be Afrikaans-speaking to be a Boer. An AWB spokesman says English-speaking people as well as French, German, Dutch and Hungarian citizens have joined the AWB. 'A Boer is a person of European descent who subscribes to the programme and constitution of the AWB.'

Forty-one residents of the Boland town of Ashton are suing the Minister of Law and Order (Adriaan Vlok) for an amount totalling R2 million; the actions result from police repression in the Ashton townships of Zolani and Oukamp between 25 May and 5 July 1990. In the biggest single claim, twenty-one-year-old Jan Gertse asks R750,000 for the loss of sight in both eyes. In an affidavit, Gertse says he was shot by police on Monday, 2 July, after he and a group of people had come from a candlelight service at the Anglican Church. Gertse also sustained shotgun wounds to the back and face. Mr Karel Opperman, twenty-seven, lost the sight of his left eye as a result of a shotgun wound . . . A Hout Bay policeman appears in Wynberg Magistrates Court in connection with abusive and threatening calls made to a resident in the area. Mr Daniels (the plaintiff) tells the court that he was called, among other things, a 'hotnot', a 'communist bastard', 'scum' and 'rubbish'. More than seventy abusive calls were recorded . . .

New Nation explains that Damien de Lange, a white ANC activist in prison, is suffering from bleeding gums as a result of vitamin deficiency; the condition is said to be caused by the low standard of food given to prisoners . . .

Sowetan carries the story of Pretoria Central prisoner 27/0202, Cosmos Maifadi, who has had both eyes gouged out and is coughing blood after being attacked last Wednesday night in his cell by a group of gangsters known as the 'Big Five'. A spokesman for the Department of Correctional Services (their new name!) yesterday confirmed that Maifadi was 'slightly injured in an incident allegedly involving a fellow prisoner and not a group of gangsters'. A Benoni woman who is intending to sell her plush home to ANC president Oliver Tambo for R850,000 is living in fear of her life. Mrs Jill McQueen, who lives in an upmarket suburb overlooking a lake, says she has received several death-threats from individuals and organizations since word of the intended sale got around . . . Dr J. P. van Zyl, superintendent of a Messina hospital, ordered police to take a seriously burned fifteen-year-old away from his establishment because there 'had been too much interference with the patient by journalists wanting to make political mileage'. The boy – who'd been soldered to a workbench by a local farmer and then 'corrected' with a blowtorch – was dragged from his bed by policemen who drove him away in a van despite his pain from severe burns and wounds . . .

The evening of 3 April finds us on the road between Stellenbosch and Simon's Town. The mountains and the sea give off heat, the skies are bathed in the lurid colours of an infected light. Colours alone must already engender a richness of mysticism in Africa – pleated blacks and pure blues, deep greens, violent reds and sharp yellows, the countless shifts of brown from water to dust.

In the car Yolande and I discuss the Wodaabe, those Fulani

nomads living along the confines of the Sahara. *Wodaabe* conveys many meanings: 'the people of the empty earth'; 'the cloud people'; 'the men of the forbidden'; 'those who live under the taboo of purity'. Myth has it that they came from Mesopotamia, crossing the Red Sea. Why not? But it doesn't matter. Their only riches are the cattle they lead. Other populations in the region despise the drifters, but they consider themselves the most beautiful people on earth.

Once a year, towards the last days of September, they gather for a festival called *Geerewol*, which marks the end of the rainy season. Like mirages they emerge from the wet desert. Then the men dolly themselves up – because this is the time when ladyfolk choose their partners; even married women are allowed to take their pick for the night. Hours are spent painting faces, outlining eyes, whitening teeth, plaiting tresses, draping robes. Codes of beauty and bearing have remained unchanged for centuries. The women look for good lovers with pleasing gestures; the boys may admit to being attracted by the grace of a silhouette and the tilt of breasts. Then the boys with the turbans and the beads twined into their hair, and reddened lips half-open to show the glitter of their teeth, and lines and daubs of yellow and blue and red and green on cheeks and chin, and wide white-staring eyes, and stretched necks, and the high-heeled shoes, weave and strut like manikins in a row.

Persistent droughts have reduced them to scarecrows. A nomad who has lost all his cattle will build an enclosure with the lyre-shaped horns and sit down in the middle to let himself perish . . .

Thursday, 4 April. The chirruping of birds, small wheeling clouds of swallows also preparing their departure; the ocean's deeper blue when the wind turns north; across the bay a luminous nearly white line as separation between water and mountain.

We have guests for lunch under the fig tree – Joëlle and Olivier Bourgois, Jakes and Phoebe Gerwel. Yolande, being the best cook in the world, has prepared a selection of salads, rice, chicken, flavoured by her secrets. A blunt black shape surfaces in the bay to make its way to port – a South African submarine made in France. I fetch the binoculars; we take turns observing the vessel, and the French ambassador thinks I stagemanaged this incident to embarrass her.

Lunch is nearly over, and we intoxicated with the beauty of the setting, when all hell breaks loose up the hill from the direction of the Xhosas. Alice comes charging down shouting furiously, clearly on the warpath. She grabs my arm to drag me towards the house. You must call the police immediately! We try to restrain her, at least to find out what it's all about.

The problem is a second woman, Pampata, who's been to visit them. We can't figure out the root of strife. I ask Jakes to calm Alice down; he is after all of the Party, should know how, and he offers a feeble conciliatory 'Sister' which she angrily brushes away. Up the hill we go.

There's a witches' concert of screeching and screaming. Bruman, who seems to have had a spot of bother with his fly, attempts to hold back a strikingly beautiful woman in a two-piece suit and beret. Pampata shakes off the arm and picks up a huge stone. Her natty suit, smeared with soil, shows the fight has already gone through an earlier physical stage. Alice stands her ground, arms akimbo, her kerchief knocked lopsided, her face a clay mask, spitting invective. Pampata moves in for the attack. Bruman is totally helpless; he fumblebuttons his fly and goes tut-tut-tut. I manage to wrest the rock from Pampata's hand but she picks up another. More threats and curses. More scraping of wings and scratching of dust.

Now Pampata takes my arm in an iron grip and frogmarches me down to the house; she orders me inside and on the telephone. I have no choice. Her employer must be called to testify – he's a naval doctor anyway. That 'country woman' up there (Alice) accuses her of having a snake between her legs! The doctor will bring the untruth to light.

I think I finally have a glimmer of understanding what this may be all about: two ladies spitting and spatting over one man (poor, placid Bruman), conflict between 'town girl' and 'country bumpkin', accusations of infidelity and man-theft, insults to clan and tribe?

The employer succeeds in soothing the feathers of the beautiful fury to the point where she relents her hold on my wrist (which is no snake). He also promises to alert the police. A policeman tele-phones to ask whaddabout de peepil, whether the trouble has been physical, is there blood, are there deads, and decides it's not worth coming out for. They must have numerous alarms every day.

We offer coffee to our slightly shaken guests under the fig tree. The wind has turned its nose, it is breathing stronger again. When they leave, chic Pampata and sturdy Alice are sitting with legs stretched flat on the ground on the incline below the hut, chatting amiably and sharing a bottle of tipsiness.

In the evening I drive into town, to Maitland where IDASA has regional offices in a well-worn building. I have to talk around 'eternal dissidence'. The offices on the top floor have a large balcony from where one can contemplate Big Wind frothing volumes of night-thoughts over the mountain.

Mark Behr is IDASA regional director. We sit in a largish room and I say to the forty-odd people present that I have not prepared a speech or any suchlike structured contribution. I shall lay myself open to questions and annotations. Before starting, does anyone present not understand Afrikaans? A young black puts up his hand to object to its being spoken, and I switch to the imperial tongue. After two minutes the young man gets up and leaves the premises all the same. Afrikaans, spoken in any other language, remains Afrikaans. Mark Behr kicks off by asking: 'Why have you betrayed the Revolution?'

Here are my notebook jottings pertaining to this give-and-take, in their pristine turbulent and chaotic surfacing:

What is eternal? What is dissident? Dissident from what? I point at functions of rebel, opponent, revolutionary, drop-out, outsider, on to exile and *zek* (as the inmates of Soviet labour camps are called). To be against the norm, orthodoxy, the canon, hegemony, politics, the State, power. Using the self as defective measuring rod. Particularly in this country with its culture of secrecy, clandestinity, manipulation, co-optation, the arbitrary, hollow moral strictures of governing élite, avant-garde cynicism, intimidation. Fractiousness a luxury?

I reassert the notion of the fuck-up as creative principle. (And a voice from the back gloomily remarks: 'Everything here is a fuck-up!') Man is the enemy of the machine, in every orderly system he is the perturbing factor, he makes dirt. The structure of capitalism demands his evacuation.

This 'differentness' is wilfully misinterpreted by some of my 'friends' who clamour for their conformal part of the pie in the sky.

Nobody in Europe is interested in Africa any longer (I announce): to Europe Africa is only a mass of human matter making a mass sport of dying. People search for the ghosts of their cattle. 'Ethics! Morality! Where are you, my beauties?' It seems self-evidently 'normal' that blacks should be killed in South Africa. Indians starving to death have nothing to do with us either. *Don't rattle your bowls so!* There is no longer any understanding of the relationship between surplus on the one hand and poverty on the other. Already in the rich part of the world people are trapped before their television screens, indulging in monologues. The programme provides the answers to unasked questions. This is capitalist utopia. Dimly in the background there's the stifled murmuring of units who don't have televisions. Give them their human looking rights! Close the windows! From halfway through the twentieth century the question of *meaning* was no longer asked, neither in art nor in literature. The importance nowadays is to empty the screens of the mind by filling them *ad infinitum* with ersatz images of life.

In the afternoon of the 5th we pack the embassy's station wagon with a carton of French wines and a change of clothes each, and set off for the Cedarberg Mountains – Yolande Golondrina, Joëlle and Olivier and their daughters Pauline and Armance. My old mountain friend of years ago, Baas Saayman, his wife Nici and daughter Sandra, have gone ahead to prepare the camping site. And Oom Frederik Joubert will be there too. For decades he's been the guide of our walks, packing our rucksacks and provisions in jute bags slung over the backs of his pack-donkeys. I haven't seen him since 1973. All his life he's lived with his brothers, pale-skinned descendants of a long-forgotten Huguenot, as 'white coloureds.' Oom Frederik is a living repository of mountain-knowledge, one of the last survivors of a time when men could still turn themselves into animals, a shaman.

Up the west coast. Milnerton. Past Bloubergstrand and Melkbosstrand. There's a 'coloured' town called Atlantis. Malmesbury. This region is known as Swartland, the Black Country. Famous for its wheat and the throat-tickling accents of its inhabitants.

Roadsigns to Dwars-in-die-weg, Somersverdriet (Obstreperous, Summer's Sadness), Die Brug, Misverstand (Misunderstanding). Moorreesburg. Piketberg.

Towards Citrusdal we start ascending. Over Piekenierskloof Pass and down again along a valley rich in citrus groves between two parallel ranges. The wind follows us all the way, dark clouds are gathering. We leave the tarred road before reaching Citrusdal. A track of reddish-brown earth leads us into a labyrinth of desolate beauty, peaks and sheer rockfaces and sombre gorges.

The Cedarberg Mountains could serve as décor for cowboy movies – yellow and ochre and orange and red outcrops eroded into fantastically shaped pillars, needles and columns and chimneys and stacks of boulders. The flood of ages hollowed caves in the cliffs. There are caverns and cathedrals with slits windowing between soaring rocks.

In the morning we visit a Bushman painting against one rockface: elephants and people walk off into eternity. From a higher vantage-point we observe the play of many rainbows lighting up the veld with a sharp dawn light, spraying arches of fireworks from the canyons. Distances are tinted indigo and Prussian blue.

We must return to town. On the highest point of Piekenierskloof Pass we stop at a roadhouse. We wander around looking at locally made shoes, dried fruit and bottled conserves offered for sale. Might as well eat lunch in the restaurant. I walk into the dining room to see if there's a table available. Two other couples are already waiting. One gent turns around to face me. His hair is grey and he wears dark glasses. He puts out a hand which I take without thinking. 'Ah, Mr B,' he says drily, 'you don't recognize me. Remember Paul Gough?'

He removes his shades and I look into the eyes of one of my erstwhile interrogators while in detention and in prison – Blue Eyes, I called him in the mumblings of my mind. He was with BOSS then (the Bureau of State Security), a cold, cruel man who got a mental erection out of persecuting his victims, playing with them the way a cat would paw a mouse. A coward and a pervert. But ensnared in the vanity of attempting to appear all-knowing and all-powerful, it transpired that he was less than bright.

My hand has been bitten! He looks me up and down, trying on

198

the half-smile of the self-satisfied torturer. 'You haven't changed, you look well,' he remarks. 'You too,' I say. 'Are you still with the same outfit?' 'Oh, no, that's been over a long time ago. I'm with National Intelligence now. We are preparing the New South Africa.'

By the door I find myself shaking with a mixture of impotent rage and terror. Exactly the sort of reaction he'd have wanted to provoke. What prevents me from ripping the bastard's innards out, supposing I could – and him from doing the same to me? I remember now that he was from hereabouts somewhere. He has the accent. His people are probably simple Boer folk. He used to taunt me with the fact that we were both from the Cape Colony. To my shame. His wife looks unpretentiously thick. They're dressed in their Pharisee best. Maybe they've been to church this morning. He must have a file on the subversive tendencies and weaknesses of God. The other man with the beefy chops and the rosy cranium has similarly cold eyes. A henchman. Murderers with their companions, out for a quiet Sunday lunch.

At table Yolande senses something amiss. I briefly inform her of their presence. We glance over to where he sits with a smirk and a black heart, stabbing at the meat on his plate. The food will turn to vomit in my stomach. Later we see them leave in a shiny Mercedes-Benz. The State looks after its own. And I ask myself: did our paths cross by accident, or was he wanting to make me aware of their surveillance? Like cockroaches they will survive all cataclysms, the original filth of our souls watching us from dark recesses.

Survival is a choice between two kinds of betrayal. Or, surviving is a slower way of committing suicide.

19

BLOOD

Early morning trip in dark to airport. Desire to turn away, drive for ever over this vast country, on condition that it stays unlit, listen to grey night voices crackling over the ether, headlamps moments spearing the luminescent eyes of shy nocturnal beasts, roll down the window and inhale the moist rumour of a nearby sea, later the dust-dry desert breath charged with stardust, on, on . . .

To Durban. Pierre Cronjé waiting at Louis Botha Airport. Good to see him on home turf when he loosens his tie and lights a cigarette. Short drive to the centre. Very much like Cape Town, this mesh of Victorian buildings and high glass towers. More Indian and black people on the streets though. First to IDASA where Pierre and Paul Graham brief me on complex local scene. Curious sensation – to be confirmed again and again – of being in a war zone. The war is mostly invisible, even if I sense it in the concerns of those I meet, hear it rippling through their conversations. People are casting around for desperate solutions to stem the violence, limit the bloodshed, find the levers that would stop the machine, contain the descent into barbarism.

Repeatedly I hear reports of killings, ambushes, hijackings, burn-outs, set battles with crazed warriors streaming over hills. And a sense of the dark hand of State institutions manipulating the hatred, organizing or triggering off the onslaughts. The warlords' names are common knowledge, their crimes public information: Samuel Jamile, Chief Khawula, David Ntombela of Sweetwaters . . . The men running them have faces: General J. A. C. Buchner, for instance, seconded from Security to command the Kwazulu Police . . . It doesn't help exposing the spalpeens. In fact, 'monitors of good faith' have to continue facilitating 'peace agreements' involving these very same people, to grasp at every legal provision in the book and reach out for every straw of influence in trying to deflect State agents from their gory path of destruction.

A quick visit to ANC offices. Rooms and corridors jammed with people come to ask for help – money, jobs, houses, legal or medical assistance, recognition. Men and women grown saltpetre-coloured in the struggle hold tattered slips of paper. Some want to tell you of their experience of prison, detention, banning, strikes, exile. The pressure by the jostling people on the ANC to provide, now that it is officially operating in the country again (a fact mistakenly equated with victory), must be overwhelming. A young militant takes me through to a quieter room. A few comrades gather round to ask for an analysis of what's happening in the 'outside world', the caving in of the Soviet Union. Notes are made, heads shaken, tongues clicked.

Lunch with lecturers of Sociology, Economics and Political Science at Natal University. Altogether different atmosphere. Rueful, waspish criticism of the liberation movement: not enlightened and rigorous enough in their handling of the national question . . . Leftist bourgeois-intellectual lily-livered more-doctrinaire-than-thou bullshit. Ah, whatever happened to the Revolution? Why did it not live up to the expectations of our superior guilty white minds? Why did it shit on the doorstep?

Afternoon run in Pierre's car over hills and valleys deeper inland, taking us through what must be the plushest suburbs anywhere – riot of cultivated tropical vegetation in flower behind high security walls; then police outposts bristling with radio masts, enclosed within their safe perimeter by electrified wire fences; and suddenly, cresting a hill, down through a patch of Kwazulu, abject poverty, pot-holed roads, burned-down schools and gutted houses, dilapidated shopfronts with glowering men shouldering a wall, scatter of fowl and goats and cattle. The killing fields. 'Only death in this place and this place we do not know': Anonymous. Sometimes Pierre stops to recount an incident and sweep a hand over a battlefield. I am looking at the future and it chills me to the bone. He chain-smokes, his eyes are bloodshot.

Towards sunset we reach home. Womenfolk are busy preparing snacks and drinks for an evening gathering. Pierre is the

Democratic Party Member of Parliament for Greytown. The guests arrive – university lecturers, Democratic Party and ANC militants, trade unionists of COSATU, the editor and journalists of *Natal Witness*, a priest or two, ordinary township-dwellers with dresses too shiny and ties too wide, soft-eyed Indians and broad-backed blacks and aftershaved whites.

I am summoned to give a talk about the perspective as seen from abroad. Lay it on thick, insist upon the fact that South Africans will have to become self-sufficient. I sketch the dissolution elsewhere in Africa, and the companion truth that the North couldn't care two rusty ha'pennies about our continent sinking in a mire of famine and plagues and imploding structures. An elderly man sits behind me in a high-backed chair, his round eyes amused behind his glasses, a smile hovering on lips adorning a short grey beard. When I've spilled my bile he is called upon to comment, and does so with witty grace whilst standing straight, even complimenting me on the impertinence of bringing harsh tidings. It is Harry Gwala, the regional ANC leader. I embrace him and only then notice that his trunk and arms are paralysed from the shoulders down. An assistant has to help him eat and drink. Pierre says it is believed that an attempt was made to poison Gwala slowly during his long incarceration on Robben Island. He survived, and he laughs. He has the reputation of being a fierce Stalinist.

People drink and talk. People drink to get drunk quickly and then talk very loudly. Like war citizens all over the globe they either break down and cry or tell stories of killing and maiming and survival as if these were hilariously funny. They mime death scenes. They laugh with tears running down their cheeks. They cannot get drunk. They rapidly go over into a language riddled with codes that only they understand. All have carried the inordinately heavy corpses of loved ones and comrades, seen children chopped to pieces, show wounds. They have counted far too many dead bodies. A weeping white woman with red blotches on her face and nails bitten to the quick clumsily tries to provoke me. She's intoxicated with despair. There is nothing one can do. So what does one do? Continue! A black lady re-enacts the gestures of a death-scare no later than last night, to the rapt appreciation of a circle of onlookers.

Barriers break down between booted, long-haired white samurais and a dog-collared ecclesiastic. Some try a song.

I cannot enter their world. They are all survivors, heroes and cowards, awaiting a more than likely premature snuffing out. I end up listening to the accounts of a young ANC activist on the run who has a heart full of ideas and plans. When he goes on endlessly I realize he too is mad, he can no longer stop the clacking tongue, his young life a scorched area of screaming numbness. We put him to bed. He shivers in his sleep. I down the umpteenth brandy: the mind refuses to cloud over.

In this place of sorrows I dream a truck full of people comes by. They stand packed together on the open back, wearing loud clothes. They sing, they sing popular ditties. They are poor down-town relatives on the female side, off to a Saturday-night dance at a neighbouring venue. There they go now, already smaller of outline and thinner of voice in the distance. All I still see are the flapping banners above their heads, on which is written, as words in the wind: 'We are going to death!'

The morning of 9 April. Pierre takes me on an extended visit to pogrom areas in the Midlands region. Blackened ruins of schools and huts, empty dispensaries, fields no longer cultivated. Clear demarcation between Inkatha and Comrades territory, sometimes just a riverbed or a dip in the valley or a fence between two fields. Refugees are a big problem. Thousands will be stampeded from a district under attack by the *impis*, flee helter-skelter with nothing but the strapped-on babies on their backs, to flood a neighbouring township – no infrastructures, no government assistance, no schools. In local parlance *inkathazo* has come to mean 'trouble'.

Youngsters live in the hills, fighting skirmishes. Revival of tra-ditional witchcraft, throwing spells, dispensing concoctions to pro-tect shivering young bodies against the gaping impact caused by bullets fired from AK-47s provided by the South African Defence Force and South African Police to chanting warriors with red head-bands. Death squads roam at will. Courts have been subverted and killers walk free with pistols on their hips. South African Army-trained 'special forces' and security police psychopaths organize ambushes and attacks with impunity. Government ministers accompany Inkatha's president, Mangosuthu Buthelezi, in helicopters over smoking battlefields.

The minds of good old-fashioned liberals like Pierre Cronjé are stretched to the limits of sanity in trying to find *mental* and *moral* and *legal* formulations that could encapsulate and explain the phenomenon. They have to operate from the premise that there are laws and legitimate institutions in this country, deal with the protagonists, bear witness, interpose themselves, save and take home traumatized orphans, transport leaking corpses in their cars. They become incoherent.

I get pathologically precise descriptions of the 'wars', and find it impossible to repeat the horrible facts, to dismount the mechanisms, to enumerate the cynical attempts at disinformation of responsible government ministers. Of what use will it be except to lengthen and sadden my litany? The land is awash in blood.

A few miles down the national highway we stop at a whitewashed cottage converted into an idyllic roadhouse. English-accented owner, waitresses with crisp aprons. We breakfast on scones and buns and home-made jams and coffee with rich yellow cream. Thousands of holiday visitors come down this artery from the north in fat cars, lobotomized by cricket scores, oblivious to the screaming death by spear and gun in the rolling green hills on either side.

In Edendale we visit Harry Gwala and his staff in the regional headquarters of the ANC. A young assistant explains matter-of-factly how in the past twenty-four hours he escaped two assassination attempts on the road. Gwala wears a bib, someone is giving him tea. In his office he has a delegation of relatives of a recently murdered chief. Telephones ring, computer screens glow, pamphlets are printed, T-shirts sold, plans for a rally finalized, a comrade secretary is applying red varnish to her nails.

Gwala shows me a letter from Buthelezi, just delivered by the hand of an envoy. It is a rambling document, quoting at length from previous statements and missives to Mandela. Buthelezi wants to have a joint tour with Mandela of the affected areas, to hoist his credibility as a national player. He accuses Gwala of sabotaging the search for peace.

Buthelezi constantly advances unverifiable figures of IFP

membership, and omits to say that no one can teach or have a house or draw a pension in Kwazulu without his membership card.

When Mandela was released from the whale, a huge welcoming rally was organized in Natal. Buthelezi wanted to outdo him. The South African Government (using Pik Botha's slush funds) spent exorbitant sums and laid on buses to organize a counter-rally. It flopped. In their wrath Inkatha *impis* ran through 'recalcitrant' townships, shooting and hacking to death scores of people.

We drive back through Pietermaritzburg, the picturesque provincial capital, to Durban. At the IDASA office a slender French-speaking lady, Maria Aletta, who teaches Afrikaans at Durban-Westville University, is waiting to take me to meet her students and colleagues. The talk oscillates between thoughts on poetry and remarks elicited on my position on language and teaching and general cultural policies. A lemon-faced Indian lecturer from another department screws up his eyes in sour disgust at my speaking Afrikaans when answering questions in Afrikaans on lines written in Afrikaans, and ostentatiously leaves the lecture room.

Maria Aletta drives me back to IDASA. It is time to leave for the airport. Mzi K, the ANC commander whom I met at Slabbert's – how very long ago it all seems now – is sitting quietly on a chair. He listens calmly to my tired blustering. Impossible to know what he thinks. His muscular frame is draped in an expensive suit, he has an empty briefcase under his arm, he's started an agency called MK Consultants, to siphon off anxious white guilt money.

Pierre flies back on the same plane. He's running over a speech he intends making in Parliament on the first occasion, once more hoping to draw national attention to the Natal bloodbath. Does he ever sleep? I find my car, relieved that it's not been stolen, and drive back to Stellenbosch where Yolande is waiting. How am I going to tell her all this? She will prepare tea, make sure I have a good night's sleep, bring me back to earth. (Learning is always better than knowing.)

In Bamako, when my name was still Bourema Diarra, my appointed bodyguard watched so closely that I saw next to nothing of life there. Thomas Nkobi was luckier – his watchdog got bored because Tom didn't speak French, so I ended up with two bothersome shadows. The film-maker Suleyman Cissé, an old acquaintance, took pity on us. He invited us to his house for a meal. We sat on the floor to share the family's food. After the meal the two policemen were prevailed upon to watch television with the flies in the next room. Suleyman winked and led Thomas and myself out the back door. He drove us to a vantage-point from where we admired the lights and small fires at our feet. We stopped at a 'dancing' for a beer. Hardly had we brought the foam to our lips when our guardian angels stormed in. I still don't understand how they found us that quickly. They were furious and turned down our offer of a drink. Nothing for it but to return to the hotel.

A security colonel waited in the foyer. He took Suleyman Cissé aside. On the spot I lost my temper, went up to the colonel and berated him for being fascist, 'worse than a South African', shouting that we had no freedom and no joy in this city, warning him to leave our friend Suleyman out of it, etc. The colonel explained that it was all for our own good. I would have nothing of it. (Later it became evident that we were being guarded not against potential assassins – though it wasn't long after the murder of Dulcie September in Paris – but to keep us away from Malian dissidents who wanted to contact us.)

In the lift up my sergeant tried to appease my ire: it wasn't meant that way at all, surely, he'd do anything to make me feel better. Soldiers with machine-guns lounged in the corridor to protect me. One the first day, next day two, and by now there was a nervous nest, so that I took the precaution of knocking on my door from the inside before opening it to leave. I went to bed. Half an hour later there was a soft rap. I opened the door and Sergeant Bodyguard walked in with a very scrawny girl in tow. He told her to wait on the bed and took me into the bathroom to confabulate that he'd thought deeply about my gripes – I had a point after all, a man must live. Out of hospitality he'd taken trouble to find this girl, 'very clean', someone from his village and not expensive at all.

I carefully explained that I regrettably had some other matters to attend to, we were on a time-consuming mission in Mali, and he left with his poor offer with the painted face. An hour passed. I was preparing night-thoughts in bed. The phone rang. Sergeant Bodyguard's conspirational voice excused itself, but there was a slight hitch, see, the lady was still downstairs and not very happy – she did after all lose a night's earnings. I think he presented the need as 'taxi-money back to the home village'. He came upstairs, I gave him a sum of money to pay for the delicate attentions so unselfishly intended, which I was by way of being prevented from enjoying. He certainly took *his* cut.

The colonel generously offered us a 'free night' the following evening and we went drinking and dancing like escaped convicts. Upon our return we found him waiting. He told us how he had personally followed us the whole evening: it had cost him so much in fuel because he had to use his own motorcar, and what about the beers he had to buy himself, to drink behind dark glasses in the joints we'd been to? Is this fair? What about the people?

20

DANCE!

Yolande and I meet Ukwezi Star at the airport. The circle of our stay in this country is closing. We take her to the harbour area for a lunch of fish and white wine. Then to Stellenbosch where I submit to an extended session with philosophy and political science students under the guidance of Johan Degenaar and Jan Duiwel. They ask incisive questions, driving me into the final dug-out of my perceptions and convictions. Johan Degenaar hums to the hidden music of words; with half-closed eyes he is on the look-out for inadvertent cracks through which new meanings may spurt. Jan Duiwel fixes me with one malicious green eye – he is a hard man to convince, let alone impress.

On the morning of the 12th I am grilled for two hours by lec-turers and senior students of the Afrikaans Department in the B. J. Vorster Building. When it is over, after they have sufficiently fingered the ink-splotched sheet of paper that must serve as substi-tute for a literary soul, once I have been reduced to incoherent babbling, the lady who organized the encounter offers me a bottle of red wine as compensation. They know my weaknesses. They also know my worth.

Saturday, 13 April. The night of the party at the residence of the French ambassador in Newlands. Yolande and Joëlle Bourgois's secretary and Alex Boraine's right hand drew up lists, sent out invitations, phoned friends. Spluttering torches planted on the lawns light up the garden, the palm trunks are smoothly grey and taper off in a discreet applause of leaves, the mountain is black, staff members wear impeccable white jackets, flower arrangements perfume the night air, long tables with snowy napkins groan under a diversity of dishes, the two barmen look as if they're suffering from

St Vitus's jig in the arms, the gendarmes at the front door have brushed their tunics, Yolande Mariposa is a splendid black-and-green butterfly, friends whom I haven't seen for thirty years surface with leathery faces and flowery ties and smiles like kites on a windy day in the Bo-Kaap.

When township music comes, these South Africans take to the floor with happy feet and pumping knees and wiggling backsides, black and brown and white in a mass of hopping and swinging humanity. Basjan Beer is talking Korean to Gabriel Polony who's talking Greek to Toetsie Star who's talking cigarette smoke to Cloete's daughter Anna who's talking lover's eyes to a youngster with a rugby scrum neck who's listening to Doep du Plessis who's laughing Afrikaans at Cloete who's talking Swahili to Rachel who's cooing bird to Jan Biltong who's talking poetry to his bottle while John Coetzee is smiling silence and Jan Duiwel roars at nobody in particular.

Our evening star arrives, Abdullah Ibrahim (as Dollar Brand has become), accompanied by two silently smiling gentlemen of his own faith. All three strict observers of Islam, they wear skullcaps. It's the month of Ramadan and they had to wait for the sun to go down. No, they won't have anything to drink, thank you, maybe a cup of tea later on. Abdullah sits down behind the piano and lowers his gaze; in the old days there would have been a smouldering cigarette and a glass of whisky within reach. His fingers start wandering over the keyboard, the syncopated notes of his past and of his dreams fill the room with a gentle beauty.

People become quiet. Maybe the younger generation does not realize the poignancy of listening to the returned Cape master, certainly one of the finest jazz pianists alive. Time stops.

It is time for me to return where I came from. Am I happy now? It is of no importance. I came, I saw, I was confused. And I made enemies, many new ones to add to those I always had. But, as George Orwell said, liberty is the right to tell people what they do not want to hear. Perhaps, again like Mr Orwell, I like my friends no better than my enemies, and certainly exaggerated with the innocence of a savage. Should I have said things with more consideration? Maybe. Anyway, I have finally become redundant. Wasn't that the true purpose? The man with self-respect should leave when he wants to. Nothing particularly noble in that. In death everyone gets an aquiline nose.

And then? Perhaps it will be like death. Certainly the spring which made me react at opportune and inopportune moments will be broken. I'll be rootless – disgruntled and frustrated even. But at least I can live the life of a wandering monk, with an umbrella full of holes.

Yolande is calling from the doorway, drawing me back to the light. Where have you been, she wants to know. There's a bathroom in the house, you know that, and peeing outside blights the flowers! Our guests are going, the music has stopped.

Basjan Beer is the last to depart, walking very carefully on unsteady legs, my little brother; he tries to whistle nonchalantly, he's lost his jacket and his wife. The gendarmes look him over with a professional eye. In France he would have been intercepted and asked for his papers.

We spend the night in the Slabberts' Rondebosch cottage. Images, sloshing around in too much wine, crowd the black hours. I dream I go through a dark landscape. Next to me walks a companion, I don't know if it's a man or a woman, it's too sombre to see. Although we are in total obscurity we encounter no obstacles, we have a light step. We converse intimately so that words are not needed – at least they don't have to be pronounced. We arrive at a dark pond. My ally explains that it is a pool of pig's piss. (I should smell the stench, but I don't.) 'This is where you can lay down the old skin, the previous one, the one that's become superfluous.' I take off my skin: it is dark and rubbery and limp like the wetsuit of a diver. I shall throw this stripped envelope into the black cauldron, where it will be dissolved.

The 15th. The wind too has finally died down. Summer is drawing to its end, but when it stops blowing, underlying heat surfaces and temperatures range around 32°C. With Joëlle and Olivier we wander through the Bo-Kaap streets, also traditionally known as the Malay Quarter or Slamse Buurt, and Schotsche Kloof. Present-day descendants of the original inhabitants prefer to call themselves Cape Muslims. Their ancestors were brought here as slaves, political exiles and convicts from Africa, Madagascar, Ceylon, India and the area today known as Indonesia. The arrivals were already followers of Islam and they shared a common tongue, Malay-Portuguese, the trading language used from Madagascar to China. In the way that the unwritten history and customs and attitudes of the vanished Khoi and San constitute an invisible presence in the make-up of South Afriquas, this disappeared language infused and became a core element of Afrikaans. Maybe Afrikaans could be seen as a new avatar of that supple lingo of seafarers, slaves and nomads – of people who constantly have to invent themselves.

The hills are steep, the houses neglected, some decayed. Most are a mixture of Cape Dutch and English Georgian styles. Many were gaily painted, the colours now faded. Sometimes one still sees, as a nearly forgotten memory, a façade with its typical curvilinear Baroque parapet, its *voorstoep*, the sash-windows, the elaborately carved front door with a separate top and bottom panel, the decorated fanlight above the door, the wrought-iron fittings. The oldest Cape mosque, the Auwal, is still in use.

When I was young and carefree the plaintive voice of the imam or muezzin floated down from the heights, and to my dream-being the startled fluttering of doves is associated with dawn. The pious Muslims living here were tailors, fishermen, cobblers and coopers.

In a wasteland we come across a *kramat*, the burial place of a saint. Actually three people are entombed there. Inside the small, white, dome-shaped structure a believer is chanting prayers, perhaps giving news to the dead. A man with a fez tells us this piece of land, overlooking the city bordered by the silvery surface-memory of the sea, used to be a Chinese cemetery. Untended graves disappeared in the soil. In the old days people still lived with the dimension of a future, but all time eventually becomes earth. Even up here, in backyards of dilapidated houses and on vacant lots under the poor shelter of scraggly trees and shrubs grown crooked in their endless resistance to the wind, squatters with babies and a dog and a tethered goat live. A mother washes herself in a pool of stagnant water. People sift through rubbish dumps.

Then we drive out to the University of the Western Cape where lunch with Jakes Gerwel and members of his staff awaits us. Students throng the corridors and cafeterias. The percentage of black students coming from homelands and mushrooming town-ships and settlements on the Cape Flats increases yearly; although still a minority in numbers they constitute the moral majority. They refuse to learn or be tutored in the native Afrikaans of the brown community. Students from the faraway *platteland*, whose parents sacrifice savings to send them here, now have to bite back their tongues.

On the 16th we have a liquid lunch in a run-down Indian res-taurant in Long Street with Baas Saayman and James Polley, organ-izer of film festivals in South Africa. Dust-filled second-hand book-shops line the pavements like Ali Baba caves, decrepit hotels with long rickety balconies on pillars topped by wooden lace-work dis-gorge human wrecks too smitten by world-weariness to walk. There's a wet glint of nostalgia in Baas Saayman's eye. He still runs a publishing house up the road, if only he can find the key, upstairs from a café where the best *roti* in town is made by a stately Malay lady, but burglars regularly pilfer the stock he never managed to pay the printers for, so that his books can be found for next to nothing in the second-hand shops. Still, riches (he says) are waiting just over the hill. Xhosa, that is the answer. Apart, that is, from the horse with the lucky number due any day now. In fact already galloping. He's going to publish books in Xhosa and they will be prescribed in their thousands! To this we raise our glasses. The only wee little hitch may be that he doesn't speak a word of Xhosa. Let this be no impediment, ladies and friends. Didn't André Brink, notorious for his total abstinence due to an anxious liver, write a book on brandy which he published? And didn't you, Mr B, write about politics? And is this not a Christian country?

The 17th. Tomorrow we leave Cape Town. Tonight we have a last meal in Newlands at the home of Suzanne and Revel Fox. The Boraines are also invited. Suzanne is having her troubles with Alice. Alice, by dint of being the beneficiary of Suzanne's largesse over a long period, has peremptorily decided that Suzanne should be responsible and provide for her and her family. Now she is demand-ing R500. Her son, in Standard 8 in the Transkei, has left a girl two years his senior with a bread in the oven. Her parents are outraged – agreed, he may be too young to marry the pregnant girl, but he must compensate for the deflowering as is customary. Why doesn't Alice's husband sell a cow, Suzanne wants to know. But this would be unthinkable for as long as there's a white ma'am to provide.

We pack everything. Even Mr Ixele is going north again, safely settled in the back of the car. (Yolande doesn't like touching the 'decapitated head'; she imagines it will start bleeding like some Catholic relic.) We ask Suzanne's permission to leave the miniature windmill in Paradise House.

21

DEPARTURE

> even though the mountains be blue
> her words I shall remember so true
> but this you should one and all know
> no memory-wind her words can blow
> away and even if my love lies far
> I'll take her with the morning star

Thursday, 18 April. The above is my approximation in the imperial tongue of a sentimental Afrikaans song. When pretenders still trotted their horses over a never-never land. We set the alarm system and lock the door of Paradise House. We stroke the trunk of the fig tree. We get into the car and drive off.

We arrive three days later, at 5 p.m., at Meadowbrook Farm, having done altogether 2,600 kilometres, and find Dian Joubert staying with the Slabberts. Our intimate supper abruptly flares with arguments moving forth and back across the plates and glasses between Slabbert and myself. Dian, Slabbert's long-time friend and also his master in sociology, appreciates with a smile in his ear. Slabbert is tired and under tremendous pressure. I am heartbroken, our debate inflamed by liquor. As I back up against unsolvable contradictions, my radical outbursts become small whimpers for an impossible revolution; Slabbert, on his side, has invested his hopes in the 'objective laws' of transition and being able to advise (or influence) key figures in all camps. We go to bed with *dronkverdriet* (maudlin drunkenness).

Tuesday, 23 April. I spend the morning at home, chewing my rancour and making notes next to the swimming pool, listening to the notes of birds too. Ah, to write on the sky and leave no traces except for echoes in the sleep of dreamers! Yolande watches me from afar; she's off shopping with Jane. Lunch and commiseration with Dian.

In the afternoon Jonna visits. Our publishing concern, Taurus, which bravely fought the hegemony of pig-thoughts and God-suckers all these years, is dying. We have to prepare the death notice. This is the New Sarth Efrica – no money, no leeway, margins mopped up by the centre, more broadly based hegemony but same mechanisms and same sadness. The time has come to let the thoughts go. The shit has hit the fan but it doesn't matter since the fan no longer works.

Slabbert and Jane have a number of influence-wielding and -welding persons (guilty rich and professional strugglers adept at milking the guilt) at their table for supper. This is where power is handed around in hushed tones as if it were the by-blow of the Holy Spirit's dalliance, and turned over with bated breath to sniff the arse and establish the sex. My mind is clearly deteriorating in a million images. I see naked people all around the table, and they're not even kings.

After supper Slabbert has quite rightly had enough of my sniggering. He points a finger of thick exasperation and accuses me of being a 'poseur', a misery sponge, a bird of doom come here for the satisfaction of high and holy moral indignation to spew disgust over the assembly, flying off to lick imagined wounds in 'exile'. I am furthermore a utopian 'revolutionary' socialist in a disguise of reasonable concern. Get drunk.

Wednesday, the 24th. In the morning I drive to Wits University for an informal session with a number of students in the Afrikaans Department. Now I really have nothing left to say. Slabbert was already gone when I got up; he left a note among the paw-paws and the pineapple slices saying we mustn't stupidly hurt one another.

I return to Meadowbrook Farm to find that Pierre Cronjé has arrived. Slabbert is in a grumpy mood. This country is gnawing at our innards: it wants to make us believe our turds are offerings to the gods. Nation-building is the contract we're all expected to sign, to guarantee to the powerful the eternal enjoyment of the fruits of their privileges.

We have a strained supper. Pierre and Slabbert have other, older scores to settle. There's a phone-call for Pierre. He listens, turns his back on us and lowers the head. A friend of his has been assassinated this afternoon together with his wife in their car on a road leading to Edendale. He weeps like a disconsolate child. I take him in my arms, his body is shaking. We drink. The ladies have withdrawn. Slabbert shouts: 'You make out as if you're the only ones who care! What makes you think I'm indifferent to the deads?'

Thursday, the 25th. At breakfast Pierre explains that the real reason for his coming to the Transvaal is to see the ANC and, perhaps, Government. He has a 'canary', a killer working for an SADF death squad. The man's been involved in bumping off targets; now he wants to come clean but he needs protection, he's afraid, he ought to know. Maybe the best tactic would be to hand him over into the safekeeping of the Minister of Justice: the only way to survive is to involve the protection of the enemy. We take leave of each other. He has to return to Durban: the 'canary' may decide to fly the coop.

Friday, 27 April 1991. Slabbert and Jane left this morning for their Swaziland farm. We thanked them for all their hospitality and their kindness, but I and Slabbert couldn't look each other in the eye.

We say goodbye to Jennifer Friday, to Chisi and Timothy and Lizzie. Doep and Ukwezi Star come to fetch us for the airport. We have a mountain of luggage, but at least Jane allowed us to leave the wooden bust we bought in Venda until we return next time. Will there be a next time? We embrace Ukwezi Star and shake Doep's hand. We are booked in, processed through immigration. Our flight is called. SAA 262. Destination Orly, France.

22

THE CONTAMINATED HEART

Africa was the subject. Did I disfigure it? Yolande reads my notes, her smile like a butterfly on my shoulder, and reminds me of the cruel passages, the unfair generalities, the white viewpoint. My excuses? None. I'm aware of the superficiality – from airport to dinner table to lecture room. But it could only ever be the glance of a moment's flight from the 'white' Tuaregs in the north to the 'brown' Afrikaners in the south.

It was a passage towards the making and the unmaking of memories. Consciously and unconsciously, deliberately and unknowingly, I robbed and raped and adulterated the memories and the imaginations of many others. Whatever moved within sight of my field of perception became absorbed immediately.

It is not easy to be a bird of prey! In the process mind became clogged with useless information. I lost my friends and my sense of direction, I discarded my dreams, I scuttled my chances of participating in the National Reconciliation on the road to a New South Africa, I forfeited the repose of belonging to 'my country' with 'my own people', I deformed my past and destroyed my future. What freedom!

An initiation demands sacrifices. Writing is an expression of the rites (and rights) of passage.

What I returned with? The satisfaction of having been back, of having made my bow and paid my respects to the ancestors. I've been to the mountain. This thing is finished. Everything is changed and all remains the same. Sea entered behind the eyelids. There is the image of having traversed a land of dust, of stopping to dig for gold and finding below the surface families of crouched people groaning and murmuring. There is also the abiding picture of a bird writing beautiful words on the sky, and of not being able to spell these concepts for myself.

That is perhaps as it ought to be. I found that one could travel from language to language, from death to life and from exile to home, but not translate from one into the other. I have furthermore come to the conclusion that revolution is inserted in the 'acting process' of creation which is an undoing, whereas politics presumes (upon) power and must therefore posit non-transformation to ensure the mediocrity of control. I also saw that politics is voracious, deadening all else, achingly projecting and manipulating the images of perception to mask the real in its unsatisfiable hunger for release from having been born.

It is a story of the crossing. When Scorpion asked Frog to take him across the river, Frog said no, because certainly you will sting me to death as we go. Scorpion said how could I ever do that? If I kill you I must go down as well. Am I mad? So they set out for the opposite bank with Scorpion on Frog's back. Halfway across Scorpion raised his poisonous tail and struck. As they started going down, Frog burbled, why did you do this? Look, I'm dying and you will drown with me. Yes, I know, said Scorpion. I'm sorry, but it can't be helped. I'm the scorpion, remember?

It is a story of the passage. Two monks came to a river where an old woman stood wringing her hands. Please take me over, she implored, I am old and frail. I can't do so, ma'am, the first monk said. We don't know this river – I may stumble and fall with you on my back and we shall both be carried off. It is too much of a responsibility. The second monk hitched up his skirts, put the old lady on his back and walked across from stone to stone. On the opposite bank he put her down and they continued their separate ways. Now the first monk remonstrated endlessly with his brother. How could you have done such a thing? Your foot may have slipped, this or that could have happened, etc. etc. The second monk said, look, I picked her up, carried her over and put her down and that was it. You are still carrying her.

It is a story of the hand. A man called Eka, hearing of the great Patriarch who was sitting in a cave, went to visit him. On arriving, the man looked in and saw the Master busy concentrating. So he waited outside. It was cold and snowing. When it grew dark, he tried to get the Master's attention. The Master, sitting like a block of wood, ignored him. After a few days of this – the snow was now up to his waist – Eka called into the cave: 'Hey! Psst! Please, my mind is not at ease. Pacify it for me!' He said this haltingly, for he was crying. Despairing of a reply, he drew his sword and cut off his left hand. The Master looked at Eka then, and he said: 'Bring your mind in here before me, and I will pacify it!' 'But when I seek my own mind,' replied Eka, heedless of the pain in his arm, 'I cannot find it.' 'There, I have pacified it,' the Master laughed. Stepping out of the snow spotted with blood, Eka prostrated himself before the Master.

The essence of initiation is imitation. Of course the book doesn't stop here. The future, like the past, is a sequence of present moments. Time will pass, taking us along, effacing us.

Later Slabbert will write to untangle the crow's nest of our relationship. Then I shall write to him. Then he will come to Paris and together we shall fly off to Dakar. We shall spend our days on Gorée in the red house where André Sow and Nathalie live. We shall lie in low armchairs and hammocks and drink Flag beer, while goats outside blether short of breath in the sand-floored alleys and slow flies crawl over our hands and blacken the sugarbowl. We shall knock our heads together and laugh about the silliness of our quarrel.

It will be during the slightly cooler season. Swallows will swoop in the wind above the sea. But especially kites, light brown in colour and with hooked bills, will hang in their hundreds above the island, sailing against the blue like the silently floating applause of hands. They're the cleaners of backyards and rubbish heaps. The whole night long the island will throb to the beat of bongas and electric guitars.

Long before daybreak, even before the goat due for sacrifice is lovingly cleansed in the sea, the imam in his mosque-tower against the hill will sing to the faithful that Allah is the Greatest and Mohammad his Prophet. Then white cocks with splashes of black tail feathers will commence their crowing. After that the goats will belch.

In darkness we shall walk down to the water and sit waiting for dawn. The morning star flashes brilliantly, a scraping of moon drifts dreamt-out on its back. The early-morning *chaloupe* emerges from the fog like a ghost vessel with a mast-light, to tie up to the landing. From the alleys children on their way to school in town appear, and people going to offices. We shall swim out to where a metal buoy with a red light bobs in the bay, there and back about a kilometre. The water is heavy and reeks of diesel oil. Untreated refuse is poured into the sea; the currents sometimes return it to the coast. We are nervous about the Grey Cadillacs (sharks), but André says they aren't dangerous. The sea-bottom is alive with fish.

Some baobabs will have flowers: enormous, lazy, light-yellow birds. On Sunday, 3 November, we shall be there for the adoration of St Charles Barromée, the island's patron. The flaked church will overflow with believers. The wooden ceiling is like a stellar vault with bunches of sparkling lightbulbs, banners with the images of saints flap in the breeze. After the service the congregation will follow in solemn procession to the water's edge the priests and altar boys carrying the man on his cross. There a white-robed cantor will precede the other voices in scripture and prayers wafted over the sea 'from where death and life come', and plead for protection for fisherfolk and sailors. (And when one now remembers the big going-away over the waters one's throat hurts.) Then the children will throw fistfuls of flower petals on the waves.

Later in the day a smaller procession of *baye fall*, ecstatic from dope, dressed in their gaudy clown-like garments, accompanied by booming drums, will dance down the hill from the castle ruins and gambol goat-like to the sea, and white maccoa ducks and white goats and chickens and black children will scatter.

We shall become part of the community. A blade with black bow-tie and golden cummerbund will bring us food at home, ground wheat and tough meat. Other people – neighbours, orphans, jobless youths – will look in to eat with us, to chat or watch television.

Ka'afir will come staggering through the sand one evening to kiss me on both cheeks with tears dribbling from below his dark glasses, and announce that the prison museum has been closed down – nobody knows what happened to Sankara's embalmed hand which was exhibited there, the one donated by a certain Walker. It looked like a bird skeleton. (Still later, in Paris, I shall receive a letter out of the blue from Walker asking me to intervene with my ex-Soviet friends to make them an offer: he wants to take Lenin's body on tour and then cut it up so that every communist cell in South Africa may have its own holiness. He also has, he will write, patented his idea of fabricating do-it-yourself amputation kits for Africa and Asia to go with the landmines.)

Slabbert and I will pursue our venture to realize the existence of a Gorée Institute, housed on the island in the gracious Maison du Soudan. Here we shall start our work for democracy, development and culture in Africa . . .

On the day of our departure our ferry-boat will be late, and we shall cross the choppy waters in a *pirogue* called *Nelson Mandela*, to arrive thoroughly soaked. Cheik Ahmadou Bamba, it is believed, returned from exile in Gabon standing on a grass prayer-mat on the waves . . .

Of course, I could continue into the future to describe how Yolande and I return once more to Gondwanaland. Mandela and De Klerk will be ruling the land hand in hand, like Zog and Zob. The country will be purple with jacarandas and hydrangeas in bloom. A neverending shivering of thunder-flashes will fork the skies around Johannesburg. In Cape Town it will be summer again. The fig tree outside Paradise House will be black with starlings and mousebirds.

The situation at 'home' will continue deteriorating. Newspapers will be stained with horrible stories. Of young white policemen on holiday killing a black youth by stoning him and pushing him into a river to drown. Of a white couple going to complain about their dog having had sex with that of a black labourer, then returning with reinforcements carrying iron bars to kill the owner of the 'kaffir bitch'. Of a black farmworker, Gabriel Mahakoe, going to a white farm, Grootstry (Big Struggle), walking into the house, taking a rifle, waiting for the owners to come, and killing the grandparents, the housewife and one daughter. When the housewife tries to give him money he will say: 'Just put the bag down, missus.' He will declare: 'I am guilty. I wanted to chop off the hand of apartheid. Unfortunately I only chopped off the fingers.' He will declaim: 'I said Africa must return, and I'm killing that thing . . . kaffir, baboon, dog – this is what we are called. I said you [missus] will forgive me, because I'm not killing you, but that thing . . .' He will explain that he had to cock the weapon each time because it was not an AK-47. He will add that he then put the gun down because his work was done. No, he will say, he did not go to rob – how could he rob dead people? He will conclude that he wanted to kill between twenty and fifty people that day, because 'Africa is becoming bitter' . . .

We shall ceremoniously drink all the ripe bottles laid away by Yolande while I was lurking 'inside', which have waited all these years – the KWV Roodeberg, the Kleindal Cabernet Sauvignon, the Swartland, the Theuniskraal Riesling, the Meerendal Shiraz '76 . . . Then we shall leave.

We are always leaving.

Where to? One day I should write a book about exile, about what it is like to live turned in upon oneself, and give a description of the blunting caused by estrangement from the intimate and the familiar. The eyes and ears are sealed with beeswax, and all the other orifices as well, so that one detects and exploits the inner echoes much more clearly. Also that one becomes constipated.

The condition is one of 'birdness', because exiles are birds driven by snowy landscapes to the city where they will be both wild and humble. Uprooted ones have few earthly possessions; they are masters at the art of packing trunks, their temporary habitations are like camels which can be loaded and offloaded but which will always be lopsided, and we can be inexplicably attached to a few books, pebbles, shells and other botherations of little value.

My conclusion, based upon observation, will be that exiles integrate the refined knack of make-believe life. We pretend 'normalcy' where we can lay no claim to it. In this manner we develop a code of tricks and stances, and perhaps we become entangled in the illusion game. Reality can be approached only through illusion – it is really a semblance thereof. A painted cloth is by way of illustration an eye-swindle, but in the absence of real reality one may as well ape being.

Exile is coming face to face with the self as mirror (or mirror as self?), and it strikes me that exiles often put pipes in their mouths to lift their hats jauntily to an imaginary mirror. Maybe the mirror is home.

In this too we are as birds: in that we speak languages which we don't understand, get terribly serious about small things, yet beat our wings to a bloody pulp against windowpanes reflecting the illusion of life outside.

Exiles are nomads of the real who need not plant or sow. We fashion ourselves – repeatedly, to make up for a fugacious self-definition – but do not contribute to the plotting of fields or the planting of orchards. The sun is something in the way, at best a beacon, never the partner with whom to farm on shares. We bring about landscapes by rapidly stroking emptiness with the eye, especially so as to mark down references to dangers and possible breaks. The landscapes which we drag along only provide the necessary play for the imagination of survival. We recognize, but cannot know. It is a blind seeing.

Such behaviour is risky: darkness may take one by surprise. Appearance is eye-wash, the art of mimesis is not only the game of hit-or-miss conventions, but also concealment and blotting out. The more edged light is, the easier impersonation will flow along, but all the more turgid those darknesses that need to be spirited away, heavier the dead things piling up behind locked doors, more numerous and scattered the tracks you cannot erase, not really, bigger the wake which you have in tow. Elimination becomes a problem.

The world is a station that can be taken on only with the corrupt memory. The eye is a caterpillar on the salad leaves of remembrance, the ear a maze, and the only remedies the ointment of a dream, the unclean souvenirs, the bird's imagination. The writer flies through language as wide and as unique as his wings. Like all birds he sings in French when in France, Afrikaans in Africa, English in London, and so forth. And always about *nigredo* and *albedo*. It's the only way to be indigenous. Those winged creatures who recite the same song wherever they go will soon be picked upon as unadapted moon-growths of a foreign culture, their warbling quenched in a burbling of blood through the slit in the crop.

These are some of the arguments I should mention: 'When wind makes bigvoice in the treetops you feel as if you're buried under the sea's sounds, you lift your eyes to stars so pale and stark, but they will for ever be strange celestial bodies swimming up there.' And: 'The coast is caressed by time.' And: 'The smaller the bird, the more sharp-whetted the voice.' And: 'Sun rises in the glass palace, higher, it sets off a tinkling of birds, on the earth a cloud lays a shadow of roses, this is the beginning of a poem.'

GLOSSARY

SOME PEOPLE, ORGANIZATIONS AND TERMS APPEARING IN THE TEXT

NOTE: some names have been disguised in the text, or given only in part. The following list is not intended to be exhaustive.

ADAM, Heribert: political scientist and Africanist of German origin.

AFRIQUA: the mixed offspring of Khoi (Hottentots) and passing sailors were known as Afriquas. Later the word was deformed to 'Griquas'. The suffix *-kwa* (*-qua*) to Hottentot names indicated 'the people, the sons, the men of . . .' (Thus *Korachokwa* meant 'the men of Kora, or Korannas'.)

ANC: African National Congress, a major and old liberation movement, now in the process of becoming an ordinary political apparatus.

AWB: Afrikaner Weerstandsbeweging – Afrikaner Resistance Movement, a crypto-fascist grouping. Its leader: Eugène Nuy Terre'Blanche.

AZANIA: name given to South Africa by Black Consciousness adherents.

BAMBA, Cheik Ahmadou: founder of Mouridism in Senegal, exiled by the French authorities on the 18th Safar 1313 of the Hegirah (21 September 1895) to Gabon, an event celebrated annually as the *Magal* in the holy city of Toubah.

BANTUSTANS: self-governing ethnic 'homelands' for South African blacks created in terms of the Apartheid system of segregation.

BEE, Lady Barbara: ANC (q.v.) official. Personal assistant to Nelson Mandela (q.v.).

BIKO, Bantu Stephen (Steve): Black Consciousness leader killed by South African security police, September 1977.

BLUM, Peter: an Afrikaans poet of fugitive origin. Died 1990.

BOESAK, Allan: one-time preacher, patron of the defunct United Democratic Front. Chairperson of the ANC (q.v.) in the Western Cape.

BORAINE, Alex: South African ex-parliamentarian. Founder and chairman of IDASA (q.v.). His wife: Jenny.

BOTHA, Pik: South African Minister of Foreign Affairs.

BOTHA, PW (Crocodile): former State President of South Africa, with the wagging finger.

BOTHA, Stoffel (Slopmouth): South African Interior Minister until 1989.

BOURGOIS, Joëlle: French ambassador to South Africa. Her husband: Olivier.

BRAND, Dollar (Abdullah Ibrahim): South African jazz master.

BREYTENBACH, Cloete: author's second brother, a photo-journalist. His wife: Brumilda. His daughter: Anna.

BREYTENBACH, Jan: author's eldest brother, a military officer. His wife: Rose. Their daughter: Angel.

BREYTENBACH, Rachel: author's sister. Her daughter: Anna-Kind.

BREYTENBACH, Sebastiaan (Basjan Beer): author's youngest brother.

BRINK, André: Afrikaans novelist, playwright, critic and academic, who also writes in English.

BROEDERBOND: League of Brothers, the semi-clandestine control mechanism grouping the white Afrikaner élite.

CAMPAORÉ, Blaise: President of Burkina Faso. Had his predecessor, Thomas Sankara (q.v.), killed.

CCB: Civil Co-operation Bureau. South African Government death squads consisting of SADF (q.v.) cadres, Military Intelligence and National Intelligence and security police operatives, hired and blackmailed killers, and other psychopathic riff-raff.

CISSÉ, Suleyman: film-maker from Mali.

COETSEE, Kobie: South African Minister of Justice.

COETZEE, John Maxwell: novelist, critic and academic.

COSATU: Congress of South African Trade Unions. In alliance with the ANC (q.v.).

CRONJÉ, Pierre: member of the South African Parliament. Former DP, now ANC (q.q.v.).

DAPPER, Olfert: (?1635–89) historian, translator and travel writer who lived all his life in Amsterdam. Published ten books during his lifetime, the most famous being his *Description of Africa*.

DE ANDRADE, Mario: Pan-Africanist politician and author.

DE BROGLIO, Chris: anti-apartheid activist in exile. Founder of the South African Non-Racial Olympic Committee (SANROC). A selfless benefactor to many outcasts.

DE BRUYN, Buljan: Afrikaans poet and academic.

DEGENAAR, Johan: philosopher and academic.

DE KLERK, Frederik Willem: South African State President, leader of the National Party. Made by the Broederbond (q.v.).

DE KOK, Ingrid: writer and academic (English).

DIOP, Cheik Anta: pioneer African historian. Dakar's university is named after him.

DIOUF, Abdou: President of Senegal.

DOS SANTOS, Marcelino: poet and vice-president of Mozambique.

DP: Democratic Party. Formerly the Progressive Party, after having been many other parties.

DRIVER, Dorothy: lecturer in English at Cape Town University, critic.

DUIWEL, Jan: Political Science lecturer at Stellenbosch University.

DU PLESSIS, Marti 'Green': book designer and writer. His wife: Hettie.

DU TOIT, André: political scientist, editor of *Die Suid-Afrikaan*. His wife: Maretha.

ENTHOVEN, Dick: businessman and ex-politician of South African birth.

FALL, Cheik Ibra: companion of Cheik Ahmadou Bamba (q.v.), patron of the *baye fall*. Buried in Toubah, Senegal.

FONDATION FRANCE-LIBERTÉS: humanitarian organization based in Paris, presided over by Daniëlle Mitterrand (q.v.).

FOX, Revel: architect and cultural leader. His wife: Suzanne, sister of Uys Krige (q.v.). Their son: Master Justin.

FRELIMO: Mozambican Liberation Front, the party ruling in Maputo.

FUGARD, Athol: South African playwright.

GADDAFI, Muammar Al: the Helmsman of Libya.

GERWEL, Jakes: academic, rector of Western Cape University. His wife: Phoebe.

GONDWANALAND: name given to a super-continent, of which South Africa was once a part, before it was fractured during what is known as the 'Continental Drift'.

GOUDINI, Coenie: Euro-African journalist.

GRAHAM, Paul: IDASA (q.v.) representative in Durban, Natal.

HENNING, Piet: advocate who defended the author during his 1975 trial. His wife: Elbie.

HEYNS, JA: political theologican. Previous moderator of the Dutch Reformed Church.

HUDDLESTON, Father Trevor: British ecclesiastic who worked in South African townships as a young man, but was expelled.

IDASA: Institute for a Democratic Alternative for South Africa, founded by Alex Boraine and Van Zyl Slabbert (q.q.v.) in 1986.

INKATHA FREEDOM PARTY: Zulu-based political formation, led by Mangosuthu Gatsha Buthelezi, in open conflict with the ANC.

JACKSON, Jesse: American politician.

JOUBERT, Dian: Sociology professor at Stellenbosch University. Translator from Greek.

KAUNDA, Kenneth: former President of Zambia.

K, Mzi: ex-commander in Umkhonto we Sizwe (MK; q.v.), now director of MK Consultants.

KA'AFIR: poet and dealer of West African origin.

KLEINSCHMIDT, Horst: South African exile working for the Defence and Aid Fund.

KRIGE, Mattheus Uys: (1910–87) Afrikaans poet and playwright who also wrote in English and translated extensively from Spanish and French.

KRUGER, Jimmy: Minister of Police at the time of Steve Biko's (q.v.) murder.

LOUW, Chris: South African journalist.

MABUZA, Enos: former Chief Minister of KaNgwane, a Bantustan (q.v.).

MACHEL, Samora: Mozambican President, killed in a mysterious aircraft crash.

MAKATINI, JF (Johnny): prominent exile leader of the ANC (q.v.). Died in 1989.

MAKEBA, Miriam: South African singer living abroad. Previously married to Stokely Carmichael, a Black Power leader in the USA.

MALAN, General Magnus (Mug): desk-warlord, ex-Minister of Defence, architect of Total Strategy to ward off communist onslaught on South Africa, creator of the Civil Co-operation Bureau (q.v.). Now Minister of the Environment.

MANDELA, Nelson (Madiba): President of the ANC (q.v.). His wife: Winnie, now estranged.

MANUEL, Trevor: ANC (q.v.) and SACP (q.v.) militant from the Western Cape, member of the ANC's National Executive Committee.

MARTINS, Helen: poet and artist who lived all her life in a small Karoo town, where she conceived of the famous 'Owl House'.

MBEKI, Thabo: Foreign Affairs spokesperson of the ANC (q.v.).

MILES, John Jonna: Afrikaans author and academic. His wife: Elsa.

MITTERRAND, Daniëlle: chairperson of Fondation France-Libertés (q.v.). Her husband: François, President of France.

MK: Umkhonto we Sizwe, 'Spear of the Nation', armed wing of the ANC (q.v.).

MOTLANA, Dr Nthato: medical doctor, businessman, community leader.

NAIDOO, Jay: Secretary-General of COSATU (q.v.).

NAUDÉ, Beyers (Oom Bey): South African preacher and anti-apartheid leader. His wife: Ilse.

NGOM, Benoit: Senegalese jurist, chairman of the African Jurist Association.

NKOBI, Thomas: treasurer of the ANC (q.v.).

OKHELA: ill-fated underground network working in support of the ANC (q.v.).

OLIVEFIRE, Gerrit: Afrikaans academic and author.

OUBAAS: father.

OUNOOI: mother.

PAC: Pan-Africanist Congress. ANC's (q.v.) breakaway and rival liberation movement.

PAHAD, Aziz: National Executive Committee member of the ANC (q.v.). Brother to Essop (q.v.).

PAHAD, Essop: Executive functionary of the SACP (q.v.). Brother to Aziz (q.v.).

RABIE, Jan Biltong: Afrikaans writer and teacher. His wife: Jabbery Wallace, well-known painter.

RAPER, Ian: Afrikaans poet and academic.

RAWLINGS, Flight-Lieutenant Jerry: ruler of Ghana.

RENAMO: Mozambican terrorist organization directed by South African Military Intelligence.

ROCARD, Michel: French Prime Minister until early 1991.

SAAYMAN, Baas Daantjie: publisher and cyclist.

SACHS, Albie: ANC (q.v.) militant, jurist and writer. Severely wounded when South African Government agents tried to kill him by car bomb in Mozambique.

SACP: South African Communist Party. Oldest communist formation on the continent. It runs the ANC (q.v.).

SADF: South African Defence Force.

SANKARA, Thomas: former President of Burkina Faso. Assassinated at the behest of Blaise Campaoré (q.v.).

SAVIMBI, Jonas: leader of UNITA (q.v.).

SCHOON, Marius: writer and ANC (q.v.) activist who spent twelve years in South African prisons.

SEPTEMBER, Dulcie: ANC (q.v.) representative killed in Paris by South African agents, March 1988.

SERFYN, Sog: journalist working for *Vrye Weekblad*.

SEROTE, Wally: poet, spokesperson for the ANC on cultural matters.

SLABBERT, Frederik van Zyl: South African politician, academic and thinker. Chairman of this and that. His wife: Jane. His daughter: Nathalie.

SLOVO, Joe: former Secretary-General of the SACP (q.v.), now its President. His dog: Revolution.

SONN, Franklin: Principal of the Peninsula Technikon, trade unionist and politician.

SOW, André: director of Gorée Institute (Centre for Democracy, Development and Culture in Africa) on Gorée Island, Senegal.

STAR, Ukwezi (Stella): old friend and buddy of Yolande (q.v.) and of the author.

TAMBO, Oliver: chairfather of the ANC (q.v.). Died 1993.

TOBE: Sowetan student leader, died in exile 1990.

TRAORÉ, General Moussa: deposed President of Mali.

TSHWETE, Steve: member of the ANC's (q.v.) National Executive Committee.

UNITA, Angolan rebel liberation organization. After independence (1975) it started a civil war on behalf of South Africa against the MPLA Marxist government which had come to power in Luanda.

U TAM'SI, Tchicaya (Felix): Congolese poet and playwright, exiled in France, where he died in 1990.

VORSTER, John (Sitting Bull): former Prime Minister of South Africa. Brought security police to supreme power in the State. Pushed out by Crocodile Botha (q.v.) as champion of the SADF (q.v.) and specifically Military Intelligence. Died 1985.

VRIOLIE, Fanie: Afrikaans poet and academic.

WADE, Abdoulaye: leader of the opposition Democratic Party in Senegal. Now a Minister of State in President Diouf's (q.v.) government.

WALKER, Jean (Jan): African adventurer and dealer of French origin. Ex-member of the late Okhela (q.v.)

WATSON, Stephen: poet and critic (English).

WILLY THE LAUGHING REVOLUTIONARY POET: Keorapetse Kgositsile. A small man with a big heart.

WOODS, Donald: South African author and newspaper editor. Spent time in exile.

YOLANDE, Mariposa Sonrisa Ruiseñor: wife and heart's partner.